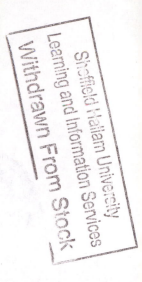

Key Themes in the Ethnography of Education

The book is dedicated to Professor Len Barton, who has done more than anyone else in Britain to build and maintain the Sociology of Education, and Otto de Campos Hutchinson born 11.04.10, who is the future of *capoeira*.

Key Themes in the Ethnography of Education

Achievements and Agendas

Sara Delamont

Los Angeles | London | New Delhi
Singapore | Washington DC

Los Angeles | London | New Delhi
Singapore | Washington DC

SAGE Publications Ltd
1 Oliver's Yard
55 City Road
London EC1Y 1SP

SAGE Publications Inc.
2455 Teller Road
Thousand Oaks, California 91320

SAGE Publications India Pvt Ltd
B 1/I 1 Mohan Cooperative Industrial Area
Mathura Road
New Delhi 110 044

SAGE Publications Asia-Pacific Pte Ltd
3 Church Street
#10-04 Samsung Hub
Singapore 049483

Editor: Chris Rojek
Editorial assistant: Gemma Shields
Production editor: Katherine Haw
Copyeditor: Kate Harrison
Indexer: Charmian Parkin
Marketing manager: Michael Ainsley
Cover design: Jen Crisp
Typeset by: C&M Digitals (P) Ltd, Chennai, India
Printed by: Replika Press Pvt. Ltd, India

© Sara Delamont 2014

First published 2014

Library of Congress Control Number: 2013936400

British Library Cataloguing in Publication data

A catalogue record for this book is available from
the British Library

ISBN 978-1-4129-0158-1
ISBN 978-1-4129-0159-8 (pbk)

contents

about the author

Sara Delamont is Reader in Sociology at Cardiff University. Her first degree was in Social Anthropology and her research has been focused on ethnographic studies, where sociological and anthropological concerns overlap. She is the sole author of nine books, including *Appetites and Identities*, *Feminist Sociology* and *Interaction in the Classroom*, and the co-author of eight others including *Key Themes in Qualitative Research* with Atkinson and Coffey, and *Fighting Familiarity* with Atkinson.

preface and acknowledgements

I need to thank all the teachers, students, and support staff in all the formal educational establishments where I and my colleagues and students have done research since 1969. In recent years I have been observing how two martial arts – *capoeira* (since 2003) and *savate* (since 2009) – are taught and learnt in the UK. That research has been conducted with Neil Stephens who has been invaluable, and *Contra-Mestre* Claudio de Campos Rosario has been the best key informant I could have had. James Southwood, a London *savate* teacher, has helped me enormously to grasp the subtleties of the French kickboxing he loves. I have been lucky to have inspiring colleagues in Cardiff, including Amanda Coffey and William Housley. I also need to thank Mrs Rosemary Bartle Jones for typing the book. Throughout my career I have shared my life – material and intellectual – with Paul Atkinson, who is the best companion and toughest critic and co-author any scholar could have.

The chapter titles are all in two parts: the classic ethnographic convention. One part is penny plain, the other is a quote from Zora Neale Hurston's (1935, 1990) *Mules and Men* – her study of African American folklore in Florida and of hoodoo (magic) in New Orleans. The chapter headings are quotes from ethnographies of educational settings, and 'horror stories', or 'urban legends' told among pupils and students about education.

Throughout the book I draw on the fieldwork I have been doing since 2003, on two martial arts, *capoeira* and *savate*, described briefly below, as well as more orthodox 'educational' research. The core of the fieldwork is observation, recorded in field notes, supplemented by: (1) informal conversations with people during classes; (2) interviews done by appointment with key informants; and (3) the collection of any 'documents' available (including CDs and DVDs). *Capoeira* is Brazilian, *savate* is French. Observation is done primarily on one teacher, Achilles, a Brazilian who has lived in the UK since January 2003, and has been teaching twice a week in Tolnbridge since April 2003. He also teaches in Cloisterham, where he lives, and his classes there are observed periodically. Any other teacher who conducts classes in Tolnbridge is also observed – whether guests teaching for Achilles or competitors – and so are Perseus, who teaches in the neighbouring city of Longhampston, and several teachers in London, including Leontis, Sophocles and Hermes.

More than 40 teachers, including several women, have been observed since the fieldwork began properly in the autumn of 2003 and I am grateful to them all. I have done much less observation of *savate* which hardly appears in this book, but the procedures are the same.

The rest of this preface is parochially British, and I suggest readers outwith the UK skip on to the Introduction.

I see a crucial link between that fieldwork and Len Barton to whom the book is dedicated. I have known Len Barton for 35 years. Here I offer him an apology, a recompense, and an expression of gratitude. I once, inadvertently, offended Len by calling him an entrepreneur. I meant it positively: as a compliment because he created arenas for us to perform in. I had in mind an impresario like D'Oyly Carte or Cameron Mackintosh rather than a capitalist business man like Freddie Laker or Richard Branson. The term entrepreneur clearly had capitalist overtones that Len, quite rightly, disliked. I hope Len is happier with my new metaphor a *Contra-Mestre* of the Sociology of Education. Here Len is six feet tall, a drop dead gorgeous African-Brazilian covered in tattoos, with dark wavy hair in dreadlocks, who can dance all night and then cartwheel into a *capoeira roda*, do a back somersault and then run round the circle clapping, singing, swinging his hips, and stamping his feet, raising the energy (*axé*) and refocusing everyone's attention on the business in hand.

There is no doubt that sociologists of education in the UK have needed a *Contra-Mestre* raising the *axé* at regular intervals since 1976. Len Barton, by running the Westhill Conferences, editing collections of papers, and founding the journals *BJSE* and *ISSE*, has been that *Contra-Mestre*. His role has been particularly important because of the absence of leadership from other, perhaps more famous or exalted figures. Precisely because Len has always created intellectual spaces, and offered unconditional enthusiasm for my research, this book begins far from conventional school classrooms, in the *apparently* 'irrelevant' world of martial arts.

It is 2 p.m. on a hot July Sunday in central London, in a Victorian building now used as a dance studio. Big air conditioning machines struggle to keep the temperature down to a level bearable for the martial arts students in a large hall. About 40 students, mostly young adults, are dressed in white trousers and matching t-shirts which proclaim the name of the club and their teacher around a picture of two men fighting, above the slogan 'Summer Festival 2009'. The students are sitting in a large circle, clapping and singing the choruses of a song in Brazilian Portuguese. About a quarter of the circle is made up of musicians: seven or eight people playing drums, tambourines, cowbells, and tall, bow-shaped instruments strung with a wire. A tall dark-skinned man is singing the verses of a song, leading the rest of the circle in a call and response vocal pattern. Surrounding the seated students are another 30–40 people standing in an outer circle: a mixture of people in martial arts kit, and those in ordinary clothes, watching the action. Many hold cameras and mobile phones, and take pictures of the 'play' in the centre of the ring. These people come and go during the five hours the ceremony lasts.

In the centre of the ring a slim white woman in her twenties is playing a game of *capoeira*: the Brazilian dance and martial art: with an African Brazilian teacher. They circle each other, she watching him warily, moving in time to the music. Each tries to test the other with kicks, and to escape, elegantly and safely, the attacks of the other. After a couple of minutes, the teacher suddenly points to something behind the young woman. Distracted, she turns to look where he is pointing, and he picks her up and puts her down on the floor so her bottom lands with a small 'thump'. The crowd whoop and cheer. The teacher pulls the student, who is herself laughing, to her feet, hugs her, leads her out of the circle through a gap by the musicians, and ties a beige and orange plaited belt round her waist. Another teacher, also a tall African-Brazilian in his 30s with dreadlocks, puts another beige and orange belt on the floor below the tall bow being played by the man singing the verses, and beckons to a slim Japanese man to come forward and squat opposite him at the foot of the instrument. They cartwheel into the centre of the circle and begin to move in time to the music.

The *bateria* struck up again, and a female student sang an opening verse (*ladainha*). Then the call and response song began, rather ragged and subdued. Gyges immediately ran round the *roda* twice, singing the chorus '*San Antonio e Protector*' (Saint Anthony the Protector) loudly and clearly so everyone could copy him, and again signalling he wanted more noise.

The 44 students gradually earned their *cordas*, and by 2.40 p.m. when one boy, ten women and seven men had been 'done', Gyges had run round the *roda* six times, and by the end of the orange and beige belts he had repeated the performance a further eight times. Each time he ran round the ring the seated students and the audience *did* sing louder, clap harder, whoop with more enthusiasm when a student fell to the floor, and cheer more lustily when a good attack or escape was executed. Gyges worked hard to keep the *ax*é high.

ix

Len has done an equivalent job for UK sociology of education. Most of us have been like students getting a *corda*; easily distracted from the ongoing welfare of the discipline after each job application, grant proposal, final report, PhD viva, or publication. Len has repeatedly refocused us on the sub-discipline as a whole, by highlighting the big themes. If I think back over the sociology of education's rocky passage since 1970 (the last time the British Sociological Association (BSA) held its annual conference on the theme of education), the need for someone to raise the *ax*é has been recurrent. Sociology of education has been, to quote Basil Bernstein, a 'pariah', marginal *both* to sociology departments and the BSA, *and* to Schools of Education and BERA (British Education Research Association). The BSA have not respected or supported the sub-field. BERA, founded in 1974, has been careful not to follow AERA (American

Education Research Association) into disciplinary divisions, so does not present a forum 'labelled' sociology of education. The conferences, and the journals, organised and sustained by Len Barton have been the main arena for sociology of education in the UK, with participation from scholars based in other countries.

I gave a paper at the first Westhill conference on the importance of traditional, peopled ethnography (Fine, 2003; Hammersley and Atkinson, 2007; Brown-Saracino, et al., 2008) for the sociology of education. *BJSE* provided space to argue that qualitative sociology of education would not advance if it shunned the American anthropology of education (Atkinson and Delamont, 1980) and that 'thick description' ethnography (Geertz, 1973) needed to be combined with the structuralist sociology of Bernstein (Atkinson, 1985) and Bourdieu (Reed-Danahay, 2005) to make progress in research on teacher education, and the intellectual socialisation of PhD students. In all those research projects the vital importance of collecting rich ethnographic data, *and* of being constantly engaged in making the familiar strange as Geer (1964), Becker (1971), and Wolcott (1981) argued in the past, followed by Lave and Wenger (1991), and Singleton (1999) and Varenne (2007a and b) have reiterated more recently. Martial arts classes are an educational setting, in which teaching and learning go on. The sociology of education can be progressed by ethnographic research in many settings, from teaching hospitals and brothels (Heyl, 1979) to pottery studios (Singleton 1998a) and *capoeira rodas*.

At exactly the period 1979–2003, when the Thatcher government was trying to close the ESRC (Economic and Social Research Council), drive all scholarly thought out of initial teacher training, and reduce the size of the higher education sector by squeezing out the social sciences, when among sociologists of education the collective *axé* had dropped, Len raised it by creating high status spaces where sociology of education could flourish. Twenty years later, Woodhead (1998) and Tooley (1998) gained extravagant publicity for philistine, ideological and badly researched attacks on the sociology of education. The BSA was entirely silent, although much of the attack focused on sociologists of education using sociological concepts such as organic solidarity and habitus. Len Barton organised the consultation about whether it was sensible to have a public debate with Tooley, which would, ironically, have given his ideas wider publicity, or not.

Overarchingly, the way in which Len is most like a *Contra-Mestre* is that he has always shown his own enthusiasm for the research others were doing, and simultaneously signalled that the quality of the sub-specialism will only ever be as good as the work and the energy everyone

x

contributes, and focuses onto and into the subject. Every paper refereed, every book review written, every conference attended has been seen as a contribution; so the accomplishment of UK sociology of education has been built out of many efforts, not just the famous books by a few stars. A *Contra-Mestre* urges everyone to sing and clap to build *axé*, Len has urged everyone to read, write and speak the sociology of education.

one

introduction: a detective of some kind

This study of Edgewood Academy extends my ongoing exploration of American high schools... I began in rural, Midwestern Mansfield and Mansfield High School (Peshkin, 1978/1994), where village life and agriculture were prominent. I continued thereafter, first in fundamentalist Christian Bethany Baptist Academy (Peshkin, 1986)... next in blue-collar Riverview and Riverview High School (Peshkin, 1991)... and finally in Indian High School (Peshkin, 1997). (Peshkin, 2001: *xi*)

Before I went to St Polycarp RC School in 1996 I was told by my cousin that the older girls gave first-years wrong directions on purpose so they got lost all the time.

The subtitle of this chapter, as of all the chapters, is a quote from Zora Neale Hurston *Mules and Men* (1935: 60). Here she compares the ethnographer to a detective: probably the first scholar to draw what is now a common analogy, but still not a bad starting point. All the chapters are introduced by a quote from an educational ethnography (the voice of the scholar) and an urban legend or scary story about school transfer (the voice of the child). The opening of Peshkin (2001) recounts a long career doing one school ethnography after another: an unusual work trajectory. The 'urban legend' reminds us that for children waiting to transfer from a primary to a secondary school, the stories they hear warn them that big secondary schools can be treacherous places where they are in danger of being tricked and misled.

While writing this book I have edited two companions. Delamont (2012a) is a four volume set of 70 articles on the ethnography of education, containing papers from Mead (1943) to Petrone (2010). Delamont (2012b) is a handbook in which 56 scholars explain the research methods for doing *Qualitative Research in Education*, from studying documents (Prior, 2012) to dancing the results (Bagley and Castro-Salazar, 2012). This book is the condensed, individual vision that drove those compilations.

The research discussed is one of the outstanding achievements of the sociology and the anthropology of education. It is a research area that depends on a qualitative method – ethnography – which is the basis of all anthropology and has been part of sociology for over a century, but only widely used in sociology of education since the late 1960s. There are previous reviews of this research (e.g. Hammersley, 1980, 1982; Atkinson, Delamont and Hammersley, 1988; Pelissier, 1991; Foley, Levinson and Hurtig, 2001). I draw on the research to outline what sociologists and anthropologists know about the everyday lives of pupils and students inside schools, colleges, and universities and what they know about the everyday lives and interaction patterns of the adults in those educational institutions. In practice that tends to mean teachers, because there has been a scandalous neglect of research on the other adults who work in educational institutions: secretaries (except Casanova, 1991), cooks, cleaners, lab technicians, nurses and so on. In the USA where school counsellors are a separate occupation, they have been studied (Cicourel and Kitsuse, 1963), but other occupations are largely ignored.

In 1971, Murray and Rosalie Wax bemoaned the lack of 'a solid body of data on the ethnography of schools' (p. 3) but at the very same time they published their lament the first steps towards creating the solid body of data they wanted to see had already been taken. In the late 1960s there were eight pioneering researchers who published ethnographies of everyday life in schools and classrooms:

1. L. M. Smith and W. Geoffrey (1968) *The Complexities of an Urban Classroom.*
2. P. Jackson (1968) *Life in Classrooms.*
3. D. Hargreaves (1967) *Social Relations in a Secondary School.*
4. H. F. Wolcott (1967) *A Kwakiutl Village and School.*
5. A.R. King (1967) *The School at Mopass.*
6. E. Leacock (1969) *Teaching and Learning in City Schools.*
7. J. Singleton (1967) *Nichu: A Japanese School.*

They were not exactly the first school ethnographies because there were earlier scattered examples or studies with some ethnographic data in them, such as Hollingshead (1947) and Stinchcombe (1964). However, those did not start a torrent of other studies: the seven monographs listed above were the beginning of a 40 year tradition.

All but one (Hargreaves) of the seven is American, although if one extended the deadline to 1970 a second UK book – Lacey (1970) – parallel to Hargreaves (1967) could be added. Focusing on the seven books highlighted here, two are about the everyday lives of exemplary elementary school teachers in the US (1 and 2), two are about the ineffectiveness and culture clash in the schooling, or miseducation, of First Americans and First Canadians (4 and 5). Singleton (1967) is the first book to detail how very differently the Japanese school system works, and Leacock (1969) exposed the mechanisms inside urban schools that were producing African-American failure in the American ghetto. Hargreaves's (1967) book explored what happened to boys in a city in the north of England who had failed the 11+ exam and were then placed in a streamed secondary modern school where most learnt nothing except to be disaffected. Lacey (1970) is an ethnography of an elite state school for boys he called *Hightown Grammar*. Despite these pioneering books, Palonsky (1975) still felt able to state in print that: 'there have been very few studies in education which have used the participant observation format'. He cited only Gordon (1957), McPherson (1972) and Cusick (1973). In his inaccurate generalisation he followed a pattern for qualitative researchers in education that persists to this day. One purpose of this book is to display the many studies that have been done.

Beyond the school but still in formal education there were parallel ethnographies of higher education by Becker, Geer, Hughes and Strauss (1961) and Becker, Geer and Hughes (1968) which formed the basis for understanding how students make sense of their experiences, paralleling the work on school pupils and foreshadowing all the subsequent ethnographies of higher education such as Moffat (1989), Sinclair (1996) and Adler and Adler (1991). Of course many people are educated or trained or socialised or enculturated in settings that are not called schools or colleges, and in ways that are not formal, and as this book progresses we shall explore the ethnographies of such enculturation too.

None of the pioneering studies treated the sex, gender, sex roles, sexuality or sexual orientation of the teacher or the pupils as problematic: those topics came later. Foley, Levinson and Hurtig (2001) is a thoughtful mapping of how the American anthropology of education developed in the 1990s to pay more attention to gender, and to be written by scholars from many more perspectives, especially 'ethnographers of color' (p. 41). Class, race, and ethnic or linguistic diversity were already apparent in the tradition.

However, if we start by focusing on the studies of formal schooling in the UK and the USA it is clear that my list mixes sociological and anthropological ethnographies, and is therefore unusual. There are two traditions in school and classroom ethnography (Atkinson and Delamont, 1980; Delamont and Atkinson, 1995; Delamont, 2012c), and the scholars in each simply ignore each other's work. The sociologies and anthropologies of education in the USA and Canada are still ignoring each others' publications as resolutely in 2012 as they have for 45 years. Because there

3

is also a resolute ethnocentricism among school ethnographers, so that Americans read nothing written outside the USA, and most non-Americans ignore much of the best American output, the big picture about schooling that could be discerned is not. It is very noticeable that, for example, Weis (2004), a sociologist, does not cite Ortner (2002, 2003), an anthropologist, or vice versa, and that the British *Journal of the Royal Anthropological Institute* reviewed Ortner (2003) but has never reviewed Weis's work.

Seven major themes are vividly present in those landmark volumes which have proved to be enduring: that is they have re-emerged in the classroom and school ethnographies ever since.

1. How schools can *create* scholastic and disciplinary difficulties and accentuate the problems they face (difficulties and problems they cannot subsequently solve) by their organisation and procedures without realising what they are doing.
2. How there can be irreconcilable culture clashes between ethnic or cultural or linguistic minorities and the mainstream government (or missionary) school system, and how such culture clashes can also arise across social classes.
3. How hard the everyday life of the classroom teacher is.
4. How classrooms are places where 'busyness' is valued.
5. How teachers make 1000 decisions every day.
6. How precarious the teacher's control regime is, even in the best run classrooms in the most elite schools.
7. How resistant to change the dominant systems of talk, of teaching, and of control over knowledge are.

The research that has confirmed, (re)discovered, and (re)examined these seven themes forms the empirical heart of the book. The methodological discussions draw on that research, and are intended to provide a guide for future scholars wishing to use ethnography in educational settings. The book aims to provide help and advice for educational researchers about how to frame research questions; think about what is important about teaching and learning and what is not; and, for those researchers who adopt qualitative methods, practical help with data gathering, reading, and writing, around the key themes. In each chapter there is an account of what is known about the topic, and what is not known (often more important and interesting) and there is a focus on the implication of that account for *future* research(ers).

The studies of formal and informal schooling that are recommended and praised in the book are predominantly examples of what Fine (2003) called 'peopled ethnography'. He set out principles for 'peopled ethno-graphy' articulating, even codifing, the methodological strategy that had guided his studies of fantasy gaming (1983), Little League baseball (1987), restaurant kitchens (1996), mushroom hunters (1998), American high school debating teams (2001), and meteorologists (2007) among many other small groups. He emphasises that he values 'interacting small groups as the primary focus of ethnographic investigation' (Brown-Saracino et al., 2008: 547). Fine was careful to state that ethnographic work at the micro-level is fundamental even when the theoretical issues to be illuminated are macro-level. In their 2008 paper, Brown-Saracino, Thurk and Fine develop the ideas to move beyond small groups, via seven pillars of 'peopled ethnography' (PE):

1. PE is theoretical: it is not just a description of a setting or culture, but can answer 'why?' and 'how?' questions and allow the identifica-tion of other settings where the theory might apply.
2. PE builds on other ethnographic studies to prevent 'blind' entry to the new fieldwork.
3. PE studies the interaction of small groups in settings where there is meaningful, ongoing, social life.
4. PE meets calls for generalisations by working on multiple research sites.
5. PE relies on extensive, in-depth fieldwork, only concluded when theoretical saturation is reached.
6. PE reports on interaction through thick description.
7. PE relies on 'analytic objectivity' (Brown-Saracino et al., 2008: 549): a distance sustained between the scholar and the members of the group under investigation.

Although Fine and his colleagues do not mention explicitly that these principles rule out autoethnography, and other more 'engaged' forms of qualitative research, they do so implicitly. My position on that is set out in Chapters 2 and 12. These principles do not address how the writing and representation of ethnography are to be done, although Fine's own work has used a 'conventional' ethnographic format. A similar manifesto for 'traditional' ethnography to that espoused by Fine and his colleagues, but one in which the issues of writing and representation are addressed is Katz (2001, 2002). He starts by pointing out that:

> Literary devices traditionally used for representing social life have been rendered deeply suspect by analyses that reveal how they implicitly construct social realities and subtly claim rhetorical authority. (Katz, 2001: 443)

5

Katz argues that the standpoints used to evaluate ethnographic data 'cut across writing styles and bridge the anthropology/sociology divide' (2001: 444). In other words, Katz believes ethnographers share a common culture. His own construction of that common culture was, however, both ethnocentric and sexist, which undermined his belief in one ethnography. Katz only cites American authors to make his point, ignoring European writers (Atkinson, 1983, 1990, 1992, 1996; Edmondson, 1984; James et al., 1997; Spencer, 1989, 2001). Katz also omits all the contributions to the debate by women scholars (e.g. Behar and Gordon, 1995; Coffey, 1999; Richardson, 1990, 1994).

Focused on what he terms 'luminous' description, Katz (2001: 462) understands the ethnographic consensus about how data are to be written up to be like the shared ideas of any group of craftspeople. By contrasting the shared understandings about what 'well presented' data of the authors from the First Chicago School of Sociology (1890–1942) look like – or rather how they read – with that of the Second Chicago School (1942–1962) (see Fine, 1995), Katz is clear that subcultures within sociology and anthropology have collectively developed 'craft concerns for qualities of description'. Katz contrasts styles of data presentation across several well known groups or traditions of ethnography. What they have in common is that they contain 'rich and varied', 'contextualised' or 'context-sensitive', and 'densely textured data' (2001: 464). He is clear, though, that a data set can only be called rich when it contains the resources to develop causal explanation.

Research aimed at producing luminous descriptions, causal explanation, and peopled ethnography is central to this book. Despite some wild claims to the contrary, such ethnography is still being done in sociology and anthropology, and good scholars are still reflecting on how and why they do it. So, for example, Papageorgiou (2007: 223) writes engagingly that 'Field research resembles bungee-jumping', meaning that once you have started there is no going back. His research field is Greek folk music and he plays the *Ud*, a traditional instrument. Of one fieldwork event he writes:

> I learned that night (and later confirmed) that appreciation of folk traditions among urban intellectuals and local villagers connected to the tradition differ radically. The former experience the performances as a pleasure. For villagers, the music recalls painful *memories* of loved ones who have departed… and a nostalgic melancholic recognition of a rapidly fading world.

His experience – a concert for villagers –

> enlightened me far more than had hundreds of interviews I had conducted with musicians and revelers until then.

That conclusion is the central message of this book: observational data are to be preferred to interview data wherever possible.

SCOPE AND PURPOSE OF THE BOOK

The aim of most of the research discussed in this book is to see how the teachers on one hand, and the pupils and students on the other, experience and understand their educational lives: that is to see their work through *their* eyes. The work on pupils and students can lead readers to criticise it for being anti-teacher (e.g. McNamara, 1980; Foster et al., 1996) but, of course, many pupils *are* anti-teacher, and even those who are happy and conformist do not necessarily share any of the perceptions of their teachers about education.

At the same time that the sociological and anthropological ethnographers were beginning to study interaction in schools and classrooms, there were also sociolinguists (Coulthard, 1974; Cazden, 1986) focusing on classroom talk, and psychologists and educational researchers who had begun to use coding schedules to measure classroom behaviour systematically (Flanders, 1970). These approaches focused on the classroom, and overwhelmingly on the teaching of academic subjects indoors in self-contained spaces. The ethnographic work was wider in its focus, covering corridors and playgrounds, sports fields and dining halls as well as the self-contained classrooms, and, following pupils off site into their homes or into the neighbourhood during their leisure activities too. For example, Spindler (2000) remembers beginning a piece of educational research in 1950, after doing research with his wife Louise on the Menominee, a native American group. He was assigned to observe the young male teacher of a class of ten year olds in a Californian elementary school. Spindler repeats that initially 'It was so boring!' because unlike the exotic, unfamiliar Menominee community, where he had been bewitched and had the spell lifted by a shaman, 'there was nothing to see, nothing to take notes on' (2000: 14). Luckily, that did not last, and Spindler spotted massive class and race inequalities in the classroom which gave his research a focus. He went to the children's home neighbourhoods, he explored the children's friendships and so on creating a 'typical' piece of school ethnography, ahead of its time.

This book violates a disciplinary boundary, between the anthropology of education and the sociology of education, in order to prioritise the use of ethnography to study educational settings broadly conceived. The core aim of the book is to pull together continuities and discontinuities in the 'findings' of 60 years of ethnography in educational settings, formal and

7

non-formal. The level of generalisation is an intermediate one. I am working at the level of concepts such as '*bricolage*', 'total institution' and 'career' rather than macro level concepts such as capitalism. The findings of ethnographic research from anthropology and sociology of education are included, but the middle order concepts are mostly more commonly used in sociology than anthropology. There are important differences between the anthropology of education, and the sociology of education, but for the purposes of this book those differences are not nearly as important as their methodological similarities.

Many of the studies mentioned are anthologised in Delamont (2012a) – a set of four volumes of classic and contemporary ethnographic studies of education. The 70 papers in these four volumes are routinely cited in this book. It is equally important that ethnographic work is theorised, and this is also a book that uses theory. Core middle-order concepts addressed in the book include awareness contexts, rites of passage and status passage, careers, total institution, stigma, gatekeepers, initial encounters (of the actors in a setting and of the ethnographer in a field site), *bricolage*, habitus, classification and framing, *flâneur*, the public and the private, the presentation of self.

The book will, in passing, challenge several myths about educational research – more by highlighting unjustly neglected studies than by reporting them at great length. For example, educational researchers are frequently told by policy-makers, journalists, politicians, etc. that 'teachers' do not read, use or value educational research. In fact there is good research to show that this is not true: Biddle and Saha (2002) show that, in the USA and Australia, they actually *do*. Another theme running through the book is that research and writing by women is as valuable as that by men, and *especially* if the women's work has been 'forgotten', then it deserves to be foregrounded.

One recurrent theme in the book is absence, or absences. This has three meanings here. First there is an emphasis on the *lacunae* in the existing educational ethnography: what has not been studied, written and remembered; second there is a focus on the absences in the ethnographies that we do have: the taken for granted things the authors have not drawn attention to; and third there is the injunction that good research is frequently generated by focusing on what is absent in the fieldsite, in the narratives of our informants, in our own fieldnotes, our own writing. The examples are taken not only from ethnographies of schools and schooling, but also from vocational and higher education, and from teaching and learning in non-formal settings such as peer instruction in skateboarding or novice witches learning to go into trance and visit other worlds. Some studies reappear in several chapters, because they contain important data across the themes. An interaction between Loïc Wacquant (2004) and the inspirational African-American boxing trainer whose gym he studied in Chicago about whether apprentice boxers should pay attention to books on boxing techniques is used in this volume to address ideas about knowledge and learning, about places and spaces, about time, about the public and the private, and about groups and identities. And, of course, it is also used to illustrate ideas about methods.

Learning and teaching go on in many settings other than schools, and some of the most evocative prose about key themes in the book is not in academic ethnographies. Some of the examples come from folklore, fiction and anthropologies not focused on education. Zora Neale Hurston was a subversive writer long before such texts were fashionable, and her research experiences among voodoo and hoodoo believers are drawn upon. Because the book was written after Hurricane Katrina hit New Orleans in 2005, the 2010 earthquake in Haiti, and during the BP and Haliburton oilwell leak that still threatens the deltas and coasts of Louisiana, Texas and Florida, several of the examples are taken from fieldwork and research on Haiti, New Orleans and in the delta. These are the setting for some of the best writing about America, especially James Lee Burke who writes beautifully about Louisana landscapes, urban and rural, and Karen McCarthy Brown's (1991) *Mama Lola* – a luminous thick description of the worlds of a Haitian voudou Priestess and her family.

THE STRUCTURE AND FORMAT OF THE BOOK

Apart from this introduction, there are ten substantive chapters and a conclusion. Chapter 2 focuses on methods, the rest are explorations of what ethnography has found and reported about learning and teaching, by direct instruction and by more subtle enculturation. Each chapter does four things: it reviews key 'findings' from the ethnography of education; it proposes possible middle-order theoretical concepts to add power to these findings; it sets out (a How To section) some innovative ideas and for gathering data on that 'topic'; it raises (A look to the future) some questions that have been neglected or remain problematic. So in Chapter 10 on 'senses and sensory materials' the most important results are explored, I theorise to illuminate them, and then the gaps and the implications for future research are explored. Delamont (2012b) showcases a wide range of qualitative methods that can be used to collect rich data in educational settings, and the 44 chapters in that volume are routinely cited.

two

one page of notes and no hypotheses: the spyglass of anthropology

I sat next to Heather at a girls' basketball game one evening. She was sitting in the bleachers with the rest of her prep friends front and center, cheering on the team, many of whom were part of their peer group. She kept glancing at the corner of the gym where several adults were standing… I asked her if she was expecting someone, and she whispered 'My dad said he might stop by and check the score. I hope he doesn't'. (Bettie, 2003: 149)

Before I went to Marswick Comprehensive in 1996 I was told by my teacher that they did not say prayers and I would go to Hell. (I went to an RC primary School.)

INTRODUCTION

In the quote from Bettie (2003) an American high school girl from a working-class family, whose school friends are all much richer, expresses the 'problems' she has with managing her life: balancing the norms and values of both her working-class home and her middle-class school-friends. Such tensions have been reported from many US high schools for 60 years. A different kind of culture clash is captured in the school transfer story: Roman Catholic primary school teachers, focusing on the ungodly atmosphere in the secular secondary school, who threaten eternal damnation.

 The first part of the chapter title is a quote from Blanche Geer's famous paper 'First days in the field' (1964) in which she demonstrated the intellectual importance of the early encounters between the fieldworker, the setting and the actors in it, and outlined the 'familiarity problem'. In the subtitle, Zora Neale Hurston (in *Mules and Men*, 1935: *xvii*) described how she was much too familiar with the African-American folklore of Eatonville, Florida until she had acquired as a student of Boas 'the spyglass of Anthropology' to look through. This chapter outlines one of two key concerns about good ethnography that run through the whole book: Good ethnography needs to fight familiarity.

Geer formulated the familiarity problem, highlighting the difficulties faced by beginner ethnographers who often find the research processes hard. These 'untrained observers... can spend a day in a hospital and come back with one page of notes and no hypotheses'. The hospital was too familiar: 'everyone knows what hospitals are like' (1964: 384). Geer's paper was a demonstration of how she 'fought' the familiarity of American college life at the start of the research project that eventually became Becker, Geer and Hughes (1968). It was simultaneously an account of how the researcher's initial encounters with a field setting can be disproportionately valuable, as long as the researcher works hard to construct and then to abandon working hypotheses (or foreshadowed problems as they are often termed), and a plea for treating the familiar (be it hospital, college or classroom) as anthropologically strange.

Geer's second point was subsequently taken up and reiterated by her collaborator, Howard Becker (1971) in a now famous statement, originally tucked away as a footnote added to a paper by the educational anthropologists Murray and Rosalie Wax (1971):

> We may have understated a little the difficulty of observing contemporary classrooms. It is not just the survey method of educational testing or any of those things that keeps people from seeing what is going on. I think, instead, that it is first and foremost a matter of it all being so familiar that it becomes impossible to single out events that occur in the classroom as things that have occurred, even when they happen right in front of you. I have not had the experience of observing in elementary and high school classrooms myself, but I have in college classrooms and it takes a tremendous effort of will and imagination to stop seeing only the things that are conventionally 'there' to be seen. I have talked to a couple of teams of research people who have sat around in classrooms trying to observe and it is like pulling teeth to get them to see or write anything beyond what 'everyone' knows. (Becker, 1971: 10)

In other words, these researchers are not working hard enough to develop good working hypotheses or foreshadowed problems, but are focusing on the familiar aspects of the setting. In the paper to which Becker added the footnote, Wax and Wax called for 'a solid body of data on the ethnography of schools' (1971: 4). We now have that solid body of data, but Becker's diagnosis still holds true. Becker and Geer followed up their own manifesto by studying learning in a range of non-educational settings such as hairdressing (Geer, 1972) but did not do any research that made schooling ethnographically 'strange'. They did, however, make medical education in the USA, and the liberal arts

11

undergraduate experience 'unfamiliar'. Geer and Becker's insightful comments have not received the attention they deserve. Over the subsequent four decades, other scholars have made parallel statements, but the problems Geer set out have persisted. The next section outlines the history of the familiarity diagnosis.

RECURRENT DIAGNOSES

A parallel statement to Becker's was being made in the same year in the UK by Michael F.D. Young (1971), who argued that educational researchers were not, in practice, defining their own research-based research problems (i.e. making education 'strange') but were accepting the problems defined by practitioners. His specific concerns about knowledge, curricula and power are central to Chapter 11. Young's impassioned call for a shift from *taking* problems to *making* them launched a short-lived, but highly controversial, flourishing of sociological research on the curriculum, called the 'new' sociology of education in the UK (Bernbaum, 1977). The wider issues implicit in Young's (1971) manifesto were not, however, taken up by Anglophone ethnographers.

A parallel disquiet to Becker's was voiced in the USA when there was renewed enthusiasm for educational ethnography (see, for example, Spindler, 1982). Wolcott published his 'Confessions of a "trained" observer' stating that: 'Central features of education are so taken for granted that they are invisible' (1981: 253). He wrote that it took a colleague from outside educational research

> to jolt me into realizing that the kinds of data teachers gather 'on' and 'for' each other so admiringly reflects the dominant society and its educator subculture. (Ibid.)

This colleague was 'particularly intrigued' by the research, very fashionable in the USA in the late 1970s, about 'time on task' and commented:

> How incredible… that teachers would measure classroom effectiveness by whether pupils appear to be busy. How like teachers to confuse 'busy-ness' and learning. (Ibid.)

The fashion for studies of pupils' 'time on task' (Denham and Lieberman, 1980) has waned, but the problem is still prevalent. Wolcott then pointed out that he and his educational research colleagues

> [h]ave not systematically encouraged our students… to go and look at something else for a while. We keep sending them back to the classroom. The only doctoral

12

student I have sent off to do fieldwork in a hospital was a nurse-educator who
returned to her faculty position in a school of nursing! (Ibid.)

Wolcott too is implicitly calling for robustly formulated working
hypotheses about educational settings and explicitly calling for scholars
to treat schools and schooling as anthropologically strange.

During the 1970s, ethnographic methods began to be more widely
accepted in educational research than they had been when Geer, Becker,
and Wax and Wax were writing (Jacob, 1987; Atkinson, Delamont and
Hammersley, 1988). While that growth took different forms in the USA
and the UK, in both countries the problems outlined by Geer and Becker
were not tackled. In 1980 Paul Atkinson and I drew attention to the gulf
between the two predominant types of ethnographic research being
done in education: by anthropologists of education in the USA, and
sociologists of education in the UK. Despite the differences between
these two ethnographic traditions, they shared a failure to make their
own education systems problematic. That gap had not been previously
documented, nor its implications explored, as Metz (1984) was later to
point out. The pattern of isolated voices raising the familiarity problem
was perpetuated when George and Louise Spindler (1982) rehearsed
similar ideas reflecting on their 30 years of fieldwork, in a paper sub-
titled 'From familiar to strange and back again'. As summarised by
Parman (1998), the Spindlers compared 'the experience of doing ethnography in familiar and "exotic" settings'.

13

> Each setting imposes its own anthropological dilemma: first how to observe
> situations so familiar that it is almost impossible to extract oneself from one's
> own cultural assumptions and be objective; the second, how to observe situations
> so different from what one is used to that one responds only to differentness.
> (1998: 305)

Parman continues that 'making the familiar strange' is 'the ultimate goal
of every anthropologist' (1998: 395). What is striking about the Spindlers'
formulation is that they, unlike Becker or Young, *do* mention some strategies to fight it, such as the use of film.

Ethnographic research on schools and classrooms continued to flourish
during the 1980s, conducted by anthropologists and sociologists. Most
repeated the pattern of failure: they did not start with robust foreshadowed problems designed to make schooling anthropologically strange;
nor did they achieve strangeness in their eventual portraits of teachers
and pupils. During the 1980s the textual conventions and rhetorical genres used to publish qualitative research came under increased scrutiny
(Clifford and Marcus, 1986; Atkinson, 1990, 1992, 1996, 2012; Spencer,

2001; Atkinson and Delamont, 2008). Educational ethnographies were one suitable set of texts for genre analysis (Delamont and Atkinson, 1990) but educational ethnographers did not reanalyse classic texts to scrutinise their assumptions, such as familiarity.

Anthropologists of education did not address the familiarity problem, nor the need for well-formulated foreshadowed problems, for nearly two decades after Wolcott (1981), which may be why Lave and Wenger (1991), and their three key concepts of legitimate peripheral participation, situated learning and communities of practice, received a lot of attention when they called for researchers to study education *outside* schools. Lave and Wenger wrote as if they were completely unaware of the anthropology of education, and the sociological calls to 'fight familiarity'. Their manifesto claims an originality for their diagnosis that it did not, in fact, have.

When, in 1999, *Anthropology of Education Quarterly* celebrated its 30th birthday, key figures returned to the topic. Hess (1999: 401) recapitulated the ideas of Wax and Wax (1971), and raised the issue of whether anthropologists of education 'are still asking good rather than trivial questions, whether we are asking the right questions' (1999: 400). John Singleton (1999) argued that after 30 years the anthropology of education still needed to be better connected to anthropological work outside schools. He wrote: 'The critical confusion of education with schooling continues to bedevil us' (1999: 457). He cited Lave and Wenger, and drew his readers' attention to his own research on apprentices learning Japanese folk pottery and ethnographies of occupational training and socialisation in Japan across a range of other, non-school, settings (Singleton, 1998b). That collection demonstrates all the points made about learning by Lave and Wenger; reinforces the importance of the Geer (1972) collection; and lives up to the calls for treating education as *not* coterminous with schools. It has, however, been resolutely ignored by educational ethnographers (Eisner and Peshkin, 1990).

I returned to the theme of fighting familiarity after an absence of several years, contrasting four types of educational research, and arguing for what I called 'Lebanon Gate' research that took researchers out of their 'comfort zone' into unchartered territories characterised by fighting familiarity and, at some intellectual risk, trying to find genuinely new insights (Delamont, 2005a). Frederick Erickson (2006: 236–7) made a parallel point when he argued, drawing on Nader (1975) that anthropologists should study 'up' rather than 'down': 'to visit and document the lives of the privileged and powerful'. He points out that 'Nader's injunction would seem especially apt for us' (anthropologists of education). Yet, with the exception of Alan Peshkin (2001), Erickson continues, this is rarely done. He could have included Proweller (1998) and Sara Lawrence Lightfoot (1983).

In 2007, Herve Varenne edited a special issue of *Teachers' College Record* on educational anthropology. In his editorial essay he remarks:

> The great paradox of work on education by social scientists is that it is mostly about schools... work on education is, paradoxically, rarely about education. (2007a: 1539)

Varenne approvingly quotes Bourgois's dictum that 'the streets are almost always more powerful than the schools' (1996: 1562).

These examples, of repeated largely ineffectual attempts to highlight a perennial problem, make depressing reading. The popularity of Lave and Wenger (1991) did not have any greater effect on ethnographers, not driving them to fight familiarity, stop focusing on schools, or devise more robust foreshadowed problems, than Geer (1964) or Becker (1971) had had. Gamradt (1998) in an intriguingly titled paper 'Romancing the gall-stone' (p. 71) reports that she met some 'outright hostility' (p. 76) from colleagues when she decided to focus on the advanced continuing professional development of surgeons rather than on schools. As she explains:

> Educational research in general remains heavily invested in the study of K-12 practitioners and students. Working on the problem of how highly successful, high-status professionals learn takes one well outside mainstream educational anthropology. Studying up represents a serious and perhaps threatening violation of convention. We are experts at the careful compassionate study of the deviant, the disadvantaged, the disenfranchised, the other. (Gamradt, 1998: 76)

In part that may be due to the general lack of clearly specified strategies for achieving the goal of fighting familiarity: the focus of the next section.

STRATEGIES TO FIGHT FAMILIARITY

This section sets out six strategies which will help ethnographers fight familiarity, particularly by providing the raw materials from which to construct robust working hypotheses or foreshadowed problems. Self-conscious strategies to create such hypotheses which enable, even require the researcher to fight familiarity are essential. The six strategies to fight familiarity proposed here are as follows:

1. Revisiting 'insightful' educational ethnographies of the past.
2. Studying learning and teaching in formal education in other cultures.

15

3. Taking the standpoint of the *researcher* who is 'other' to view the educational process, for example, by doing ethnography from the standpoint of participants from a different social class, a different race or ethnicity, a different gender, or a different sexual orientation.

4. Taking the viewpoint of actors other than the commonest types of 'teachers' and 'students' in ordinary state schools. This can mean focusing on unusual settings in the school system, such as schools for learning disabled pupils, or the deaf or blind, or in the UK Welsh or Gaelic medium schools, or 'other' actors in ordinary schools such as secretaries, laboratory technicians, campus police, cooks.

5. Studying learning and teaching outside formal education settings.

6. Using intermediate theoretical concepts from other areas of the discipline to re-energise educational ethnography (for example, the concept of the *flâneur*).

In other publications, ethnomethodology has been proposed as a seventh strategy (Delamont, 1981; Delamont and Atkinson 1995; Varenne, 2007a and 2007b). That approach, originating with Garfinkel (1967), is not explored here because it requires a radical rethinking of social science far beyond the scope of this book. I now offer powerful examples of how each of the six strategies can serve to strengthen educational ethnography addressing two agendas; firstly fighting familiarity in general, and secondly fighting *fashion*. The educational sciences 'forget' research very quickly and consistently reinvent the same wheels. Educational research urgently needs to cultivate the *longue durée*.

1. revisit the insightful educational ethnographies of the past

Educational researchers in general, and educational ethnographers are no exception, operate with a very short timescapes or time horizons. Fashions come and go, terminology changes so that previous research seems obsolete, and work is quickly forgotten. It is salutary to revisit apparently obsolete, neglected, out of print ethnographies, using them as a lens through which contemporary educational settings can be re-envisioned. Here I offer three specific examples of currently neglected work that, if reread, offer ways to fight familiarity, and develop powerful foreshadowed problems for contemporary research. My three themes are: urban schooling; age as a factor in teacher–pupil relations; and uneasy relations between teachers and educational 'innovators'. An equivalent example about the hidden injuries of class in the US High

School is central to Chapter 8. Many others could be substituted, as, for example, Foley's (1996) critical reflections on the 'silent' Indian.

The first example of a research area where greater attention to the findings of earlier researchers would, at a stroke, improve the current studies, is urban schooling in the USA. A leading journal, *Teaching and Teacher Education*, carried many papers during the years 2000–2010 focused on how ill-prepared newly qualified teachers were for the multi-racial, multi-lingual, poor students they were required to face in urban schools. These papers showed no historical understanding of the problem they addressed, which has certainly existed since the 1950s, and been studied by excellent researchers. Apparently forgotten is a series of papers by Becker and Geer on Chicago public school teachers published in the 1950s and 1960s, (Becker 1952a, 1952b; Geer 1966a, 1966b). In those articles, all the issues about the difficulties of teaching poor children in American city-centre schools were vividly described. The papers by Merryfield (2000), Sconzert et al. (2000), Mueller and O'Connor (2007) and Siwatu (2007), for example, all lack any recognition that similar problems arose in the USA 50 years ago. If scholars today recognised the deep-seated and longstanding gulf in America between the recruits to inner city teaching and the lives of the pupils they are required to teach, in terms of class, race, language, experiences of poverty, violence, bad housing, poor health and diet, and a highly developed set of skills and knowledges we can gloss as 'street-smarts' their teachers lack, the diagnoses and the solutions proposed would be better. Lois, one of the African-American college students studied by Winkle-Wagner (2009), left her teacher preparation course at a mainly white midwestern university because she decided it was not trying to bridge that gap. She remarked that all the lecturers skipped the chapters in the text books on 'diversity'.

The second example is grounded in the research on age as a factor in teacher–pupil relations in the American high school, with a consequent 'anti-pupil' rhetoric of 'decline' souring education. Warren Peterson (1964) published research on how three cohorts of women teachers in US high schools related to students and to the curriculum. The women interviewed were then in their 20s, 40s and 60s. The careful attention to gender and age is exemplary, and was years ahead of its time. Issues of the interaction effects of age and sex on teacher beliefs and practices were clearly fundamental to teaching *then* and are equally important in recent decades. Peterson's teachers who were in their 60s were entirely convinced that the students they had taught 40 years before were infinitely superior, and tackled a much more demanding curriculum, than their pupils in the 1960s. It appeared to the paper's readers, however,

17

that the change was as much in the teachers' shared life experiences with their early pupils, and their 'distance' from those they were facing when they were in their 60s. The older women were lamenting the loss of their own youth and energy, as much as any decline in American schooling, exactly the way Herzfeld (1983) found older Cretans bemoaning 'semantic slippage and moral fall'. The research on memories and memorials is explored in Chapter 5, but the importance of age differences and associated beliefs can be seen as perennial. For example, Datnow's (1997, 1998) careful study of how one powerful group of older white men destroyed a school reform reveals the complex interactions between age, sex, and power in the school hierarchy five decades after Peterson's work.

A third area is where attention to important research from earlier eras concerns attempts to 'reform' schools and curricula. In 1977 Wolcott published an insightful research study on the uneasy relationship(s) between classroom teachers and the educational technocrats introducing waves of 'reforms'. Wolcott's careful, painstaking investigation revealed that the two groups worked in different occupational sectors, with contrasting occupational cultures and little or no appreciation of each other's goals or practices. Any scholar setting out to research attempts to drive through any type of school reform would learn a good deal from that relatively unknown work recently reprinted (Wolcott, 1997 [2005]).

These three examples are sufficient to show how close inspection of any classic ethnography from 30 or 40 years ago will inevitably lead to the formation of several working hypotheses about continuity and change. If these working hypotheses, when pursued, seem to produce findings of continuities, then the reasons for the persistences can be explored. If there seem to have been social changes, then documenting them will, in itself, improve the modern ethnography.

2. formal education in other cultures

It may seem paradoxical that educational ethnographers are frequently parochial, and fail to read, cite and *use* ethnographies of schooling and higher education in other cultures. Exemplary scholarship that would be sovereign in the fight against familiarity and the formulation of foreshadowed problems is ghettoised and neglected. Such research done by fellow countrymen and countrywomen is ghettoised into 'the anthropology of education' or 'comparative education', equivalent research done by scholars from other countries is not registered at all.

There are many examples of neglected studies that, if studied and utilised, would enrich American and British school ethnography. There are three ethnographies of schooling in France (Anderson-Levitt, 1987, 1989; McDonald, 1989; Reed-Danahay, 1996) which illustrate this point. McDonald's fieldwork in Brittany includes data on the Breton language school movement (called *diwan*, or seed) rarely cited by Anglophone ethnographers yet packed with contrastive and comparative material, which should be read by those focused on bilingual or mother tongue schooling. Reed-Danahay and Anderson Levitt's (1991) comparative article about French teachers' conceptions of how difficult it is to teach in the 'backward countryside' and in the 'troubled city' has resonance for the USA. Spindler and Spindler (1982) published an account of German schooling in the 1950s that is rarely cited but would generate good foreshadowed problems.

Singleton's *Nichu* (1967), about a Japanese secondary school, is a salutary contrast for Americans: those adolescents did *no* paid work, *no* household chores and had *no* social life at all. In contrast is the one study that highlighted the paradox of the American high school as a basis for parties, sport and hanging out, rather than academic work. Gibson's (1988) ethnography about Punjabi immigrant high school pupils in California who did not have paid jobs or 'party' (though they did do many chores for their families) showed that the teachers regarded them as maladjusted because they did not attend the class picnic or the prom. How intriguing that *teachers* would demand that adolescents 'party' and do paid work, rather than do homework, in order to be 'good Americans'.

An Australian analysis of how a whole school of clever boys lived out a principled rejection of the school curriculum is also a salutary read. Bullivant's (1978) ethnography of Chassidic Orthodox Lubavitcher Jewish boys in an Australian high school, who 'knew' that the Australian state curriculum contained 'nonsense' (because it contradicted the bible) but scored high marks in it anyway, has lots to teach us all. How did a school produce such high exam marks from a pupil group entirely resistant to the curriculum?

19

3. take the standpoint of the 'other'

Taking the standpoint of the 'other' is a valuable research strategy. All educational researchers should try to understand how the setting is perceived by, and experienced by, people who come to it, and live in it, from standpoints other than their own. This is partly an ethical and political point, drawing upon Becker's (1967, 1970) classic question 'Whose side are we on?'. His core concerns are relevant in 2014, although a contemporary scholar may find its unproblematic treatment of the researcher a little perplexing. Atkinson, Coffey and Delamont (2003) explore how that paper should be read in a new century. For my purposes here, the word to be emphasised is 'we'. Too often the ethnographer has been a straight, highly educated, middle-class white or Jewish man from the USA. With only a few exceptions the research has been done from that standpoint (but see Foley, Levinson and Hurtig, 2001 for a gradual change in this). Work by gay and lesbian authors, by women, and by non-whites has been less common, and, once done, less widely known. The work from other countries that does get known in the USA also tends to be by straight white men. For example, the only two British ethnographers regularly cited in the American literature are Lacey (1970) and Willis (1977), when, for example, Cecile Wright's (1996) work, from the standpoint of an African-Caribbean woman, provides a far more useful comparator for American writers. The *Handbook* edited by Denzin, Lincoln and Smith (2008), focusing on critical and indigenous methods, could provide fresh approaches for future ethnographers as long as the caveats expressed by Foley et al. (2001: 48–49) are recognised.

4. study unusual schools, or other actors in the usual schools

20 The vast majority of educational ethnographies focus on pupils between the ages of 6 and 18 in state schools. Researchers rarely focus on schools for those with physical or mental disabilities, on the expensive schools that educate the children of the elite; on rural schools rather than urban and suburban ones. The few studies of religious schools, for Jews, Catholics, Evangelicals, Protestants or Muslims are not used for contrastive purposes as they should be. In the UK there are Welsh and Gaelic medium schools yet the very existence of these is not known by most ethnographers and there are no ethnographic monographs on them, nor are there scholarly evidenced-based comparisons of everyday life inside them and in English-medium schools. Educational ethnography would be far better if the research on the unusual, exceptional settings were systematically drawn upon to provide contrasts that force the researchers in the 'normal' school to think about it in novel ways.

An alternative way to achieve that critical distance in mainstream schools is to focus on non-teacher and non-pupil actors in the 'normal' setting. Ursula Casanova's (1991) ethnography focusing on secretaries in Arizona elementary schools is a (rare) example of such a study. Finding a view of an educational institution from the school office, or the nurses' room, or the cupboard where the cleaners are based, is unusual in educational research. Yet in the sociology of health and illness it has been done regularly since Roth (1963) studied a TB sanatorium working as an orderly.

5. education outside 'education'

Many settings outside formal schooling and universities are the location for teaching and learning. When there is research on that teaching and learning it rarely crosses into the mainstream of educational research, and many such settings have hardly been studied at all. That is why this book focuses on higher education and non-formal settings as well as schools. The explanatory power of ethnographic research on learning and teaching away from formal institutions was one reason for the popularity of Lave and Wenger, and their concepts of communities of practice (COP) and Legitimate Peripheral Participation (LPP). In 1988 at a conference in San Diego they presented their first formulation of the ideas published in 1991 as *Situated Learning*, stating:

> 'schooling is usually assumed to be a more effective and advanced institution for educational transmissions than (supposedly) previous forms such as apprenticeship'. (1991: 61)

Lave and Wenger argued that this generally unexamined belief should be made problematic in two ways. Firstly, apprenticeships and other learning models should *not* be assumed to be less effective and advanced than schooling. Secondly, research on learning and teaching in non-school settings was badly needed. They had decided to 'take a fresh look at learning' (1991: 39) because 'issues of learning and schooling' have 'become too deeply interrelated in our culture in general' (pp. 39–40). Their longer-term goal was to rethink 'schooling from the perspective afforded by legitimate peripheral participation' (p. 41). Lave and Wenger therefore focused on five case studies of apprenticeships not in the education system of the USA at all: American newcomers to Alcoholics Anonymous; American apprentice butchers; American naval quartermasters; Gola and Vai tailors in Liberia; and midwives among the Yucatec.

Spindler (1967) had argued for exactly the same strategy for many years: cultural transmissions in Palau, Ulithi, Hano, Tiwi, Gopalpur, Inuit, Sansuron, Guadalcanal, Anatolia, and a Philippine *barrio* were rehearsed to encourage American educational ethnographers to think outside the box of the school.

Since the original book was published in 1991, Lave and Wenger have taken separate intellectual paths, and there has not been a concentrated programme of ethnographic research and publication on learning in non-school settings. The concepts of LPP and CoP have, rather, been mainstreamed into conventional educational research (see, for example, Timmons-Flores, 2009). This kind of mainstreaming does not provide

21

the robust foreshadowed problems and weapon to fight familiarity that the original book promised. The potential insights from the application of Lave and Wenger's ideas to a variety of unusual educational settings was shown in a special issue of *Teaching and Teacher Education* (Vol. 26 No. 1) in 2010, which include research on, among others, prisons, Hindu priests, skateboarding and *capoeira*. Paul Atkinson and I (Delamont and Atkinson, 1995) drew on such disparate examples of teaching and learning outside schools and higher education as trainee mediums in Brazilian *umbanda* (Leacock and Leacock, 1975), *capoeira* academies in Salvador de Bahia (Lewis, 1992; Downey, 2005), a madam training novice prostitutes to maximise their earnings (Heyl, 1979), sword-swallowing and fire-eating (Mannix, 1951) and an Albanian Bektaski Tekke (monastery) in Michigan (Trix ,1993). These are entirely parallel to the Lave and Wenger case studies both in their apparently 'exotic' and therefore apparently irrelevant focus, and in the insights they actually provide for mainstream schooling.

Instead of repeating these parallels, I have used a new example to illustrate my argument: focused on self-esteem and self-efficacy beliefs among experienced and novice teachers. Teacher self-efficacy beliefs have been a focus for considerable research effort in the past decade and are a regular topic of academic papers in *Teaching and Teacher Education*. The subject would benefit from ethnographic research: do teachers or student teachers with a hightened sense of self-efficacy *behave* differently in the classroom, the faculty lounge, or staffroom, the yard or playground, or on the playing fields, when compared with their less well-endowed colleagues? The large body of research is only based on what teachers say about their self-efficacy beliefs, or what they write on questionnaires, rather than how they act, and interact, and react in their workplace. High quality ethnographic work on those with high levels of self-efficacy in education, and in other contexts, would strengthen the area immeasurably. The published research on teachers and self-efficacy also lacks imaginative ideas about how the low levels of self-efficacy beliefs in novice or experienced teachers might be raised. Yet there are bodies of research in settings away from schools or teacher education programmes on how learners experience a raised sense of self-efficacy. In the ethnographic literature on neopaganism, and especially that on feminist Wicca, there *is* a body of research on self-efficacy and its creation, accentuation and retention, which provides a challenge to the prevalent ideas in the educator subculture.

Magliocco (2004) researched a variety of neopagan groups in the San Francisco Bay area, including the famous Reclaiming Witchcraft Movement founded by Starhawk. For the purposes of making the beliefs of teachers anthropologically strange, Magliocco's account of how her conversion to, and research on, neopaganism transformed her own sense of self-efficacy is particularly vivid and thought-provoking. The best example is one private ritual she describes (2004: 117–118) arranged for her precisely to create and strengthen her self-efficacy belief. Magliocco was at the time divorced, desperately homesick for the site and people of her doctoral fieldwork in Sardinia and the 'authentic' research she had done there. She had been moving around the USA in a variety of temporary posts for nine years, trying to get a tenure-track appointment. Her closest friends in a small neopagan coven in which she was apprenticed helped her devise a ritual that would change her:

> ...from a stranger to a native, from an outsider to an insider, from a position of insecurity and rootlessness to one of security, prosperity and belonging, through a series of symbolic transformations. (Magliocco, 2004: 118)

The room was set up with four altars at the compass points, also signifing earth, air, fire and water. Magliocco entered the circle in the heavy clothing she had worn in the Midwest, carrying symbols of her old life. She then moved round the four altars. At each she shed some of the winter clothing and discarded the symbols of her old life. At each altar her friends handed her symbols of the new life she wanted such as 'hawk feathers, symbolic of intellectual freedom and my ability to soar' (p. 118). Small items of Californian food and drink were taken, to put California into her body, and they planted a rose bush to signify groundedness. Magliocco describes this as 'a piece of performance art that enacted, through the use of symbols and actions, changes I wanted to see in my own life' (p. 118).

A fortnight after this ritual Magliocco got called to interview at a Californian university for a tenure-track post, and was eventually appointed. Her pagan friends were confident that the ritual was instrumental in getting the job, but *only* because she had already made several job applications in California. They believe that magic only 'works' if the sensible steps to produce the desired outcome are taken in the material world. It is not necessary to have any neopagan beliefs to accept that the ritual could have helped transform Magliocco into a more employable university teacher. The efforts expended by her Californian friends, in themselves, could be empowering. A sceptical reader, with no belief at all in the magic, could well decide that Magliocco went to the interview in a more positive, confident, empowered frame of mind: in other words she had a greater sense of self-efficacy, and that was an important factor in her self-presentation, and therefore she was in a better position to impress an appointing committee with her employability.

Greenwood (2000), who did a parallel research project in the UK, describes a Samhain (Halloween) ritual in a feminist coven. In the pagan calendar Samhain is the end of the old year, and is a time to celebrate new beginnings, and one element of the ritual Greenwood describes involved calling out everything negative the participants were leaving behind in the old year while facing a mirror. Participants then re-entered the circle made up of the rest of the coven by jumping over a fire. It is clear from the fieldwork that such rituals are empowering for participants who believe in them. The ethnographic examples from Magliocco's and Greenwood's work are examples of increasing the self-efficacy beliefs of women, but the neopagan research includes similar stories about men. For example, Greenwood (2000: 132–134) is an account of how success in magic transformed the self-efficacy of a man she calls Chrys.

Parallel examples from a religious tradition entirely different from neopaganism will serve to make the same point. David Smilde's (2007) ethnography of converts to evangelical Protestantism in the urban slums of Caracas covers similar ground. Men who chose to convert – to be born again – experience a massive growth in self-efficacy, enabling them to kick drugs, stop gambling, end affairs and break off their social relationships with members of violent gangs. Researchers have found informants', and their own, self-efficacy beliefs revolutionised by conversions, rituals, rites of passage and other revelatory experiences, from which educational reformers who want to raise the self-efficacy of teachers could learn.

I offer these examples of successful ways of changing people's self-efficacy beliefs that ethnographers have reported in fields very *unfamiliar* to educational researchers; neopaganism and Latin-American evangelical christianity. My argument is that understanding change in self-efficacy in an *unfamiliar* sphere generates foreshadowed problems, or working hypotheses, that can challenge familiarity. Instead of focusing repeatedly on self-efficacy in preservice teacher education programmes, studying the phenomenon in another milieu, especially one where it *can* be radically improved, could produce strategies for changing the self-efficacy beliefs of trainee teachers.

6. using theoretical concepts

The ethnographic work of sociologists and anthropologists of education has not been noted for deploying the middle order theoretical concepts that the wider disciplines do. Useful concepts, such as the *flâneur*, the poetics of manhood, and tournaments of value are used throughout the book to move beyond the ethnographic description. The deployment of such middle order theoretical concepts is intended here to challenge familiarity. The concept of the *flâneur* is used in Chapter 6 to refocus what a 'deviant, school refusing' boy in Coalthorpe was actually doing when to the growing frustration of his teachers he repeatedly failed to 'find' his science class. While there was a fashion for deploying the concept of the *flâneur* in British sociology a decade ago it did not get picked up in educational ethnography, despite its potential explanatory power.

three

places and spaces: a group on the store porch

In New Orleans, there were fortune tellers and fire eaters at the cathedral; second-line parades and jazz funerals, nuns on the bus; John the Conqueror and Stop Evil Floor Wash in the grocery store; chicory coffee and *beignets* at the French market and okra gumbo at the Napoleon House; St Expedite in the mortuary chapel and the Blessed Virgin Mary in the front yard... It was funky and decadent and beautiful and slightly dangerous. (Long, 2006: *xv*)

Before I went to (secondary) school at Birleton School I was told that there was a ghost in the bell tower that rings the bell after midnight.

The opening quote is from a book about the Witch Queen of New Orleans, Marie Laveau: but its main purpose here is to take the reader to New Orleans. It does not matter what second-line parades and *beignets* are (the latter are a sweet, icing sugar dusted, light doughnut sold to eat with the strong chicory flavoured New Orleans coffee): the point is to contrast the city with the cold, dull, colourless, characterless places where the author was sitting when she starts to write the book and where the readers are likely to be ensconced when they begin to read it. Nor does it 'matter' whether there really was a ghost in the bell tower at Birleton: the 'point' of the story was to contrast the old, mysterious buildings of the big secondary school with the friendly local primary school and to scare the child about to transfer to Birleton. In this chapter the central theme is the importance of understanding, and evoking, places and space in educational ethnography. The chapter title from Zora Neale Hurston's *Mules and Men* (1935: 7), emphasises how a place can be exactly right for data collection. In her case, the African-Americans gathered on the shaded porch of the township store were to be her first informants in Eatonville, Florida.

This chapter outlines the main conclusions ethnographic research allows us to reach about place and space in educational settings; it makes practical suggestions for gathering data in such settings on the spatial theme; and finally highlights some locational aspects of education settings we know too little about. It is structured around some core concepts from sociology and anthropology, including the *flâneur,* boundaries, the public and the private, places of memory, 'this' world and 'other' worlds. The chapter deals with ethnographers' spaces and places first, and then moves on to what they have discovered about space and place as important to and for learning and teaching.

THE ETHNOGRAPHER'S PLACES AND SPACES

One of the first ways in which ethnographic research is different from other educational investigations is that the scholar goes, physically, to the spaces and places where the data are to be collected, and spends time there. In the resultant written accounts, the reader is also taken to those spaces and places. One of the surviving differences between sociological ethnographers and anthropological fieldworkers is that anthropologists are more likely to believe they should live, i.e. eat and sleep, in their field setting for extended periods, rather than visit it for data collection. Wolcott (2002b), comparing anthropological ethnography with travel writing, argues that because 'first-hand experience and intimate, long-term acquaintance' are regarded as central to *anthropological* field-work, there are problems of acceptance if the researcher does not live in the setting. The coming of cyberspaces has widened the concept of 'going to' a place, as Boellstorff's (2008) research in the virtual world of Second Life makes clear. His avatar 'lived' in Second Life and conducted research there, issuing consent forms in the virtual world. If virtual ethnography (Ruhleder, 2000) and 'observation' in virtual worlds (Markham, 1998), are slightly problematic, commuting to the field on an urban subway certainly does not 'count'. Wolcott reports that he was surprised to discover that Spradley's (1969) famous study of James Seidid, a Kwakiutl from Alert Bay, British Columbia, was conducted by Spradley as a commuter from Seattle. He visited to do interviews but did not live among the First Canadians. Wolcott, a student of George Spindler's, never doubted that he had to live for a year in a remote village in Alert Bay (Wolcott, 1967) to 'legitimate' himself and his research.

Generally academic credibility as an anthropologist is grounded in the scholar's long-term, resident fieldwork. In the UK in the period before 1970, serious anthropologists had to have done their data collection abroad; British fieldwork did not really 'count'. In America and Canada it was generally acceptable to do the research in the home country if the culture under scrutiny was 'foreign' or 'exotic', such as Wolcott's Kwakiutl village in Alert Bay, but the 'sacred' space of professional anthropology, the learned society, could not be entered if the topic was not deemed sufficiently anthropological. He also reported that when he and his fellow Stanford graduates (trained by Spindler) and those from Columbia (trained by Kimball), applied to join the American Anthropological Association they were all rejected as a group, because their doctorates were in education not anthropology.

For ethnographers in both sociology and anthropology today there is less concern about whether the fieldsite was 'abroad', or 'exotic' or required long-term immersion, but the scholar needs to establish the authenticity of their data collection by vivid evocations of the spaces and places they have observed. So, for example, a passage such as the following is *de rigeur*:

> Sticks beating, hands beating, the rumble of bass drums so bass they sound for all the world like thunder, the rapid-fire crackling of a stick so sharp on a skin so tight it sounds for all the world like gunfire… it's Salvador, Bahia, Brazil, and it's the Afrocentric carnival organisation Olodum rehearsing in Pelourinho (Pelo), the old square in which slaves were pilloried, now a preserved 'historic district', and tourist center. (Browning, 1998: 1)

Browning is aiming to describe the Brazilian city of Salvador de Bahia, the home of the re-Africanised Brazilian carnival, source community of much of the African-Brazilian musical innovation of the past 50 years including Olodum, and the soil in which practitioners believe they can find the roots of *capoeira* the African-Brazilian dance and martial art. The classic ethnographies of how *capoeira* is taught and learnt (Lewis, 1992 and Downey, 2005) were both conducted in Salvador, as was the study by Willson (2010).

The 'serious' ethnographer, of an urban neighbourhood, a school or a university dormitory (Moffat, 1989), has to use his or her written texts to establish that the insights are authentic, because they come from time spent in that location, and that the fieldwork was *work*. In other words, the ethnographic account must not seem to have been written by a *flâneur*. The idea of the *flâneur* spans this chapter, Chapter 6 on movement, and Chapter 4 on time, it is briefly explained here, because it is not widely used in educational research. *The flâneur* was originally a type of man who evolved in Paris after 1800, when the urban revolution was in full swing. He hung about observing the daily life of the city, especially watching the workers at work. The *flâneur* himself did not work, although he might be planning to paint or write novels or poetry or plays. He frequented cafes and restaurants, enjoyed window shopping, and was amused by gossip, changes in fashion, and avant-garde developments in the arts. Elizabeth Wilson (2001) is a useful introduction to the concept, drawing on the original analyses by

Siegfried Kracauer and Walter Benjamin. Crucially the *flâneur* is the onlooker, the watcher, the observer, and his gaze both embodies modernity and objectifies women. British sociology became interested in the idea of the *flâneur* in the 1990s, around speculations about who, or what, could the *flâneur* be in a postmodern city. Tester (1994a, 1994b) edited the collection of papers that put the concept firmly on the sociological agenda. There are three aspects of the sociological concern with the *flâneur* that are relevant to educational ethnography.

Firstly, and relevant in this chapter, and Chapters 4 and 6, is the gender of the *flâneur*. The French term is masculine, and much of the discussion is clearly about men. No respectable woman could have strolled around Paris in 1807 and been seen as a 'fine person' or an artist: such a woman would have been categorised as a whore. Wilson (2001) is adamant that while the *flâneur* takes possession of the city by his gaze, among the objects he possesses are the women he observes. The *flâneur*, for Wilson, is an apparently powerful sociological idea that on examination becomes a concept that excludes women, objectifies women, and a theoretical idea that is a boys' game. This makes the concept of the *flâneur* problematic for educational researchers: male ethnographers need to be careful neither to objectify women themselves nor to adopt the male gaze of *flâneur* informants in the setting of their choice.

However, precisely because the *flâneur* is a man who has infinite time (because he does not work) and spatial freedom (because of the many public spaces in the modern city), so the concept can usefully be deployed to focus on some important aspects of both time and space in educational settings. The researcher can productively search out *flâneurs* in the school, college or other setting, following their gaze with his or her own. Focusing on those who manage not to be constrained by spatial rules or timetables will make those constraints and schedules 'visible' to the researcher. Thirdly, because many educational settings are resolutely modern, rather than postmodern, the concept may be more useful in educational sociology or anthropology in 2014 than it is in current urban sociology or anthropology. In the next chapter the freedom of the *flâneur* from time constraints is the key theme, here the focus is space and place.

The locations where the ethnographer chooses to spend their time determine the view of the setting that is eventually published. If the researcher is male, and chooses to spend time where men or boys are, that has consequences for the way the space is understood. There are criticisms that too much urban ethnography has been done by men on male spaces. Lyn Lofland's (1975) feminist critique of American urban sociology centred on the invisibility of women in the published accounts, partly because the male anthropologists and sociologists had chosen to study street corners and bars, rather than shops, beauty salons, day-nurseries at collection times, or churches. Elizabeth Wilson (1991, 2001) also raised the problems with a whole social science literature of urban ethnographies done by, and about men. There is a good deal of detailed ethnographic research on how, in many cultures, space is strongly gendered, and it is not acceptable for men and women to be in the same spaces. If a person of the 'wrong' sex has to be in the 'wrong' place, there are conventions about clothing, speed and trajectories for movement and direction of gaze, to signal to those watching that there is a clear purpose for the breach. In many educational settings a gender bias may have operated, and in school research there are certainly gendered areas where ethnographers did not go. Lavatories, changing rooms and 'medical' areas are the most obvious. The only time I ever entered a boys' changing room was when some boys came out to find an adult to stop a fight and I was the only adult they could see.

The focus in this chapter is primarily on the way(s) in which places and spaces are an important aspect of the research, because they are part and, usually an important part, of the informants' identity, sense of self and their social world. Savage (2010) criticises many British sociological researchers of the 1950s, 1960s and 1970s for failing to listen when their informants stressed locality as important in their lives. He proposes that the selective inattention occurred because location was not so central for the scholars *or* the research sites were too alien for the investigators to conceive that anyone could feel 'at home' there. This is an error we can all avoid. Of course a place can be wrong for an ethnography. Michael Herzfeld tried to do a study in a village on Rhodes which proved a poor choice (Herzfeld, 1985: 282). For the researcher it can be too dangerous, too dirty, too unhealthy, too emotionally distressing, or even too dull.

When the place and space are right, good ethnographic research is a magic carpet ride for the reader, taking her into strange worlds. When we read about young Mexican-American women at Waretown High (Bettie, 2003) or young French-Algerian women in the Lyceé Lureat (Raissiguier, 1994) or skateboarders learning to survive 'heckling' and 'snaking' in the Franklin (Michigan) Skate Park (Petrone, 2010) or young people being 'reformed' by sailing on Tall Ships (McCulloch, 2007) or novice graffiti painters in Mexico City (Valle and Weiss, 2010), we not only read about learning and teaching, we also experience strange places. One of the important tasks for the researcher is to record salient features of the 'places and spaces' where learning and teaching take place, both formal instruction and informal enculturation, and then write about them so that readers can see them in their mind's eyes.

The quotes from Long (2006) about New Orleans and Browning (1998) about Bahia are both accounts of locations which are more exotic and mythical than the places where the majority of their readers live and work. One danger for the ethnographer is to fall in love with the mythological location themselves. To illustrate that danger, consider a similar evocation of place, this time the Mississippi Delta, where the Blues began.

> On Old Highway 61 in Mississippi, between Lula and Robinsville in the heart of the Delta, stand the remains of a wooden railroad bridge partially submerged in a murky swamp. The air enveloping the bridge is sticky and fetid, thick with the smell of decayed vegetation, and the dark, stagnant water stretches far into the distance, engulfing the trees. To look at the scene is to peer at an eerie, apparently timeless landscape, primordial and untouched by history, the world Noah might have glimpsed after the flood. (Hamilton, 2007: 1)

Hamilton took a photograph of the bridge in 1999, which is reproduced in her book. As a scholar of American history, she was self-consciously reflecting on her own investigative processes. Her aim was to research the many pilgrimages made by white Europeans and Americans in search of 'authentic' Delta Blues. Her aim was to write a detailed scholarly dispassionate, disinterested, account of the pilgrims and their myth-making: for all pilgrims, all seekers, make myths as they go – as Candace Slater (1986, 1990) has shown for pilgrims to the shrine of Padre Cicero in north-east Brazil, and to the tomb of Fray (Brother) Leopoldo in Granada, Spain. Hamilton intended to scrutinise the myths about African-American Delta Blues perpetrated by whites in search of authenticity. As she puts it, her aim was: 'to get a handle on the pilgrim experience' (2007: 1). But she found herself smelling, seeing, feeling, and photographing, the place. She goes on:

> As I made my way south – past the bridge to Clarksdale, Tutwiler, Itta Bena, Parchman, all the places whose names resonate in accounts of blues history – I found myself wholly caught up in that story. (2007: 2)

Once back in London, Hamilton was able to refocus herself, and as she points out:

> every landscape is a work of the mind, shaped by the memories, the obsessions of its observers. (p.3)

To help her readers locate the scholarly processes Hamilton went through, she gives a brief biography. She was at high school in San Diego in 1977, and a fan of the New York Dolls when she first heard the name of Robert Johnson, although she did not listen to any of his

31

recordings (and there are only 29 recorded songs known) until 15 years later. Johnson, the most legendary, mythologised and revered of the Black men whose singing and playing developed into the musical genre known today as the Blues, was born in 1911 and died, in mysterious circumstances but certainly violently, in 1938. The histories of Delta Blues valorise the African-American men whose voices were recorded there by white talent scouts and folklorists. She writes that:

> the Delta Blues has provided a luminous focus for a rewriting of African-American history. (Hamilton, 2007: 7)

Evocation of places, if well done, can provide luminous foci for all ethnographers as Katz (2001, 2002) proposes. This can be easier to achieve for anthropologists who have studied coral islands, painted deserts and emerald forests, and other beautiful settings, or harsh terrains. Atkinson (1996) argued that graphic evocations of the fieldwork site are commonplace in ethnographic accounts, used simultaneously to establish the credibility of the research and researcher; to help the reader imagine the place; *and* to contrast the fieldwork site with locations the reader knows. Atkinson created a fictional arrival story, about a village in western Crete where he, Michael Herzfeld and Greg Eaves collected folk songs in 1967 (reproduced in Atkinson, Delamont and Housley, 2008: 147–148). An educational equivalent occurs in Delamont and Galton (1986) when Ashburton, an English Midlands town is described:

> A new traffic scheme shunts us round the town centre, difficult to get at... A thriving cattle market... a thumping great brewery dominates the town. On the outskirts, the relentless march of the new Ashburton proceeds across the open countryside. It is Saturday afternoon, and migrants from the slums of Birmingham and London are moving treasured belongings into the new villages... (1986: 8–10)

Here, Galton and myself contrasted two schools (for pupils of ages 9–13) that were the focus for the ethnography. Firstly, Gryll Grange, a purpose-built show school opened in 1972, single-storey, with a great deal of glass and ample playing fields. And secondly, in contrast, Guy Mannering was in an old building, and had been several types of school before becoming a mixed 9–13 middle school. We wrote about two other buildings visible in Ashburton.

> In one area of the old city the visitor can see St Bridget's Middle School in a set of Victorian buildings, where notices still hang reading 'St Bridget's Secondary Modern School for Girls', and the twin arches over the school gates onto Cripplegate still bear the legends 'Boys' and 'Girls and Infants' carved in the stone when the building was erected in 1870. Similarly in the very centre of the city

there still stands, where Linenmarket Street meets Cheesemonger Row, the original 1770 building which once housed Josiah Martlet and Obadiah Heep's SPCK elementary school. This was an elementary school at least till 1945, and [in 1977] housed a pre-school play group.

For a British reader the whole history of mass schooling for the working classes was visible on the old buildings, from the Christian charity of the Society for the Promotion of Christian Knowledge (SPCK), through the first compulsory schools of the 1870 Act, on to the schools after the 1944 Act when compulsory secondary education was imposed on the working classes, to the post Plowden Report (1967) Piaget-influenced three tier comprehensive system of lower (5–9 years) middle (9–13 years) and upper (12–18 years) schools. Guy Mannering had been newly built as a girls' Secondary Modern School sometime in the 1950s or early 1960s, moving from the red brick terraces of Balaclava Road to a greener site, but its previous incarnation was clear from the large number of cookery rooms, laundry rooms, needlework rooms, and the contents of the library. Almost all the books were aimed at girls: stories of ballets, histories of fashion, biographies of Elizabeth Fry and Florence Nightingale, novels about girls' boarding schools, ballerinas and ponies. No one, least of all me, who wrote those evocations of Ashburton schools, could possibly think that Gryll Grange and Guy Mannering were 'exotic', or that the description of Ashburton was mesmorising, but they serve the same function for the reader as Long on New Orleans.

As Katz (2001, 2002) pointed out, we can all aim at luminosity. Leaving prosaic Ashburton to return to the mythological landscapes of New Orleans and the Delta, following Long and Hamilton, the novelist Ace Atkins (1998) wrote a detective story about a quest to find some previously unknown late recordings made by Robert Johnson. Atkins's text transports the reader into the same mythical landscape that Hamilton evoked, and on into the realms of magic and African-American religion. In the legends, which are all that survive because there are no written records, Johnson is 'believed' to have sold his soul to the Devil at a crossroads (see de Vos, 2011). It is much more likely that Johnson was a believer in the African-American religion hoodoo (Hurston, 1935), and if he ever invoked any supernatural power at any crossroads he probably called Legbas, the spirit who opens the gate to the spirit world rather than the Christian Satan. This trickster god is common to Haitian voudou, Cuban Santeria and Brazilian Candomblé as well as hoodoo, and all African origin religions in which initiated devotees are possessed by

33

spirits called *orishas* (*orixas* in Brazil). Formal ceremonies in these religions invoke Legbas to open the portal (like a Stargate) to enable the *orichas* to come to our world, and possess their medium(s). In the USA, in the areas to which the African slaves were taken, 'hoodoo' was the secret religion.

Zora Neale Hurston (1935) collected the folklore of hoodoo, whose most famous practitioner was Marie Laveau, the 'witch queen of New Orleans'. She has been the subject of many types of texts: pop songs, three novels, a film, plus plays, a musical and an opera. This century there has been a scholarly text by an anthropologist, Martha Ward (2004) and an investigation by an art historian Carolyn Morrow Long (2006). In the fiction about the Delta and New Orleans – by Atkins and by the great master James Lee Burke (1995), in the myth debunking work of Hamilton, and in Long's scholarly investigations of Marie Laveau – all the authors explore and invoke the landscapes and the places, past and present, either the real or that of the other world(s) of voudou. Good educational ethnographers need to write about spaces and places with the same openness to the actual and the imagined; the real and the mythological; to this world and the otherworlds, but rarely do. It is, for example, as important to understand and explore the cyberworlds important to school pupils as it is to describe the physics lab.

The evocation of place is frequently linked to the history, or mythology, of the site. Reed-Danahay's study of schooling in a French village locates 'her' ethnography in space (up in the Massif Central) and in a *long* time frame (from the Roman empire represented by a 2000 year old temple, through a long period of rural pastoralism, and up to the present contemporary tourism):

> Lavaille is a French commune on the Massif Central... and is nestled in a mountain valley. Most visitors to Lavaille reach it either by train or by highway, both of which wind up into the mountains of Auvergne... There used to be a temple to Mercury on the top of the Puy-de-Dome... the remains of many shepherd huts still stand... now a popular summit for hang-gliding. (Reed-Danahay, 1996: 4–5)

In this way the spatial setting of her school ethnography is located in a deep past, which is contrastive for her American readers. Their school days did not take place in the shadow of a Roman shrine.

We now turn from the importance of place for the ethnographer, and the ways in which it is invoked for readers, to the research on how spaces and places are experienced by students and pupils in formal education, and learners in informal enculturation.

· LEARNING TAKES PLACE IN SPACE

The urban legend about transfer to secondary school which opened the chapter invoked the 'strangeness' of the secondary school. Birleton's building is old enough, or large and grand enough, to have a bell tower, and unknown enough to have a ghost. When children in the UK reach the top of their primary (elementary) schools, and face their transfer to secondary education, many of their 'rational' anxieties and wilder 'irrational' fears are centred on spatial issues. Space and place for pupils and students means exploring their home neighbourhood, the environs of the school or college, the open air spaces of the institution such as the playing fields and the playground, the public spaces of the institution such as the corridors, dining hall, library etc., the more private spaces of the classrooms and lecture halls, and the 'private' areas like lavatories. Given the apprehensions about school transfer it is important to remember that powerful adults, especially policy-makers, generally hold strongly positive ideas about the personal and educational benefits of changing places, leaving familiar localities, meeting strangers. Elite British families are committed to sending their children to boarding schools; and their student children to universities that require them to live away from home. The positive value of 'keeping close' (Barker, 1972; Pugsley, 2004; Mannay, 2013) is a working-class one, as Ball (1994, 2000), Gewirtz, Ball and Bowe (1995), Ball, Maguire and Macrae (2000) showed in their work on school 'choice'.

Spaces and places may be imagined as well as real, remembered as well as current, and stories about 'other worlds' can be powerful in many people's lives. Knapp and Knapp (1976: 248–249) argued that 'the neighbourhood story... gives a certain glamour – some literary resonance – to the otherwise unremarkable places where children grow up'. In that category was a vivid story they collected in one Kansas City school where 'the former principal was buried under the mound at the base of the flagpole, which came right out of her grave' (p. 249). The American folklore scholar Bill Ellis (2001) makes a similar point about an American tradition where every community has some 'scarey' place (such as a murder site, or burnt-out ruin) to which pre-adolescent boys make a journey to 'test' themselves. The River Phoenix film *Stand by Me* centres on such a quest. Its poignancy derives from the contrast between the absent older men in Vietnam, and the self-imposed 'ordeal' of the boys. When there are moral panics about satanic child abuse or similar dangers, these centre on the destination of such quests. So even in conventional settings the ethnographer may

35

find she has been offered entry to some 'other' world. This can be the conventional culture shock of all good ethnography, but might be more than that. The ethnographers who have not only studied modern neopagan witchcraft, but have learnt it and been initiated, have been, themselves, transported to other worlds: they have learnt to go there. This research is explained later in the chapter.

In the ORACLE project (Delamont and Galton, 1986) data from an ethnography of children in three English cities were gathered in their final year in their first schools, and their initial year in the secondary school. Children transferred to six 'big' schools, which were at the heart of the study. At the same period Measor and Woods (1984) were conducting a much more in-depth project following one cohort of children through the whole of their last year in primary school and the following one in Old Town Comprehensive. The spaces and places in and around the transfer schools were acutely relevant for the children, and the themes of boundaries, especially between public and private became prominent. As the children crossed the boundary between 'baby' school and 'big' school they anticipated locational and spatial attractions in their new institutions, as well as expressing anxieties about them.

The bigger secondary schools with specialist facilities and equipment were an attraction for many children, especially when they had been on a visit and seen sports halls and cookery kitchens for themselves. One of the Measor and Woods children said:

> They have got great big sports halls like down the town in the leisure centre, they have got a great big place where you play basketball... (p. 41)

and,

> The good thing was in a big school there is loads of equipment especially metal-work equipment. (p.41)

In the ORACLE project one girl, Bronwen, told the team that on her full day's experience of her new school:

> I liked games because we do the disco's (discus) but we didn't do the disco's at our old school – are (sic) old school didn't have a gym nor a woodwork room or a metalwork room for design.

Equally important were the fears provoked by the new space and place: not often obvious to an adult researcher who had been in and out of many schools. Concerns about the secondary school buildings focused mainly on their size and complexity, because the destination schools were much bigger than their current schools, and were two or more storeys high rather than being single storey. In a later ethnography, conducted in 1999 and 2000 in England and south Wales the same anxieties about the locations of the new schools and their spatial arrangements surfaced. Two of the girls moving told Mellor (2003) that it would be: 'Scary' (Anna), because as Gemma elaborated 'we'll probably get lost'. One 11 year old boy, Henry, generally keen on his imminent move, reflected:

> They'll be hundreds and hundreds of people there, so it'll be a lot different. 'Cos it's a lot bigger it'll take us a long time to find our way around.

Mellor argues that many of the children were worried about the size of their next school, and the new, bigger spaces they must occupy. Particular areas which were thought to be frightening were science labs, showers and lavatories. The Roman Catholic children moving had been shocked to learn, after a day spent at the secondary school as a Year 7 class, that there was a condom machine in the boys' changing rooms. The spaces of the new school offered not only greater complexities, but also a new sexual geography. Showers and lavatories were known to be relative adult-free spaces, so private for pupils, but therefore sites of bodily exposure and potential danger from bullies.

Behind these 'rational' anxieties lies the rich subterranean children's culture. The fears about science and science laboratories are that *live* rats or mice, possibly pregnant, have to be dissected and that, if you are a boy, you may disgrace yourself by fainting. Behind the fears about PE is the myth of the five or ten mile cross country run. Boys worry that if they cannot do the run they will be revealed as wimps to their male peers and the staff and/or be beaten by the teacher.

Changing places is frequently believed to be, in itself, educational or even life-changing. Martha Ward (1999), an anthropologist based in New Orleans, ran a summer school for her students for several years in a castle in the Italian Tirol (high in the Alps where the language is close to German). She has written entertainingly about how the American undergraduates were shocked to discover a world without unlimited hot water, where alcohol and drugs were hard to obtain and not routinely used, and formal manners were needed to interact with the resident owners of the *Schloss*.

School pupils experience their educational buildings rather differently from teachers, partly because their legitimate use of much of the space is restricted by adults. There is research which focuses on space *inside* classrooms, on the corridors, the playground (or yard), the playing fields, and in the neighbourhood round the school. The perception of children and adolescents is often, when investigated, found to be very different from that of adults such as teachers or parents, and from the researcher's. Two American examples will illustrate this.

Raley (2006) studied Pacifica College Prep School, an unusually successful high school in a small city near San Francisco serving a low income community of African-American, Latino and other ethnic minorities. He had chosen it deliberately because it was a successful school: its graduating class went to college. Raley shadowed students inside and outside the school and drove round the neighbourhood listening to them. He found that a core concept in the young people's world view was that Pacifica was a 'safe' place where they could not only be themselves, but they were able to experiment with 'other selves' without being reprimanded, ostracised or punished. To the reader the location, in Bayview, a city with a high murder rate and a reputation as a tough place, sounds very dangerous, but it is understood by the Pacifica students in a complete reversal of the 'majority' view. The students described most of Bayview as safe, and the affluent, low crime city across the motorway as not safe *for them*, just as the new Starbucks, built for commuters en route to Silicon valley, is unsafe *for Bayview adolescents*. 'Safety was a dimension of local cultural structure' (2006: 133) for the ethnic minority adolescents, and one reason for the success of Pacifica was that it was a safe space for them.

38

Seyer-Ochs (2006) conducted an ethnography of a high school in the Fillmore district of San Francisco, which included getting over 250 young people to draw maps of their neighbourhood. The Fillmore is where the poor residents of San Francisco live: indeed the young people Seyer-Ochs worked with called it a ghetto. The Fillmore African-American high school students are a minority at Jefferson High, which is 65 per cent Asian-American (Chinese, Vietnamese and other South East Asians). The different races did not, in practice, attend 'the same' high school: the Asians were mainly in the high achieving Advanced Placement track, the African-Americans mainly in the Special Education and At-Risk tracks. Seyer-Ochs was interested in the lived landscapes of the Fillmore students and she collected their maps to gain that understanding. Key features of the lived landscape for the African-American students are the limits of the territory of the Knock Out Posse (KOP) – a drug-dealing gang. Anthony and Sky, two of her key informants, saw the neighbourhood primarily in terms of where the KOP were and were not active, where the police were, and, indicating the ever present gang violence, where the funeral parlours were. As her fieldwork progressed, Seyer-Ochs learned a great deal about where she could and could not go, depending on who was with her. As a teacher at the high school before shifting to be a researcher she had been entirely ignorant of the different geographies of the catchment area, which the various students had to have expert knowledge of in order to survive.

These are both anthropological projects and the anthropology of education has been particularly good at setting schools in their communities, including the spatial elements and sense of place. Both sociologists and anthropologists have been attentive to the ways in which school children make sense of the places where they are educated. One recent example is that of Gustafson (2009) who observed the use of the Hill School playground (yard) in a Swedish study of spatial strategies outside lessons among children aged 11–13. Two girls, Karin and Isabella, for example, had a location behind the physical education building where they sat together, refusing to mix with anyone else. They had created a private space for themselves in an essentially public area by their self-set boundary. The basketball court was seen as a no-go area by nearly all the pupils of the school except for 'the rowdy sixth-graders' (2009: 13) and the immigrants, who played hip-hop music and spoke 'new Swedish', a youth dialect, there. One space called the 'king pitch' because a game called king is played there, was a mixed-use area of the playground, popular with most children. For Gustafson the use of the outdoor space is a core element in the identity work the children do.

Nigel Thrift's (2006) development of the concept of 'performative architecture' is one way to force ourselves to *think*, as social scientists, about the complex relationships between school or university design and the learning that is planned for those spaces. The Kensington School trilogy – an ethnography of a progressive school in an unusual new building – is, essentially an example of Thrift's core concept researched in the 1970s (Smith and Keith, 1971; Smith, Kleine, Prunty and Dwyer, 1986; Smith, Prunty, Dwyer and Kleine, 1987; and Smith, Dwyer, Prunty and Kleine, 1988). The Kensington trilogy is never cited in current books and papers, but the ways in which the ethnographic team found out how the architecture changed the performances of the teachers and the pupils pre-figured the ideas that Thrift has since explored and elaborated. In a development of Thrift's ideas Stephens, Atkinson and Glasner (2008) analysed a research laboratory and the inter-relationship between its architecture, and the rules about entry and exit, dress, hygiene, and conduct that enabled the products of the laboratory to be labelled as sterile. Central to Thrift's theory, and the empirical work on Kensington School and the research laboratory, is the importance of boundaries. In Kensington the architecture had removed the boundary walls of the traditional classrooms, as part of a deliberate social policy to change pedagogical relations. In the laboratory very strong boundaries were enforced about access to the most sterile areas.

39

The restricted access to the most sterile area ensured that it was a privileged space, essentially the least public part of the whole institution.

There are also key boundaries between the public and the private, the secular and the sacred, the mentionable and the unmentionable, that can cause tensions in school. Some parents in America want very clear boundaries between the school (which represents the State) and the family, and so have fierce objections to schools opening up discussions of the home. In Rose (1988) the focus is parents who had set up evangelical private schools for their children in order to create and maintain an absolute boundary between them and the 'dangerous' influences that they were convinced permeated the American public school. Peshkin's (1986) ethnography of a fundamentalist Christian school discovered equally strong boundaries around the community the institution served (teachers, parents and pupils) that separated it from the rest of the world, including Peshkin, a Jew. Finding where the actors in a setting draw *their* boundaries is a central task of the ethnographer, especially when it is ideas that are being kept in or out. Some American parents want to ensure that the school does not introduce any 'dangerous' or 'subversive' ideas via the children's reading matter, objecting, for example, to books with fantasy, witchcraft, magic or non-Christian ideas in them. Shirley Heath (1982, 1983) found her working-class white families in Roadville, a settlement in the Piedmont Carolinas, did not want their children to learn via materials in which animals talked or wore clothes, or any fairy stories, or anything that was not a simple narrative about ordinary people doing ordinary things.

Space inside the classroom always needs to be studied. Just as Wolcott needed a colleague to query the educational researchers' tendency to equate 'busyness' with 'learning' (see page 12), many aspects of space inside classrooms are only seen as odd or problematic to an outsider. During the ORACLE transfer project (Delamont and Galton, 1986: 160–161) we found that an 'invisible' organisational feature of the two 12–18 schools had spatial consequences. In both Melin Court and Waverly the registers were sex-segregated. All the boys were listed in alphabetical order first, then all the girls. In the practical, technical lessons of woodwork, metalwork, and technical drawing, which took place in specialist rooms with tools and instruments the masters used the register to assign seats which were intended to be 'permanent'. Each seat was numbered and the box of specialist equipment was allocated by that number to the student. At the beginning of the lesson the child in seat seven was required to check the inventory of Box Seven, and report to the teacher if any item were missing. That process was repeated at the end of the lesson. In the classes we saw there were more pupils than desk spaces with boxes. In every one the master assigned seats from the register, so all the boys got seats, but the last six to eight girls did not. The overspill were seated at the sides of the room, without a box of equipment and told that in each class they should see who was absent, and have that child's seat for that week's lesson. The last six to eight girls on the class register therefore faced having to sit next to two different boys each class, and being asked to take responsibility for a different box each week. It is hard to imagine a strategy more calculated to make the 12 year old girls feel conspicuous, unsettled and out of place in those rooms: yet it was unlikely that all the masters intended their seating strategy to have that effect.

Thus far the chapter has been focused primarily on actual physical places and spaces in which the researcher and the informants are co-located. It now turns to imagined locations.

PLACES AND SPACES IN THE MIND'S EYE

Many aspects of pupils' and students' education live on into adulthood as memories of the locations in which the education took place. Peshkin's (1997) phrase 'places of memory' is not only evocative, but also useful. For many contemporary school pupils and students it is not landscapes of memory, but cyberspaces that need to be studied because of their importance in the lives of informants. One of the biggest developments in ethnography over the past 15 years has been 'observation' in cyberspace. Scholars like Markham (1998), Kendall (2000), Miller and Slater who researched the impact of cyberspace for residents of Barbados (2000), Scott (2004, 2007), Williams (2006), and Boellstorff (2008) have joined virtual worlds to study behaviour there, or set up data collection in cyberspace. In educational research there have been projects on using internet resources to provide in-service education, and discussion groups for teachers, but there have not yet been ethnographies of school pupils, students or other learners and teachers in cyberspace.

Given that the peer pressures that are known to exist in American and British schools and colleges in the face-to-face environments are now being aggravated and spread over 365 days of the year by mobile phone use, and on social networking sites, the importance of educational ethnography in the cyberspaces is obvious. The study of a Newark High School cohort by Ortner (2002, 2003) 40 years after they graduated from it, which emphasises how the peer groups (cliques) and the peer cultures still remained vivid in the minds of adults approaching

41

retirement, who only had to live in the culture for a few hours each day, reveals how much more oppressive, or life-enhancing, such cultures can be when they impose themselves in cyberspace as well as real space. (See Chapter 4 and Chapter 7.)

There are two reasons for focusing on how to study 'secret', 'other', or imaginary worlds. Ethnographies have established that all children have a folklore, a set of urban legends, and a repertoire of jokes etc. that is kept secret from teachers, parents and other adults (Fine, 1981; Bauman, 1982; Best, 1983; Measor and Woods 1983, 1984). There are equivalents among students, especially medical students, (Hafferty, 1988, 1991) which are not shared with lecturers. Much of children's behaviour in school, and elements of student culture, are fashioned because of these urban legends, and so the ethnographer needs to be aware of the probability of their existence, and devise strategies to gain access to them.

Much more important is to understand the possibility that pupils or students and their families may have shared, long-held, and powerfully all-encompassing cosmological, religious or magical beliefs that are powerful – far more powerful than anything expounded by teachers or lecturers. This is clear from a study of Hmong Americans by Rosiek (2006) explored in Chapter 11, and from Peshkin's (1997) study of Hopi culture in the Pueblo. These themes re-occur throughout the book, and are only mentioned here to alert the reader.

42

HOW TO... RESEARCH SPACE AND PLACE

One aspect of places and spaces that ethnographies need to focus upon and record is their soundscape(s) (Hall, Lashua and Coffey, 2008). After a project on young people they argued that researchers should pay much greater attention to noise; for including rather than excluding it in the interactions, and for recording interviews by walking with young people through *their* landscape(s) hearing and seeing them during the interviews. Chapter 9 expands this idea. In formal and informal education settings careful attention to space and place always pays off. Record details of the environs of the setting, including methods of approach you do not use yourself. If you go to the fieldsite by car, look to see how the learners get there.

One good question in school fieldwork is whether the teachers do, or would, consider living in the neighbourhood. When inside buildings, detailed notes on the architecture, furnishings, and cleanliness are useful. When observing interaction, mapping where people are standing, sitting, lying, etc. is valuable. And, of course, note where *you* are sitting or standing and check the impact of that location on the data collection. If you always sit in the same place, does that distort the observations? Discovering where teachers go at lunch time, or where truants hang out, is usually a sensible use of the researcher's time. If there are places of memory that matter, informants are usually glad to talk about them. In higher education research the same questions should be posed.

More of a problem is how to get access to secret worlds. If access is granted it is how to write about them ethically, precisely because they are secret. Zora Neale Hurston (1935) underwent the learning experience of apprenticeship to seven African-American religious practitioners in New Orleans, 'the hoodoo capital of America' (p. 183). She was initiated by four of her teachers, although she is careful to say very little about the secret procedures, *except that they are secret*. Since Hurston, other anthropologists have followed in her footsteps, learning about the beliefs and practices of Haitian voudou (McCarthy Brown, 1991), Cuban Santería (Murphy, 1993) and Brazilian Candomblé (Wafer, 1991). In a parallel set of investigations, women who were ethnographers in neopagan feminist witchcraft learnt how to practice that craft, were initiated into its mysteries and discovered how to write credible academic accounts of their work without revealing any secrets (Delamont, 2010). There are lessons for ethnographers given access to the secret worlds of children, or students, or teachers in those case studies: lessons from the learning of secret matters by those researchers for the access, rapport, the data collection, the reflections and the writing up, of educational ethnographies.

43

A LOOK TO THE FUTURE

the research we need

What are the absences in the research on places and spaces? Hanna (1982) pointed out that lavatories in American schools were an adult-free space. Teachers rarely entered them, and researchers do not routinely do so. All educational institutions have spaces where some of the teachers, or learners, or other people, can go and do go, and others where they cannot or do not. It is important. Researchers need to ensure that they map these from the various perspectives of the different actors, and explore as many of them as they can. The research on spaces and places in higher education is seriously lacking. Overall, educational ethnographies have wonderful opportunities to treat space and place much more imaginatively, and in much more theorised ways, using all the portable audio and visual devices now available.

Educational ethnographies have not yet developed research on education in cyberspace: compared to Scott, Williams, Kendall, etc. relatively little research has been done there. Perhaps even more serious is the relative lack of ethnographic work on pupils' and students' uses of social networking sites, and gaming.

four

time and timescapes: 'we were to dance three hours'

Here are these girls from other teams. They're combing their hair, they're in the bleachers, they're eating or reading *Seventeen* magazine. My girls were under the bleachers doing their homework between games. (Peshkin, 2001: 24)

Before I went to Priors' End School in Ledbury in 1996 my friend told me teachers gave out detentions for not writing quickly enough.

These two quotes encapsulate core aspects of time in educational contexts. Peshkin (2001) is an ethnography of an expensive private high school in Arizona he calls Edgewood Academy. In the quote, the female volleyball coach is contrasting the girls in the Edgewood team with those from the other seven squads they were competing against at a tournament. The core point is how they used the time between their matches: the Edgewood pupils maximised their time, by sitting under the bleachers (the seating for spectators) doing their homework. In contrast, the urban legend is about the immediacy of a school task that looms large in everyday life: writing. In a deeper sense it is about the ways in which the child's speed of working is subject to the surveillance, and even the attempted control, of adults. The pupil has little or no choice, and if they do not move at the speed the teacher wants (write quickly enough) it is *their* time that is taken from them (detention). Between those two types of pupil time, 'discretionary' and highly controlled, are the time and timescapes of the chapter. The length of time Zora Neale Hurston (in *Mules and Men,* 1935: 242) had to dance at a hoodoo ceremony in New Orleans – 'we were to dance three hours' – reminds us how time is implicated in all enculturations, not just in formal education.

All learning and teaching, whether formal or informal, is situated in a series of temporal arrangements, individual, familial, organisational, and societal. Yet educational research has not had a scholar focused on time of the theoretical standing of Adam (1990), or the perspicacity of Roth (1963) or Zerubavel (1979, 1981, 2003) – two scholars of time in hospitals. This chapter outlines the main conclusions that the ethnographic work on education allows to be drawn. The 'How to…' section provides practical advice on how to ensure that ethnographic work is properly sensitive to issues of time, and 'A Look to the Future' draws attention to the gaps in the educational research record.

RESEARCHERS' TIME

There are two sets of key issues about time and timescapes in educational settings: the researchers' and the actors'. Most of this chapter is about the micro and macro timings of actors in educational settings rather than researchers' time, but the latter is important. Both have a 'micro' dimension ('what happens *now*?'), and a 'macro' dimension ('where is my career going?'). For the researcher, the micro level would include a decision about where to look in the laboratory or to sit in a staffroom (faculty lounge) in the next five minutes; the macro would be whether to plan to spend the next six, or twelve months doing fieldwork, or even imagining a lifetime of research on *and in* the same culture. Seeger (2008), for example, has worked on the same Brazilian indigenous group, especially their music, for 38 years.

46

One recurrent finding of ethnographic research in educational settings is that, to the pupils and the teachers, we investigators look like *flâneurs*. We hang around watching. We are not working, we have no schedule, we are floaters on the surface of the busy institution. Our ethnographic presence is endlessly puzzling to the actors. What *are* we doing? What are we *writing*? Why don't we go away? The person who is there, but has no known role, is an equivalent of the *flâneur*. Keiko Ikeda (1998) did an ethnography of American high school reunions. She attended eight in the Champaign-Urbana area, as well as the meetings of the organising committees, and did interviews. She says that where the older people (30 years or more out of school) introduced her formally as a researcher, younger people did not. She also commented that:

> A lot of people were puzzled by my presence and wondered whether there had been a Japanese American in their class whom they could not recognise. (Ikeda, 1998: 30)

Some thought she was a journalist from the local paper because of her notebook and camera. While she does not use the concept, it is clear that her presence at those gatherings had equivalences to the classic *flâneur* in the cityscape.

The type of education being studied determines the researcher's time to a high degree.

Those studying boarding schools have *de facto* chosen to spend longer periods of the day in the setting, seeing life in the institution after lessons are over (King, 1967). Within school hours, however defined, good ethnographers think carefully about sampling by time, so that all the school day, and week, is covered. If the focus is the pupils', or staffs', experience of the place, then this ensures that it is fully covered. Organising researcher time in higher education is more complex: Moffat (1989) and Sabin (2007) lived in dorms (in UK terms, a hall of residence) to focus on students' lives outside class. That is very unlike Phillips (1982) on law students, which focused on their class time, not their social lives. There is no right or wrong here, but the researcher's time needs to be spent in ways driven by the research questions, and written up accordingly.

Most educational researchers will have some ideas before fieldwork about the likely official schedules of education institutions. Research in other contexts can throw up very unfamiliar timescapes, and members' taken for granted concepts of lifecycles and enculturations can be very 'strange'. One such setting was studied by Salz (1998). He spent 16 years studying a prominent theatrical family, the Sengoro Shigeyama in Kyoto, who have been famous actors in *No* and *Kyogen* (two traditional forms of serious and funny plays) for 600 years. In 1998 the head of the family (the *iemoto*) was the 25th generation to be a star. By observation of the family's contemporary work, and oral history interviews with two key informants – the leading actor Sengoro and his brother Sennojo – Salz (1998: 88 (Table 1)) could reconstruct male socialisation going back a century. Few educational researchers are lucky enough to be able to reconstruct enculturation for even 30 years and very few educational systems have been as stable over such a long period. However, all ethnographers can collect data on times past, especially focused on the stages of the pupil and the teacher career, and what is deemed age-appropriate behaviour, which can provide good contrasts with what can be seen today, or help the understanding of continuities. It is always important to focus on participants' time and timescapes, and how they understand them.

PARTICIPANTS' TIME AND TIMESCAPES

The discussion of time and the lives of pupils and teachers moves from rites of passage or, as Glaser and Strauss (1967) termed them sociologically, status passages, through what is considered 'normal', acceptable and 'impossible' for people of various ages across different cultures, and then focuses on time inside and outside education institutions.

rites of passage

When people move through life, their status changes. Being a student is a status passage from being a school pupil to being a graduate. If there is a ritual to mark a status passage the anthropological term 'rite of passage' is useful. The graduation ceremony is a secular rite of passage, a church wedding is a religious one. Children, adolescents, and adults in many cultures experience status passage, and some have rites of passage as they move through the life course. One such series, from a particularly specialised, and to British and American *educational* researchers, an exotic enculturation, is lovingly chronicled in the work of Salz (1998) on an all-male Japanese theatrical dynasty, and in particular how the boys are socialised, and proceed through the stages of their acting careers.

Different cultures have very different ideas about what children can or cannot be taught to do at particular ages. *No* and *Kyogen* acting involve a lifetime of training, and specific skills and practices are acquired at particular ages. In *Kyogen* subculture boys are taught formal movements, songs, dances, speeches and performances from a very early age. Each stage is marked by the debut in a significant role, which is age-related and age-appropriate. A brief summary of the key public performances appropriate to each age is as follows. The child (aged 3–5) performs as a boy mimicking an old man, and then as a monkey. For a teenager of 14 or 15 years there are two roles in *No* plays, which require secret learning and solo performance. Around aged 20 the young actor is trained for, and then performs (as an equivalent of 'finals' and graduation from university), an appearance as an adult, in the role of a Fox who has been magically transformed into a Priest (for the long first act) and then back into a Fox for the second act. Other traditional plays with demanding roles for a man of 25 to 30 and for an old man are also career stages. At each age, the actor has to learn to sing, dance and act in specific traditional ways, to perform in particular roles in hallowed plays. Sennojo was Salz's key informant and collaborator. He began acting in public in 1926 at two years and seven months, taught by his grandfather. This stage (the *hivaki*: opening) is treated by the family as particularly precious status passage. In 1967 four generations of the men from the family played the four roles together: Lord, Servant, Animal Trainer and Monkey. That year, the Monkey was played by Masakuri Shigeyama, his father played the servant, his grandfather, Sengoro, acted the Lord, and his great grandfather the Trainer.

That world seems entirely detached from British, or American, schooling. However, treating the accounts of children about their status passages as seriously as Salz does the accounts of his Japanese actors, yields valuable insights applicable to learners in any education system. Ideas about when it is appropriate for adults to take up particular educational roles also vary from culture to culture, and have varied over time. In the USA today it is not unusual for an adult of 50 not to have a *tenured* academic post (e.g. Shumar, 1997; Poulos, 2010). Yet when the University of Chicago began in 1894, Albion Small was head of sociology at 28, and the President, William Rainey Harper, was 34. In the UK school system there has been research on transfer (i.e. status passage) from home to pre-school; from home or pre-school to school; from primary to secondary school; and from school into 'work'. There is very little published on transfer to university or other higher education, and no studies of graduation from higher education. In the USA there are more formal ceremonies than in the UK, such as graduation from junior high and high school. The pupil or student perspective on these transfers or status passages is threaded through this book, because it relates to time, space, bodies, movements and narratives. Here the main point is that the ages at which it is considered appropriate for children to be able to do certain things, which varies across cultures, determines when transfers are made and what happens differently at the next stage, just as, in the Japanese theatrical tradition, the boy was expected to be able to perform specific roles at specific ages.

In the work on British primary to secondary transfer which has been conducted for 40 years, continuities in the children's perspectives are readily apparent. David Mellor and I (Mellor and Delamont, 2011) compare transfer studies from the 1970s and the 2000s. All the projects found that many of the children felt they were outgrowing the curricula, social environment, and physical facilities of their current school, and it was appropriate to move to a new arena. To quote a child in Bryan's (1980) study: 'I know why we have to change, because we need more knowledge, 12 is the right age'. Here an eleven year old crystallises his own sense of mental and physical maturity. In 2003 some children also locate their own individual trajectory through time with a family timescape. One boy, George, going to a Boys' Grammar School, told Mellor: 'My dad and my granddad have been there, so I want to follow them and keep the line going.' That is not a 600 year history of a family and an enculturation, but it is a 60 year one. Ethnographers need to keep an ear open for such continuities.

The chapter now focuses on the related topic of different cultural conceptualisations of what people of various ages can, and cannot do, before considering the control of pupils' and students' time by educational institutions (and perhaps their parents in the case of younger pupils). It then moves on to time in the lives of teachers and university staff.

49

age appropriate?

There is no consensus across cultures about what activities are appropriate or inappropriate for humans at different ages; nor about how many hours a year are essential or desirable for formal education. Each society with formal education has its own model of the best use of children's time, and their capabilities. For the pupils, their own chronological age and physical size run alongside the timescapes of the school, the lesson, the day, the week, the school year, and their time in that school. Anderson-Levitt (1996) draws a sharp contrast between the conceptions of time embedded in children's 'progress' that are normal in French and American schools, although they have three features in common:

1. Batch rather than individual teaching.
2. A compulsory starting age for school.
3. Graded instruction.

Children in both countries are sorted by chronological age and 'mental age', measured in months, leading to judgements of children being 'advanced' and 'mature' or 'backward' and 'babyish'.

Anderson-Levitt's ethnography, conducted in Villefleurie (her pseudonym for a medium-sized city in central France) included detailed work in three reception classes (in USA terms First Grade). French children are legally required to start their first year of schooling in the calendar year in which they will turn six. That is, on 1 January, all children who will be six before the following 31 December must be prepared to start school on 1 September. On the opening day of the school year, the youngest children are five years nine months, and the oldest are six years and nine months. However, parents can request that their children start school a year early, at four years and nine months. In the three classes which Anderson-Levitt studied, it was mainly professionals who had made the request successfully. Promotion to the next grade is based on success at reading, so in September 1978 she found the oldest child in the bottom form was seven years and six months old, and the youngest four years ten months. The teachers said they expected the older children in their reception class (the January children who are nearly seven) to be more 'teachable' than the December children (who are not yet six), but because they also expected the children from the higher social classes to be more gifted, *in fact* the specific children they named as the best were the youngest ones, who had entered at four years nine months from professional homes. The oldest children were repeating the year, and so were already 'marked by failure' (Anderson-Levitt, 1996: 59).

who controls time?

One striking feature of formal educational institutions is that the adults, and especially the management, control the *time* of the pupils or students, although they may not control their *timescapes*. If the researcher appears to the teachers and pupils to be a *flâneur*, it is because the time of most children in school is heavily scheduled, leaving few opportunities for them to observe, reflect or be creative. School teachers are also tightly scheduled and their time surveilled by a variety of external authorities and pressures.

Arnetha Ball (2002: 72) (in a literature review on classroom talk) points out that American pupils spend six or seven hours per school day over 12 years on school premises, including 7000 hours in classrooms. However, it would be wrong to treat Ball's summary as universal even for Americans, far less for the rest of the world. In the USA, some pupils face a far longer 'school' day. As Deyhle (1998) points out, there are Navaho children who have a bus ride of four hours to school, and four hours back again (1998: 45). Pupils who face such a long bus ride would normally be boarded at their school during the week (King, 1967; Peshkin, 1997), but there are young people forced to travel for two hours each way to attend school every day. The American school day is much shorter than those in most comparable countries, as is the school year. A pupil in Japan or France spends more time in school, and, if remotely academic, many more hours doing school work outside the school building. There are very different cultural assumptions about how a student or pupil of any particular age should spend their day, their week, their year. America has shorter school days, less homework, and more days of vacation than those in many other countries, partly because of the assumption that adolescents will have paid work (and that many of their teachers will also hold second jobs).

Orellana and Thorne (1998) drew on Zerubavel's ideas of the 'politics of time' whilst studying one school system (Los Angeles) which had teachers and pupils divided into three different cohorts who attended school on different cycles. The schools were open all the year round, with different patterns of terms and vacations. This had enormous consequences for the families, who found the patterns confusing, could have children allocated to different cohorts and had to make complicated arrangements for out of school child care. The legal school year in the USA is 180 days, but Los Angeles had gained approval to shorten that to 176 days to fit the three cohort pattern, making up the time by adding an extra 40 minutes to the school day.

Karweit (1981) found that the length of the school year in the USA varied from one state to another between 175 and 184 days. However, in

51

practice schools were not open on all those days because of weather conditions, teacher strikes, and financial or fuel shortages. Even in one US state the school day varied a good deal. In Maryland, Karweit reported the length of the elementary school day varied from 240 to 410 minutes, and the high school day from 300 to 375 minutes. In England, Hilsum and Cane (1971) found that across one Local Education Authority the primary school day varied from 375 minutes to 430 minutes. A child at the latter received effectively four more weeks of schooling every year from age 7 to age 11. Such discrepancies do not necessarily mean that the day is full of equally intensive learning: it could be that the shorter school day has more academic work going on. In the UK, the Scottish school year (and that of Leicestershire) are different from most of England and in Wales. Scotland finishes its school year earlier in the summer, and starts the autumn term in early August. Elite private schools have shorter terms than state schools, just as Oxbridge only offers undergraduate lectures and classes for 24 weeks a year, while most universities expect students to be present for 30 weeks, or more.

It is useful to focus on the annual, termly, weekly, and daily patterns of school life. Inside any school there is a cycle. At the Lutavitcher (Orthodox Jewish) School in Melbourne studied by Bullivant (1978) there was the 'normal' Australian cycle of terms, tests, exams and speech night. However, the religious cycle was much more important, moving through *Purim*, Passover, *Tammuz*, *Rosh Hashanah*, *Yom Kippur*, *Succos* and *Simchas Torch*. Bullivant, a non-Jew, was surprised by the impact of Jewish festivals, and commented that:

> on the day before Rosh Hashanah work is clearly impossible. In any case lessons finish at 1 p.m. (Bullivant, 1978: 174)

Burnett (1969) analysed the cycle of an American high school, with Halloween, Thanksgiving, Valentine's Day, Homecoming, Class Picnic and the Junior Prom as its highlights. In Gibson's (1988) study of Punjabi Sikhs in a California high school, the *lack* of involvement with that 'social' cycle of 'American' festivals marked out the Sikhs as 'poorly integrated' in the eyes of the staff and fellow students. In many American high schools the annual cycle of the sports fixtures (gridiron, basketball or perhaps track athletics) is more important than any academic scheduling (Bissinger, 1990). The annual cycle of UK schools is based on an agricultural year, but the three term year is relatively modern. Dorothea Beale (1904) introduced three terms as one of her reforms at Cheltenham Ladies College after 1858 and it was then widely copied.

Parallel to the schedules organised, or not organised, for children, there are differences in the temporal dimensions of teaching in schools and higher education between nations, between sectors in the same nation (e.g. between government and private schools) that the researcher needs to understand. Darmanin (1990) found that children in Maltese state schools spent more time praying than children in the private schools run by the Roman Catholic Church, who spent more time on lessons.

Staff management of classes relates to two aspects of *pupil* time – the association of speed with ability and the ways in which time is used to mark work from 'pleasure' (or at least non-work). For pupils, tasks which have to be finished are work, not leisure or pleasure. For staff and students, the speed at which tasks are completed is a proxy for ability.

Ball, Hull, Skelton and Tudor (1984) focused on time, in a paper called 'the tyranny of the "devil's mill"'. For teachers there are pressures to get their classes through each lesson, week, term, and year, and inside each class to ensure that no one gets too far behind *or ahead*. The more academic the school the more likely the teacher is to feel pressured to 'complete' the work. Wolcott's (1967) account of teaching Kwakiutl children on an island off British Columbia stressed that they were deprived because no teacher ever operated with serious attention to a programme of work. The devastating criticism of the shoddy education provided to the Kwakiutl children is exemplified by the *lack* of managerial and pedagogic attention to the 'devil's mill'. There was no continuity of teachers, none of the staff posted there followed the Canadian education scheduling with any urgency or consistency. No child had a steady progression through a consistent curriculum. The temporal constraints and opportunities of a Vancouver school were never present on the island. King (1967) reported exactly the same lack of 'urgency' in the teaching at Mopass, the Native Canadian School he studied. It was no wonder that the achievements of the children were so low.

Inside classrooms we have over 50 years of research on how the time is spent, and it is primarily teacher-centred and the main role for the pupil is, theoretically, to listen. One citation will cover this. Arnetha Ball (2002: 71) is a summary of research on the temporal elements of US schooling, and the percentages of its discourse and activities that are teacher talk and whole-class tasks. Two-thirds of all American class time is spent on teacher-centred activities, such as: taking tests; discussing written assignments; preparation for, and clear up after, assignments, lecturing, explaining and reading aloud. Half of the time spent in classrooms is teacher talk. In the elementary school, two-thirds of the time is spent on whole-class activities, and three-quarters of the time in high-school classes is whole-class teaching in lock step. Those figures are remarkably constant over a century and show no change since classroom research began in the 1950s. Ball's conclusions were, essentially, similar to those reached by Flanders (1970) three decades before.

Once the focus switches from the inside of the classroom to life outside school, the data are much sparser, and receive more attention here. One aspect of pupil time is the division between school and non-school. Pupils whose parents have no clear division between work and home respond differently to homework from those who have experienced work as a non-home phenomenon, for whom the home is a place of leisure. Pupils in households where no one is in scheduled paid employment are the least likely to be able to 'manage' either punctual school attendance or homework. Educational researchers very rarely do ethnography in homes, and especially in the parental homes of higher education students. When such research is conducted, differences of class and race are often vividly 'exposed', as in the work of Heath (1982, 1983). Class differences in the use(s) of children's time were vivid in Lareau's (2003) unusual ethnography of 12 families in the USA. The families were part of a larger project on 88 children, initially recruited at the age of seven to eight, in an urban and a suburban school, that served middle-class, working-class and very poor families. The researchers 'followed' the children: watching television, in church, in the street, at organised activities, and included at least one overnight stay in their home. They found two ways in which the childhoods and schooldays of middle-class families (both Anglo and African-American) differed from the working-class families. One was about the child's sense of agency, illustrated by a middle-class, African-American boy, Alexander Williams, aged ten, on the way to see his paediatrician. In the car, Alexander's mother gets him to focus on what he wants to ask the doctor when they get to the appointment. Laureau (2003: 122–127) shows how Alexander has a sense of agency which is mobilised in his discussions with 'his' doctor.

More relevant to this chapter is the amount of organisation and control over children's movements and time exercised in different social classes. Lareau is clear that children learn very different skills between the ages of five and 15 because of the ways in which their time is, or is not, controlled by adults, and that these skills are closely related to, for example, being able to get part-time work when in high school. A child who has learnt to be organised by many different adults (piano teacher, swimming coach, soccer referees, etc.) is much more 'employable' at 15 than one who has spent their childhood only with family and peer group. The middle-class families organised their children's time outside school, filling it with sport, music, dance, drama, youth groups (e.g. Scouts) and other adult-led, scheduled, rule governed, activities. One boy, Garrett Tallinger, did soccer, swimming, baseball, saxaphone and piano. As one of three sons, Garrett's schedule is juggled with those of the other two boys, and the parents are ceaselessly driving them to and from classes, matches, recitals and more practices. They have little or no unsupervised, unstructured time, and, Lareau reported, were often exhausted. In contrast, the working-class children had control over their own time. So she contrasts Garrett with an African-American boy, Tyrec Taylor. His out of school time was all spent with a group of friends in his neighbourhood, organising their own time, space and norms of peer interaction. Tyrec's mother has rules, but school, a summer play scheme, and church are the only adult-scheduled activities in his life.

The research on digital technologies outside school has not yet included ethnographic studies in the home: most of the data are self-reports by young people. One American study found class gaps in the amount of time young people were spending with digital technologies, so that working-class children spent 90 minutes more per day exposed to media than middle-class ones. Victoria Rideout, the author, concluded that digital technologies were not 'closing the achievement gap' but were 'widening the time-wasting gap' (*The New York Times*, 10/6/2012). We need detailed ethnographic studies such as Lareau's to see exactly what is happening.

Lareau's work got wide exposure to the general public because it was showcased in Gladwell's (2009) bestseller about success, *Outliers*. He gave her seven pages of respectful summary, something most educational researchers never get. The research that Gladwell summarised which received even more press coverage was also about time. He drew on a paper by Ericsson, Krampe and Tesch-Romer (1993) about violin students at the Berlin Academy of Music. All of these students had started the violin around the age of five, and all played well enough at 19 to get into the elite college. The staff assessed the students' likely careers as (1) competent players who would not have professional careers but were going to be music teachers in schools; (2) students who were good and might be professional musicians; and (3) the stars, who were expected to be soloists, even world-class soloists. All the students were asked to report on how many hours per week they had practised the violin since their first lesson. They all reported that, as children between five and eight, when their time was most controlled, they had practised for two to three hours each week. What the students reported about practise began to diverge when recalling their lives from the age of eight or so onwards. The 'star' students said that they had begun to practise six hours a week at nine, eight hours at 12, 16 hours by aged 14, and by the time of the research, they did 30 hours of practice every week. Gladwell summarises the data by totalling the practice hours across

12 years: the prospective teachers had practised for 'just over 4000 hours'; the good students for 8000 hours, and the 'elite performers had each totalled 10,000 hours of practice' (2009: 39). The increased proficiency produced by the practice would create a virtuous circle for the young violinist, encouraging more practice.

The implications of this for school ethnography need to be carefully considered. Turning from the pupil or student to the teachers, for the educational researcher who is studying inside a school or university, the long cycle of the teacher's career (see Chapter 5) and the pressures of managing the daily schedule are the two most researched temporal topics. Ball and his colleagues (1984) focused on how British teachers are caught between the 'curriculum time' of the syllabus to be covered, the 'biological' or 'motivational' time of the pupils' working speeds, and the calendar of the school. These operate differently in various types of class:

> With 'good classes' the problems of curriculum knowledge predominate, 'getting through the syllabus', time usually passes too quickly; with 'poorer classes' the problems of social time predominate, 'getting through the lesson', time usually passes too slowly. (Ball et al., 1984: 56)

Matching the work expected against what the class can complete in the lesson is a skill. Rutter et al. (1979) found that, in the poorly performing secondary schools, teachers were frequently late for their classes and time in the lessons was 'wasted' handing out pencils, rulers, exercise books and so on and then collecting them in at the end. Thus in the schools where teaching and learning time were most needed, the pupils got less instruction and worked shorter hours. This finding from a large project was vividly present in the six schools studied during the ORACLE Project (Delamont and Galton, 1986). We recorded examples of teachers regularly arriving late, particularly in the streamed schools when the class was a low ability one. In the schools with mixed ability classes there was no pattern of teacher lateness. In the streamed schools, teachers were prompt when due to face a 'high' group, and late when scheduled for a 'low' class. So in one day at Kenilworth (a Bridgehampton middle school) a low band first year group experienced Mr Pardoe being nine minutes late for a science lesson, and Mr Gordon ten minutes late for English. One boy told the researcher that Mr Pardoe had been ten minutes late for their previous science class. Another low ability class had both an RE and a geography lesson start ten minutes later than scheduled (Delamont and Galton, 1980: 149). The 11 year olds who most needed to be learning in a structured environment, because they were the least likely to start work in the absence of the teacher, were actually getting less teaching, day in and day out.

The same phenomenon was even more apparent in the Welsh schools where I studied the mainstreaming of pupils with learning difficulties (Delamont and Atkinson, 1995: 180–186). At all the comprehensive schools in the project, teachers started the remedial classes late and finished them early, distributed equipment at the beginnings and collected it at the ends, and gave the children time off academic work to chat. The pupils were regularly late for class, and begged to stop work and to leave early, as well as requesting lavatory visits throughout classes. Organisational delays, and disruptions for special occasions such as Saint's days in the Roman Catholic comprehensives, were accentuated in the special classes we observed, and in ordinary classes attended by our target pupils and low ability children from the mainstream such as 'B Track PE' or 'Non-Exam Track Woodwork', by late starts, early finishes, and delays for equipping pupils with pens, pencils, rulers and erasers. A typical lesson observed at Burminster, for example, when Mrs Hislop was planning to do part of an exam syllabus with the fourth year, opened in the following way:

9.15 Arrive with the teacher. She gives out pencils and rulers to those in need. Another teacher comes in and they all stand... He leaves...

9.20 Begins lesson on law and order.

The bell for the end of this double humanities lesson was scheduled for 10.20, but at:

10.16 The teacher tells them that they can finish this next week. The class begins to pack up.

Thus both ends of this lesson were curtailed.

Similar late starts and early finishes were commonly observed in all nine schools. For example at Fosse, when following Lallage, we noted:

9.15 Registration in the class's home base.

9.25 Class go to assembly.

9.40 Class arrive at Room 2 for RE with Mr Scaife. Their exercise books are given out. Then Lallage is asked to give out the text books. Then Mr Scaife asked 'hands up who needs pencils' and gives a pencil to all those who raise their hands.

9.45 Mr Scaife begins an oral revision of what they have learnt about Moses so far...

At 10.16 Mr Scaife was called away to the telephone, and at 10.21 the class was interrupted by an ESL teacher who collected a Bangladeshi girl and took her away for her individual 'English as a second language' lesson. At 10.48 Mr Scaife told the class they need only do 'two minutes' more work and could then have 'five minutes to yourself'. The time from 10.50 until the bell at 10.55 was spent collecting in all the pencils, rulers, erasers, felt pens, tracing paper, text books, worksheets and exercise books issued during the double period, and then the pupils were allowed to put on their coats, collect their bags, and talk among themselves.

Pupils we were following were frequently allowed to have free time at the ends of lessons as a reward. Sometimes they were allowed to leave the room and go early to lunch, break, or their homes. For example at Clipperstone, a class of boys whose PE had already been curtailed, had English with their form master later in the day, and he let them leave the school ten minutes before the bell went. The relaxed attitude to time-keeping and the large amount of time spent giving out and collecting equipment seemed to be further exploited by the pupils themselves. They were equally likely to arrive late and try to leave early. At Artinswell, for example, in Mrs Scudder's class:

> 10.30 The three boys are getting ready to leave the room.
>
> 'The bell's gone, Miss' they say.
>
> 'It has not gone'
>
> 'Has gone, Miss'
>
> They start to open the door and push through it. Mrs Scudder says angrily
>
> 'Since when have you left this classroom without permission? The rest of the pupils have now joined the others by the door, and as the bell finally goes; they all scramble out of the door.

Similarly at Gorston Hall in a fourth year maths class:

> At 2.21 Mr Bullivant says 'finish off the sum you're on'. Lots of pupils immediately stand up and carry their books out to the front. They put their coats on and gather by the door. Someone opens it and starts to leave. Mr Bullivant goes over, and shuts the door. At 2.25 the buzzer goes and they are allowed to leave.

During our observations we found that pupils' lateness was a recurrent problem for the staff. For example at Rushfield in Mrs Lavater's class:

> Darcy, Monoj and Krishan are all late. Mrs Lavater asks those present if Darcy is in school. Fatima says Darcy was in assembly, Llewellyn calls out that Fatima herself was not in assembly.
>
> Mrs Lavater says, scornfully 'Fatima goes to *Muslim* assembly – so does Darcy' (i.e. not the Christian assembly Llewellyn attends).
>
> Darcy arrives, and then asks if he can go the lavatory.

Target pupils and their classmates were frequently late for class in all the schools. At Sharway Downs one morning, observation started in the second year special class:

9.00 Bell. I go up to 2nd year form room. Only 5 boys and 2 girls are there on time. Mr Whaddon starts to take the register. One girl says that Adriana is in the building. Boys say that Trefor isn't and that he is going to be expelled.

9.06 Clodagh and Lysette arrive.

9.10 The bell goes for assembly, as Adriana arrives in the room (she seems to have been crying). We go to assembly.

At Fosse School even when all the pupils were present, teaching could not begin immediately. Mrs Barralty confiscated Rodney's jewellery, and gave out pens, pencils and rulers to those who did not have them. Then Eirlys was sent to the Secretary's office with the register, and when she returned, she was asked to hand out a worksheet. Then Mrs Barralty said:

'Anyone chewing – you know the rule in this class. Get rid of it now, please'. Giles goes out to the bin and spits out something. At 2.01 Mrs Barralty begins to explain the task.

At Cynllaith School the remedial form were going to go on a trip, and one boy, Chris, told the observer he could not go. Mr Wymondham told him to explain why he could not, and Chris grinning says he is going to Tenerife for a month. Mr Wymondham says he has offered to go along as a tutor: 'One hour English with you, and the rest debauchery by myself!' Chris had learning difficulties, and a month in Tenerife, in school term, was inconceivable for a secondary pupil of high ability.

In the late 1970s and early 1980s there was a wave of enthusiasm in American educational research for measuring how much of a pupil's classroom life was focused on academic work (Denham and Lieberman, 1980). Observers measured 'time on task', and argued that the more effective teachers were those who maximised the childrens' engagement. There was a data collection problem, in that the observers coded which children appeared to be busy because it is not feasible to measure the focus of their attention. So a child staring out of the window was coded as 'off task' and one writing as 'on task', when the former could have been working out a spelling or doing mental arithmetic and the latter writing 'Miss Gomez smells bad' on a note to a friend. As critics said at the time, this research confused busyness with learning, and potentially disregarded children's thinking by prioritising 'doing'. The research went out of fashion, and is now forgotten. However, the idea behind it was important, and ethnographers do well to concentrate on how time is used by all the participants in a setting, whether in a formal lesson or in non-formal context, such as people practising break-dancing in the street.

For those 'teaching' in formal institutions there can be markedly different amounts of time actually spent instructing anyone. In the UK as a school teacher or university lecturer gets more experienced it is common for their contact hours with pupils or students to decline. Similarly in Greece, in the State schools, the longer a teacher has served, the fewer hours they have to work; however, that 'free' time is usually spent teaching in a private school because salaries are too low to live on. In general in the UK, the older the client group being taught, and the more prestigious the institution, the more control over scheduling and the smaller the 'class' becomes. At one extreme the PhD supervision or the Oxbridge one-to-one tutorial scheduled by the teacher for her convenience; at the other the primary teacher with a timetable largely imposed on her from above, with compulsory elements such as the 'literacy hour', and so on. The senior management probably have longer planning horizons than classroom teachers do. The school time of adults who are not classroom teachers may be very different. The cleaners and the caretakers (janitors) work very different hours. The office staff have more clearly defined 'working hours', with less overspill covering voluntary activities such as sports coaching or taking pupils on trips (see Casanova, 1991).

60

Detailed ethnographic attention to time in higher education is sparse, and needs to be done across all the disciplines. The university student's experience of time is dependent on the subject they are studying. Science, technology, engineering and medical courses (STEM) typically involve much more intensive work in the university: more lectures, more workshops working on problems, and more hours in the laboratory or at the field station. Students studying humanities and social sciences routinely have fewer hours timetabled for formal classes, but are expected to cover far more on their own, probably in their 'own' space.

Staff timetables are similar. A scientist spends longer at the university because the laboratory is essential to the research, while a philosopher can do philosophy in her garden. Jokes frequently convey illuminating messages about settings and actors, as Chapter 9 shows. The most frequently told joke about the physicist or engineer turns on precisely that point. In a typical version three male academics are asked whether it is better to have a wife or a mistress. The law lecturer says a wife, the creative writing teacher says a mistress, but the physicist (or engineer) says 'Both'. Asked to explain he says: 'Each of them thinks you are with the other woman and you can spend all your time in the lab'. The long hours that have to be spent on university premises are one reason that STEM careers are harder to fit in alongside day care and school hours than the humanities or social science career that can sometimes be carried forward off the premises. Another big distinction that cuts across the STEM versus non-STEM disciplinary divide is the physical locations where data are gathered. A laboratory subject may require long hours on the university premises. Non-laboratory research, such as collection of soil samples, or drawing up cores from the seabed, or ethnography of old people's homes is research that cannot be done in the university. It involves the academic leaving the university for periods of time, mostly in the so-called 'holidays'. It is in the 'vacation', that journalists love to portray as holiday, that the laboratory scientist puts in the really long uninterrupted hours, and other scholars can be away doing fieldwork, or visits to archives, or on a dig or in an art collection.

The ethnographic research on academics in the UK is sparse, and robust data on how the time elements of their lives have, or have not changed over 30 years are not available. There is a good deal of rhetorical discussion of audit cultures and increasing pressure on time but few data. It is possible that the rhetorical material is a classic example of a threnody for a lost golden age, a theme explored in Chapter 5.

HOW TO... RESEARCH TIME AND TIMESCAPES

There is a strong tendency for the researcher's timeframe to be much shorter than that of the participants'. The researcher may have a timetable if on a funded project or be working for a higher degree and will have plans to leave, analyse the data, and publish. The ethnographer may spend a few weeks or months in a setting which has existed for many years before her arrival and will continue for many years afterwards. Using older studies, to frame research questions, makes sense. There are several important things to bear in mind about how to do ethnography around the theme of time. If the field setting operates 24 hours a day, seven days a week, 52 weeks a year, then the ethnographer needs to think hard about how to sample what happens over the 24 hours, over the week, over the seasons, over the year. Most educational research has been done in day schools, so the fieldwork has been done only in the school day, between Monday and Friday, during school terms. It is rare to focus on how pupils, or teachers, use their time off the premises, or on what happens on the premises outside the normal 'school day'. These are illuminating things to focus on. Equally, grasping the time 'frames' of the different actors in a setting is a useful way of fighting familiarity. Other cultures may frame the year, the week, the 'child' differently.

A LOOK TO THE FUTURE

what we do not yet know

What are the absences in the research on time and timescapes? Researchers often over-estimate the amount of social change: assuming that 'everything' must be different, and that older studies are now unimportant, because they capture a world we have lost. The past is thought to be a foreign country. Few studies give much sense of the past as it lived by the current actors. The most urgent task at the time of writing is to get an ethnographic grasp of time spent in cyberspace by learners and teachers in both compulsory and voluntary enculturations. Enthusiasts for, for example, a martial art such as *savate* may be spending more time watching it in cyberspace than actually changing their own bodies, but we simply do not know for whom that is true, and what the consequences are. The avatar ethnographer is urgently needed in the *dojos* of cyberspace.

five

memories and memorials: a diploma and a chevrolet

Newark, New Jersey, the originary site of this study, is a commercial and port city across the Hudson River from New York City. In the 1950s it had a population of about 500,000… It was very mixed in racial and ethnic terms…Weequahic became known as a predominantly Jewish neighbourhood. The most famous graduate of Weequahic High School is Philip Roth. (Ortner, 2003: 2–3)

Before I went to Emerley Hill School in Ledlington in 1997 I was told that there had been a fire in the school, and the whole attic had been burnt. A girl had been caught in the fire and died and she used to haunt the attic and the stairwell.

This chapter focuses on the importance of the study of memories and memorials in educational ethnography. The subtitle refers to what Zora Neale Hurston (1935: 2) had acquired while away from Florida in 'the North' at college (a diploma and a Chevrolet) – significant in her biography but irrelevant to the old African American men on the store porch who were to be her key informants in the collection of folklore. The ethnographer and those being studied both have their own cultural acquisitions, such as memories, before the investigation begins. In this scary school story, the past of the girls' boarding school is preserved in a ghost story, which tells of a danger facing incoming pupils many years later.

For Americans, like those followed up by Ortner (2003), the high school experience throws a long shadow over adult life. The traditional custom of the high school reunion (Ikeda, 1998) and the university equivalent, ensure that those American adults who choose to participate revisit their 'education' long after it has concluded. Ortner looks back from 1998 to the high school and city she left in 1958. She reports how, for those 200+ of her classmates whom she was able to trace, Weequahic High School memories still loomed very large. Those who had been successful and enjoyed school recalled the golden days of their achievements: social, sporting and academic. Those who had been unhappy reported the worst days of their lives, still 'burned like a tattoo' on their adult identities. Forty years is a long time for a set of peer relationships and hostilities to affect a person and a good ethnographer needs to be alert for evidence that informants are influenced by such memories.

Crosnoe (2011: 241) reflecting on the massacre at Columbine High School, quotes Matt Stone, the man who created the TV cartoon series *South Park*. He grew up in the affluent suburb of Denver served by Columbine High School, and in the documentary by Michael Moore (1999), *Bowling for Columbine*, Stone said that *if only* the two murderers had known that their misery was temporary, their rage might have been less intense. If they:

> could have just known *during* high school what they would most likely have discovered *after* high school, what most adults have discovered, that all of those seemingly momentous social struggles and identity crises that go on in high school are temporary.

Crosnoe says the same thing had occurred to him, commenting:

> You just had to wait two years or so… everything that seems so bad now would not seem so bad any more.

Ortner and Ikeda's research leads me to doubt the truth of this comment, but even if it were 'true', the timescapes of American 14–18 year olds do *not* extend beyond high school.

This chapter deals with learners and their timescapes, then with teachers and theirs, with both sections focusing on formal and informal educational contexts. It then moves on to more inchoate ideas about golden ages which are often mythical, or partial, but can be powerful determinants of behaviours in the present. There is a section on the timescapes of ethnographers, and then sections on how to study memories and memorials, and on what we do not know.

Long-term ethnographic research is not new but usually takes the form of a study followed by a *restudy* later, rather than continuous fieldwork over 30 or 40 years. One of the best ethnographies of an American high school in its community setting – *Elmtown's Youth* (Hollingshead, 1947) and *Elmtown Revisited* (Hollingshead, 1975) – were done and published long ago to capture social change. Wolcott (2002) reflected on the *Sneaky Kid* research which initially took place earlier in his career (Wolcott, 1983). Recently, Heath (2012) has published on 30 years of investigations that began in Trackton and Roadville where she studied the children and then the grandchildren of 300 families from the Piedmont Carolinas from 1969 onwards. Her research began when de-segregation and equal rights were the newly achieved result of the civil rights movement. Trackton was an African-American community of 16 families with a wider network of 130 families in a 20-mile radius. Roadville, three miles away, was a neighbourhood of 12 white families with an extension of 146 families. The nearest city was Alberta and, as it grew in the 1980s, both Trackton and Roadville were wiped out by its expansion. Heath followed her key informants physically and virtually across the USA from 1969 up to 2007. In the UK, one example of a study and restudy is the ORACLE project which was 'redone' after 20 years. The original project was carried out from 1975 to 1981, with the ethnographic work done in 1977 and 1978 (Delamont and Galton, 1986). The second ORACLE project was conducted in 1997 and 1998 in two of the same cities, and four of the same secondary schools (Hargreaves and Galton, 2002). The long ethnography of a Japanese theatrical dynasty, by Salz (1998), discussed in Chapter 4, entirely dwarfs any school or university project. Few educational researchers are lucky enough to be able to reconstruct enculturation for even 30 years and very few educational systems have been stable over such a long period.

When such restudies are done, the ethnographer(s) will have their memories and memorials, as well as a better understanding of those they find in the setting. Of course, one danger of a restudy is being blinded by one's own memories and not noticing that the setting's actors at the second engagement may have no memories at all, or very different ones. When I revisited the two Coalthorpe 12–18 schools only a few years after the first ORACLE fieldwork I was surprised that teachers I had observed trying to contain difficult pupils in the 1978 intake had entirely forgotten that I had been a witness to their valiant attempts to teach some problematic children. My vivid memories were not 'shared' *and theirs were much more important for the research.*

In the two sections that follow, on learners and then on teachers and other adults, the central text is Peshkin (1997) and his core concept of communities of memory. The specific Peshkin ethnography is of a Native American Pueblo community and its schooling where he chronicles how the Native Americans hold 'to *their* cultural ideals' (emphasis mine) despite all the pressure from the dominant American society, and that their steadfastness 'is an unballyhooed triumph of faith' (1997: 115).

65

LEARNERS' MEMORIES AND MEMORIALS

When researchers failed to treat children as rational actors in educational settings, little attention was paid to their memories and memorials. With the rise in serious ethnographic work on children and childhood (James, 2001; Renold, 2005) it became more normal to consider that even young children might have important memories and memorials. This section is mostly about older people's memories of their childhoods, but a good ethnographer of children will attempt to collect their memories of their (to the adult researcher) very recent past. The research on different American families by Lareau (2003) which stressed the class variations in the ways children's lives were or were not scheduled, was explored in Chapter 4. One of her key findings was about how children acquired or failed to acquire a sense of agency, and a repertoire of skills for relating to a range of adults other than parents and teachers. In this chapter the focus is more on learners' sense of memory, their place in long lineages, and how memorials are understood. These vary across cultures, and within societies across social classes, in ways that parallel Lareau's findings about the consequences of different parental attitudes to children's time. There are differences between the memories that a young child or adolescent can have for themselves, and those of a person of 60 such as Ortner's informants, but a child may have been enculturated to share family or community memories. One of these is the place that education has for a child and its parents in the ongoing 'tradition' of the family as with David Mellor's 11 year old boy facing transfer to secondary school in the south east of England (quoted on page 49).

Lesley Pugsley's (1998: 74) 18 year olds thinking about higher education were located by their parents into family timescapes. In the upper middle class families these were educational, in the working class family about matrilineal kinship. Pugsley (1998: 74) quotes a typical mother from a family at ease with the stratified higher education system:

> My husband is in the university, and his father was a professor at the university... we just feel it would be better for her to go to Cambridge.

Here the family is presented as inextricably linked to higher education (HE): the family and university are part of a joint story. In contrast is a working-class family where the mother's response to Pugsley's questions about parental ideas around 'choice' of HE was:

> No we haven't done any of that studying like. We don't understand any of it. This is the first one with all the brains, aren't you? She is the first of my mother's grandchildren to go to university so we are all really proud of her. (Pugsley, 1998: 79)

The memory is entirely about a three generation extended family, centred, in contrast to the previous one, on the descent line through women. The point of the story is that, up to now, higher education has played no part in that family's memories. Here the Welsh 'mam' – the young woman's grandmother – is central to the family story, not the university system, or the careers of the men.

Parallel data, from an interview study, about white, middle-class families in England who deliberately chose to send their children to state comprehensive schools are the latest to show a desire that their off-spring should learn to mix with peers of all classes and ethnicities. That theme in parental talk is central to Chapter 9, but one reason for the parents' views is central here. For many of Reay, Crozier and James's (2011) parents, the memories of *their* schooling determined the choices made for their children. So John Levy, who 'got sent away to a prep boarding school' (2011: 31) at the age of seven, and then at 13 to a famous elite boys' boarding school, said that while 'it was what families like ours did' (p. 31), the experience was 'brutal and brutalising' (p. 31) and worse, 'incredibly limited socially, a sort of complacent sameness' (p. 32). So John Levy 'never wanted that for my own children' (p. 32). Here a family history, the memories of how he and his brother had been educated, led him and his partner to decide they would not use private or selective schooling for their children. Similarly, Sarah Rhymes recalled her university as 'full of public school children' (2011: 33), whose 'arrogance' she found unbearable – that memory had made her determined not to send her daughter to a private school 'on principle' (p. 33). In another case, the deceased father's dislike of his elite grammar school still determined his widow's decision to educate their child in a comprehensive so that he is 'getting out into the world' (p. 34).

Peshkin (1997: 8–11) opens his analysis of Native American school-ing in New Mexico with the sentence 'memory reverberates in our lives', and the concepts of places of memory and communities of memory. He sought to understand how memory featured in the adolescents' experi-ences of going to 'Whiteman's school'. 'Whiteman' being a term Peshkin adopted from King's (1967) *The School at Mopass*. Peshkin studied Indian High School over 3 years, including 11 months when he lived on the campus; a 100 acre site of 34 buildings – a Native American space on the outskirts of a city. Indian High School is a weekly boarding insti-tution, i.e. the students go home on Friday and return on Sunday. Peshkin's analysis of the adolescents' lives centres on the shared tribal memory of the Pueblo, and the future-oriented, individualistic school ethos, antagonistic to Pueblo values. There is no *memory*, individual, familial or tribal, of schooling being relevant, useful, or integrating. Pueblo collective memory shapes the adolescents, Indian High does not.

TEACHERS' AND THE OTHER ADULTS' MEMORIES

Before exploring the findings on teachers' and other adults' memories and memorials, it is salutary to recognise that these may be related to space and place, and mobility, as well as time and memory. This is par-ticularly true of refugees and migrants, especially those 'in exile'. Many people, especially those displaced, may have greater attachment to, and spend more time, in their heads, with their memories, dreams and plans, at localities that are physically gone, from which they are exiled, than they do in real locations. Loizos (1981), whose original research took place in a Greek Cypriot village that became part of 'Turkish' Cyprus after the invasion of 1974, conducted one of the pioneering studies of exiles. Displaced from their village, the Cypriots were far more embedded in the place of memory than they were in their 'new' homes. Salamone (1986) found that Greeks on Ammoulioni, exiled from Izmir in 1920, still had keys to 'their' houses in that city 50 years later. The refugees were convinced, and are convinced, that the lost urban way of life was more cultured, richer, more civilised and more truly 'Greek' than the lifestyle of the Greeks in Greece either in 1922 or those in 1982 who were peasants rather than city folk and still lived a rural life. Similarly when Herzfeld (1991) did fieldwork on Rethemnos on the Greek island of Crete in the 1970s, the school playgrounds rang with 'refugee' as an insult, although the actual adult refugees had arrived in 1922. If that seems too detached from any educational setting, reading either Ortner (2002) or Ikeda (1998) on high school reunions in middle America – events which are both real events in real time but also visits to places of memory – shows the 'relevance' of Salamone and Herzfeld.

68

Teachers, higher education staff and other adults generally have memories of their own careers, and of their place in the history of their workplace and their specialisation. In the following quote from a professional musician, the speaker locates himself in relation to the memories and memorials of others, and how he can benefit from them:

> I see Dennis as a link with the great names of the past, and I do not mean that as being overwhelmed with nostalgia. I just think that, realistically, he knew people that do not exist anymore. He played for Beecham, he played for Pierre Monteux, big names like that. Yeah, he is a link with the past. It's like when he played for Adrian Boult. Well, here was a man who knew Elgar. (Cottrell, 2004: 41)

Cottrell is quoting a musician who sets his career, and particularly his learning and socialisation, into a lineage. He values what he can learn from Dennis, because Dennis learnt things from an earlier generation, including in Sir Adrian Boult's case, knowing Elgar. This is not formal education, but the intangible learning that comes by association with, and paying attention to, our elders.

When school teachers are studied they usually offer memories of their decision to teach, their training, the institutions they have worked in, and their colleagues. But, because different education systems have different career structures for teachers, the important memories in, for example, Denmark are not the same as Canada. The timescape of a career teacher in the UK is likely to include changing schools in order to get promotion and salary increases, or to find a different school ethos, more congenial colleagues, and more satisfying work. In Germany, where teachers are in a national pay system where the structure is flatter, and more money arrives with length of service, the first type of move is not practised and would not be in the timescape of the teacher.

For teachers some school years may be particularly significant such as their first, or their first in that school, their first as a Deputy Head or Head, and at the other end, their last. During the ORACLE project (Delamont and Galton, 1986) we saw Mr Le Grand in his last year of teaching, introducing nine year olds to the library and the bible at Guy Mannering middle school in Ashburton for the last time, after a 35-year career. At the other Ashburton School, Gryll Grange, Mr Hogg, the Head of lower school and senior PE master, died during the year of the research, and all the observers collected memories of him from his former colleagues. He had also become enshrined in a joke that is typical of the oral culture of schools (see Chapter 9 p. 138)

In the 1980s, sociologists of education began to gather life histories from school teachers and argue for their analysis as part of any serious sociological or anthropological understanding of schools and classrooms. There was a parallel move to include curriculum history alongside ethnography, which is addressed in Chapter 11. In the same era, several collections of autobiographies by academics were published, although these generally focus more on their research than on their teaching. The autobiographies and life histories of ethnographers and educational researchers are discussed in the next section. One of the most carefully constructed studies of teachers was done in two areas of England: in a post-industrial city in the north and a seaside resort in the south, and on teachers in contrasting disciplines (art and science), by Sikes, Measor and Woods (1982). There was no doubt that the 'working life' histories of the teachers had affects on their classroom practices every day of their lives.

Similarly, in research on PhD supervision (Delamont, Atkinson and Parry, 2000), the supervisors used their life stories, especially their memories of how they had been supervised when they were themselves doctoral students, as the frame to explain how they supervised their students. So Dr Kenway, a geographer, told us 'I decided I'd keep a very close eye on graduate students because I felt remarkably scarred by my own experience'. In a parallel quote, Dr Mincing, a natural scientist, described his experience as a PhD student:

> My supervisor… hadn't had any experience of PhD students before and he took on four at the same time. And we all sat there in this room for the first year virtually doing nothing, twiddling our thumbs and accomplishing very little indeed.

Dr Mincing stressed that precisely because all four of them were new, they did not try to get more direction, nor to report their supervisor's 'neglect' to anyone.

> I had no idea what a supervisor was supposed to do. As far as I was concerned that was what a PhD was about.

Now a supervisor himself, Dr Mincing described a supervising style he used that was about providing *training* for the students: 'training means supervision'. The contrastive rhetoric (Hargreaves, 1984) used by most of the supervisors we interviewed often took this form: distinguishing between their memories of an unhelpful supervisor when they were students and their aim to be much more helpful. Frequently these memories were stories of learning. As Dr Morrow, a geographer, said:

> Something I know about myself, I'm not very good at commenting on verbal discussions – I need something in writing, however scrappy.

70　In the case of the teachers' life histories and memories, and in those gathered from doctoral supervision, it is vital for the researcher to recognise that such interview data are not literally true, they are accounts of the past as the narrator sees it and chooses to tell it, and have to be understood as rhetorical performances. Story-telling, including life-history-telling, has culturally specific formats, and the data will be inevitably 'produced' in that form. This is the main theme of Chapter 9 but is acutely relevant here.

One of the most important things an ethnographer does is take memories and memorials seriously, whether or not the informants in a setting do. A good example of this comes from Casanova's (2010) enquiry into the reasons for the success of Cibola High School in Yuma, Arizona. For over 20 years it has consistently graduated all its population of Latino(a) adolescents and sent a high proportion (90 per cent) on to higher education when most US high schools serve Latino(a) students poorly, and send few to college. One reason for its success, Casanova argues, is that the staff have a clear sense of the school's mission and its history. The school began with an unusually high set of expectations for the Latino(a) students, and had clear strategies for achieving 100 per cent graduation. Memories of the original staff team from 1986 were vividly 'present' in the lives of the teachers when

Casanova began her study in 2004. Staff members used the inspirational leadership of the first head teacher, and the original head counsellor, to 'explain' to her how their working lives were focused on lifting the achievement and aspiration of the students.

There has been less research on the memories of those who leave teaching although those data would be a splendid resource with which to challenge familiarity, and should be collected. Heath's longitudinal involvement with the Piedmont Carolinas in the years since de-segregation is characterised by an exodus from teaching.

> The majority of those who had stayed in their classrooms through the first decade of de-segregation now explored careers that were opening for the first time to women. Management, finance, small business development, and advanced education recruited black and white women of determination, creativity, and change-making spirit... (Heath, 2012: 18)

A comparative ethnography of current classroom practices, and a set of life-history interviews with those who left the profession, would be an excellent project in the Carolinas.

MEMORIES AND MEMORIALS IN ETHNOGRAPHIC LIVES

The growth in scholarly autobiographies, and accounts of involvement in particular educational projects, such as those collected in Burgess (1984, 1985a, 1985b), Walford (1994), and de Marrais (1998), has been remarkable in the past 30 years. Almost every published ethnography of a school setting has its 'how I did it' narrative often in a separate edited collection of such 'confessions'. There are far fewer such narratives about ethnography in other settings, such as laboratories or hospitals; and the anthropological autobiographies often stress the exotic strangeness of the field setting in ways which may not make their applicability for an educational research apparent. The best reflexive writing by anthropologists, such as Herzfeld (2009) on the importance of the *researcher's* gesture and embodiment, has important lessons for educational researchers. Atkinson (1996) is an analytic approach to a set of autobiographical memories by ethnographers who had done their fieldwork in America, and there is an urgent need for a parallel analysis of the memories represented in the many 'how I did the research for my ethnography of an urban high school' collections. Among the recent examples is the autobiography reluctantly written by Heath (2012) which recalls her childhood in a monocultural rural area of Carolina, and the culture shock of a move to a city in Florida, and a multicultural high school. Her memory, designed to explain her research preoccupations, is illuminating. From that experience, the reader can see how she could later decide to study varieties of American English and their educational consequences.

> At the secondary school in south Florida, I met my first Puerto Ricans, Cubans, Filipinos, Jews, and self-proclaimed atheists. Entirely unprepared for academics I found myself in a strange new world where other students laughed at my accent, sneered at my clothes, and marvelled at all that I did not know. (Heath, 2012: 179)

These memories, and others like them, lead us gently from 'real' lives to myths of golden ages.

GOLDEN AGES: MYTHICAL TIME

There are several 'mythical' aspects to time. These can include imagined histories for institutions, customs, events, 'mythical charters', the Rebecca syndrome (named after Daphne du Maurier's famous novel about a second wife whose life in Manderley, the first wife's home, with Rebecca's sinister housekeeper, is dominated, and entirely overshadowed by others' memories of the first wife, to whom she feels entirely inferior). In education, one of the most powerful contrastive rhetorics is the idea that the pupils or students or young people generally were much better behaved, more scholarly, more respectful *then*. In educational research, Peterson (1964) uncovered the way(s) in which American women high school teachers in their 20s, 40s, and 60s regarded their students. As the women saw it, each cohort of the students had become steadily less academic and more childish as they had aged. The women of 60 recalled wonderful students from the 1920s when their careers began, tolerable students from the 1940s and were convinced that the high school students of the 1960s were idle, disrespectful and faced an intellectually impoverished curriculum. The women of 40 remembered the high school students of the 1940s as wonderful, and were less enthusiastic about those of the 1960s. The women in their 20s were very positive about the contemporary cohort. Of course, no reader can possibly 'judge' whether the students had actually changed, or that the teachers had become more distant from their charges as the age gap between them increased and their energy and idealism lessened. Herzfeld's (1983) work on moral slippage and myths of the golden age addresses this, based on Cretan peasants lamenting the slack morals of young people in the 1970s, when all the evidence Herzfeld could uncover suggested *no changes* in key indicators of 'morality'.

Many beliefs about things being far worse today than they were yesterday, like many ideas about 'traditional', 'hallowed', or 'ancient' customs, clothing, songs, sporting prowess, sex roles, educational standards, or cricket, are rhetorically powerful laments for a golden age that rarely took the form imagined by those lamenting it. As Marquese (1994) points out, the whole history of cricket discourse has been a threnody for the past. When the famous poem 'At Lord's' (Thompson, 1937/2007) was originally written in the late nineteenth century, by an opium addicted failed medical student, it was a lament for the 'golden age' cricket of his youth in Lancashire (the 1870s). Its refrain of 'Oh my Hornby and my Barlow long ago!' evoked the two greatest players he had seen depicted as ghosts running for ever between dimly perceived wickets. For Thompson, that had been the best cricket ever, and the game had deteriorated since. Marquese shows carefully how every generation in the UK since has claimed sadly that cricket's golden age has passed, while cricket continues to produce addicts attracted to something they find mesmerising.

Such beliefs are entirely impervious to evidence, however distinguished the historian who gathers it. Ronald Hutton (2006a) for example, has shown how resistant to historical evidence is the belief that highland Scotsmen have worn kilts in their clan tartan at least since the reign of Macbeth. Tartans were in fact invented, as was the kilt, in the period 1740–1822. Similarly, Hutton (2006b) addresses the archaeology and history of Glastonbury, but is realistic and resigned that a factual account will have no impact upon the myths about holy grails, King Arthur, or ley lines. In earlier work, Hutton (1999) carefully showed how the origins of today's neopagan witchcraft lie not in Pre-Roman, or Pre-Christian Britain or medieval Hungary, but in a set of ideas and practices that was deliberately and self-consciously created around the Second World War by Gerald Gardner. Such scholarship has not displaced the faith of many practitioners that they are part of an old religion dating back into prehistory.

In sport and education such myths, and their imperviousness to any evidence, are particularly prevalent. Many young men who play *capoeira* have heard a story that it originated in Angola (which is probably true) in a zebra dance in which young warriors fought, like male zebras, for access to the most desirable brides. As Assunção (2005) shows, there is no evidence at all that there ever was a zebra dance in Angola, but that does not stop the story being spread and its veracity widely held among men playing *capoeira*.

For the researcher the 'truth' lacks importance: the power and persistence of the belief at the time of the fieldwork is what matters. If the teachers in a school believe that the previous Principal ran that institution well, and things were better, then that is the social fact to which the ethnographer must attend. If a coven of neopagan feminist witches believe that their rituals have been handed down orally from wise women who worshipped a mother goddess in pre-Roman Britain or from Hungary in 1200 CE, that is socially more important than any 'facts'.

HOW TO... RESEARCH MEMORIES AND MEMORIALS

Many ethnographers use oral history, and/or documents to investigate times past. Generally, educational researchers have not been engaged in the same setting(s) or with the same informants for long periods, compared to, for example, some anthropologists. Burgess (1983) studied Bishop McGregor School twice, but Seeger (2008) spent 37 years studying one Brazilian indigenous group. What is a long-term ethnography? If I say I have been studying *capoeira* since 2003, the ethnography sounds long. If I say that I have watched 600 classes, that also sounds a lot. However, when some of those were only one hour, and most 90 minutes, and classes only run for 44 weeks of the year, the total fieldwork is very short compared to, for example, an anthropologist who lived 24 hours a day in a field setting for nine or 12 months. My 5,400 hours is only equivalent to 225 periods of 24 hours, or 550 12-hour days, which does not sound long at all.

If the project is to explore schooling in general, then fieldwork in different institutions can be cumulative and comparative, simultaneously. Peshkin spent his career focusing on different schools, rather than restudying the same one. He began his American research in the rural Midwest (Mansfield), then observed a fundamentalist Christian school (Bethany Baptist Academy), an urban working-class high school (Riverview), then he studied an 'Indian' high school and finally Edgewood. That covered his career from 1972 to his death and he drew on his memories which ensured he paid attention to the memories of his informants.

The key things for the ethnographer to do are to be patient when memories are produced, and listen to them carefully. Additionally it is wise to look at memorials. Are rooms named for people who are long gone? Are there trophies and prizes that link to the past? Does the institution display its past with honour boards, war memorials, photographs, portraits, etc.? Is there a contrastive rhetoric about 'then' and 'now'? Are there nostalgic words about golden ages? Attention to such things will always be rewarding, especially if current students and teachers do not 'notice' them at all.

A LOOK TO THE FUTURE

what we do not know

The importance of landscapes of memory, and of other types of memory and memorials, has not been explored in the ethnography of higher education, and, outside anthropology, in studies of informal education. The ethnographies of schooling are generally neglectful of the actors' memories. The simple answer to the question 'What do we not know?' is 'everything'. If there is one way in which educational ethnography can be improved it is to concentrate on landscapes of memory. Earlier in the chapter I proposed more research on those who have left teaching, as one way to fight familiarity, and that is my 'priority' research task.

six

movement and mobilities: heading my toenails

In one rural school, the children went for a walk and ended up running among crumbling ruins, perching precariously on the edge of a deep pond, and finally, lying down in the middle of a road. (McDonald, 1989: 199)

Before I went to Aldminster [a public school] in 1995 I was told by my friends that everyone was snobs who took helicopters to school.

The focus of this chapter on movement and mobility and their crucial opposites, stillness and immobility, may seem novel and 'recent'. The vogue for mobile methods and the calls by, for example, Urry (2007), for greater attention to mobilities, can lead us to believe they were neglected. In fact, they have always been central to educational ethnography. 'Heading my toenails' is a splendidly poetic way of describing 'setting out for'. In this quote used as the subtitle of this chapter, Zora Neale Hurston (*Mules and Men*, 1935: 183) was going to New Orleans to study hoodoo, the African-American system of magic, after a period gathering folklore in Florida. This chapter focuses on researchers 'heading their toenails', and on the participants in educational institutions and informal settings heading theirs.

McDonald's fieldwork was conducted in rural Brittany, a region of France where an ancient language, Breton, was, by the 1960s, in danger of dying out. A movement grew up to save Breton, and one strategy was to create nursery and infant schools where the language used was Breton, not French. In the quote at the head of the chapter, McDonald was writing about the regimes found in the Breton language nursery and elementary schools that had been set up in opposition to the state schools where French was used. The point of the observation quoted was that the *diwan* schools movement (the word literally means 'seed') was not only about producing pupils who were fluent in Breton, but also children who had experienced a childhood without the restrictions on movement that characterised the French State schools. The counter-cultural nature of *diwan* education is captured in the undisciplined, even dangerous, freedom of movement of the children. Part of McDonald's research focused on which parents chose to enrol their children in these schools, and why. The physical environment, and the possibilities of movement for children, turned out to be a central factor in the accounts given about school choice. Most of the parents who chose to send their children to *diwan* were not just committed to the survival of Breton, they were also hostile to 'traditional' French schooling with its emphasis on physical constraint.

In the 'urban legend' by contrast, the unimaginable riches of the pupils at the expensive fee-paying school are encapsulated in the absurd idea that they come to school not by car, bike, train or bus, but by helicopter. In other words, the boys at Aldminster are so rich that they move in ways entirely unlike pupils in ordinary schools. It is, of course, no coincidence that the rite of passage pupils experience when they move from a small primary (elementary) school to a much larger secondary, generates a rich set of fantasy stories, such as this one, and that some of them focus on travel to school and others on movement in the new school. In Mellor's (2003) work, the pupils facing transfer used the idea of travelling to the new school on the train or on a public bus as one way in which the new 'teenager' status would be marked. At St Troughton's, following the 'taster' visit to St Baker's, this wanting to be seen as, and seeing themselves as teenagers already was a common theme of 'independence' throughout Mellor's (DM) conversations with Year 6 pupils.

DM:	So how did you get to St. Baker's, did you go together?
Jodi:	On the bus.
Damian:	Yeah, we got the proper bus.
DM:	How was it?
Kerry and Jodi:	Scary.
Damian:	Nah, it was ok.
Ryan:	We sat at the front though.
DM:	Was it scary because of the older kids on there?
Jodi:	Yeah.
Damian:	But we'll be the ones getting the bus soon.
DM:	Did you want to sit at the back?
Ryan:	They were year 8s and 9s.
Jodi:	Older than that.

Ryan:	No.
Jodi:	Yes they were 'cos Amy Philips is in year 10.
DM:	Are you looking forward to getting the bus when you start there?
Jodi:	Sort of. It'll mean we're more like proper... ya'know, like high school and that.
Damian:	Teenagers.
DM:	You'll be teenagers?
Damian:	Yeah, like that.

In this extract the 11 year olds are clear that their future mobility is a mark of their impending status passage. Similarly, one girl, Nadine, told Mellor about going to the comprehensive, Smithfields: 'I think I will feel more independent because I have to get the train all by myself'.

This chapter looks at research on movement in the environs of the school, in the yard, in corridors, in classes of contrasting subjects where movement may be required and those where it is forbidden, and finally where movement is a punishment, and illicit movement is an escape. So it explores what educational ethnographers have learnt about movement and mobilities in educational contexts; offers practical ideas about studying mobilities and using mobile methods such as the go-along; and highlights some *lacunae* in the educational research literature around movements and mobilities.

There is no research on the movements and mobilities of teachers and lecturers, either inside institutions or on travel to and from them. The movements and mobilities of pupils on buses, and, in the USA, being car-pooled (Adler and Adler, 1998) are better covered by researchers than those of students in higher education. However, ethnographers are less likely to focus their data-gathering on journeys to school, or moving around the institutions, or on lessons focused on moving, than on classes where the learners are expected to be *immobile*.

In this chapter, concepts such as *rites de passage*, liminality, status passage, rhythms, seasonality and the mobilities paradigm are deployed. A core concept is liminality, and its relation to the ideas of status passage (Glaser and Strauss, 1967) or rites of passage (Van Gennep, 1909). A status passage is a period during which your status changes: so, for example, an engagement is the status passage between being single and being married, just as the period between filing for divorce and getting the decree absolute is the status passage from being married to being a divorcee. When a culture has one or more rituals to mark the start or finish of a status passage, the term *rite of passage* is a useful one. An engagement party can mark the beginning of the conventional British status passage from being single to being married, and the wedding ceremony and the honeymoon mark the end of it. If the new status is secret, or involves being given access to secrets, the term initiation is frequently used. Many anthropological studies of *rites de passage* have focused on initiations. Initiation rites are often the subject of myths or urban legends, for example, that to join a particular gang you have to have killed someone.

British state education does not have many secret societies, and few initiation rites, but the primary–secondary transfer is the focus for a rich mythology as we have seen throughout the book. Merton (2005) has explored the rites of passage of suburban American girls as they move from grade school (primary school in the UK) to junior high school. The most infamous rites of passage in education settings are American: central in fraternities and sororities that provide housing. The men and women who are 'pledged' are students who choose to apply to them and if they get accepted, after formal interviews and initiation tests (called 'hazing'), these fraternities and sororities command life-long allegiance from their keenest adherents. Jones (2004) is a study of the initiation ceremonies used in African-American fraternities in US universities (discussed in more detail in Chapter 7).

Many leisure activities have rites of passage: martial arts, for example, often have tests to determine if a learner can move 'up' to the next belt, or, in *savate*, gloves. In the Wing Chun Kung Fu Association studied by Jennings, Brown and Sparkes (2010) the students can progress up a hierarchy of coloured silk sashes to black, and then to a series of graduations of black sash. The research team contained three levels of expertise, inversely related to their academic statuses. Jennings had been learning since 2002 (i.e. eight years) and had the black sash. Brown had been training for five years. In the university, Brown was Jennings's doctoral supervisor; in Wing Chun Jennings was Brown's teacher, because of their relative time, and qualifications, in the martial art. In the South East Asian martial arts there is often a formalised set of behaviours that lowly practitioners have to show to those more advanced (Twigger, 1989).

The core concepts used in the rest of the chapter are taken from John Urry's (2007) seminal work on *Mobilities*, plus the idea of the *flâneur* (Tester, 1994a, 1994b). A central ethnographic method is the 'go-along' (Kusenbach, 2003, 2012; Hall, Lashua and Coffey, 2008). While educational researchers have paid some degree of attention to movement and mobilities the general vogue for mobile methods in other specialisms across sociology and anthropology, and the work of Urry in particular,

79

have not yet shown up in educational ethnography explicitly labelled as 'work on mobility' or 'mobile methods'. The neglect by educational researchers of the new mobilities paradigm is matched by the lack of attention paid by mobility researchers to formal or informal education. For example, in the collection on mobilities edited by Fincham, McGuinness and Murray (2010) there is a paper on children, but no paper on education, formal or informal. John Urry wrote that 'It sometimes seems as if all the world is on the move' (2007: 3) and set out what he called 'the mobilities paradigm'. He does not index education, does not address educational institutions or processes at all apart from one paragraph on universities (p. 244), but there is no doubt that the ideas proposed are potentially valuable for the ethnography of educational settings and processes, and that learning and teaching are often focused on moving, or not moving in prescribed and proscribed ways.

Urry (2007: 40–43) sets out nine 'mobile methods': that is, 'methods on the move' needed to implement the mobilities paradigm. These are:

1. the study of transfer points or liminal places;
2. the study of 'places' that themselves move (such as ships);
3. the study of objects that can be followed around;
4. the study of memories of movements past;
5. the study of imagined and anticipated movement;
6. the study of virtual movement (through, for example, blogs);
7. the study of time–space diaries;
8. the study of moving informants by moving with them; and
9. the study of observing moving bodies.

Urry's book illustrates these nine methodological imperatives with a variety of projects and while his are not educational or specifically ethnographic, as this chapter shows, his nine imperatives will all improve our understanding of teaching and learning.

I have used an example from the ethnography of *capoeira* classes (Stephens and Delamont, 2010), and then one from an ethnography of a boarding school for First Canadian children (King, 1967) to emphasise the relevance of Urry's ideas. In the *capoeira* research, which is focused on how learners of the Brazilian martial art are enculturated into its habitus, we draw on Urry's nine mobile methods to explore types of mobilities found at *capoeira* festivals. British *capoeira* groups have festivals called *Batizados* (Baptisms) two or three times a year, at which novice students are brought into the group (literally 'baptised') and more advanced students are promoted to the next belt in the hierarchy. These festivals are educational events because master classes are

80

a prominent feature of them, and mobilities are central because they are focused on *capoeira* movements. Clearly, research on *capoeira batizados* and on *capoeira* itself is very specific but it can be used to explore general features of that paradigm in an educational setting.

The focus on *capoeira* festivals also illustrates the potential of Urry's proposals for adjusting research to accommodate the 'world on the move'. Focusing upon the *batizado* is a study of transfer points or liminal spaces conducted by two ethnographers moving with their informants and studying moving bodies. A *capoeira* festival is a transfer point or liminal place (Method 1) because novices are 'baptised' into *capoeira* and other students are promoted to the next grade. While any one festival does not move as a ship or coach does, there are many different festivals held in many places every year, and teachers, students (and researchers) are mobile around them (Method 2) and objects, especially essential musical instruments, are taken from one festival to the next by the teachers (Method 3). The centre point of our *capoeira* and the mobilities paradigm paper (Stephens and Delamont, 2010) is an analysis of how one specific movement, a kick called an *armada*, can repay very detailed micro ethnographic attention (Method 9). We provide an analysis of 18 possible 'meanings' that can be attached to one kick, all of which will routinely be on display during any *capoeira* festival. Any other *capoeira* move, whether attack or escape, could have been used in the same way, because all movements have multiple meanings. Observing these multiple meanings, and in Neil Stephens's case, performing 13 of them, in private practice, in lessons, and in *roda* play, involved both of us in mobile research (Method 8) on a set of mobilities. Our research aim is to understand *capoeira* as it is taught and learnt outside Brazil. To attain our goal we had, of necessity, to move ourselves. We both had to be able to see the teachers' and students' kicks and to avoid being kicked ourselves.

We placed less emphasis on Urry's other strategies, but they are implicit in the data on *batizados*. Students and teachers have memories of *batizados* that form the topic of many conversations for years afterwards and are preserved on DVDs made at the events (Method 4). Before *batizados* they are anticipated and imagined (indeed such anticipation motivates routine training) (Method 5). Experiences at *batizados* are the subject of numerous blogs, emails, Facebook pages, etc. (Method 6), and of time–space diaries (Method 7).

Capoeira learners are encultured not only into the physical skills of the activity, but also into their multiple meanings, the status passages and the global mobilities of the whole *capoeira* culture. A learner in the UK will acquire a different mental map of the UK, Europe, and, of course, Brazil. The same is true of any subculture. Marion's (2008) ethnography of professional American ballroom dancers includes, for British readers, exactly such an example. Very few Americans have a mental map of the UK that focuses on Blackpool, and very few ethnographies of American society have index entries for Blackpool as 'a site of liminality' (Marion, 2008: 200). But the movements of dancers on the dance floors of California or Idaho can lead to competition in Blackpool. Marion did not draw on Urry, and rather than rework his study of bodies moving on the dance floor and through space to different ballrooms using Urry, I return to an orthodox ethnography of a boarding school.

Focusing on Urry's agenda is illuminating in all settings and subcultures. Urry's proposed nine mobile methods were published 40 years after King's (1967) ethnography of a boarding school, but their potential power for making schooling strange is apparent when King's work is read 'through' Urry's lens. A. Richard King (1967) did an ethnography of a residential school for First Canadian children at Mopass in the 'Yukon Territory of Northwest Canada' (p. *vii*). King's rhetorical style is, by current standards, 'dated': he writes of 'Indians'. However, he had known the Yukon since 1939 when, trying to establish a pioneering airline to serve Alaska, he crashed there. The study of the residential school took place between 1960–1964, and when he wrote the book he was in charge of developing teacher education in Afghanistan for the Teachers College of Columbia University. So King himself had experienced a great detail of mobility, and it is a major theme in the study of the school at Mopass, although not expressed in the terms that Urry would immediately recognise.

Two things about Mopass are striking when a mobilities lens is used. School systems in industrialised societies are places where movement upwards through a hierarchy of grades is expected. Being kept back or retained to repeat a year is stigmatising in mainstream culture. In many systems promotion depends on test scores, and here Mopass was entirely delinquent as an institution. First, King (1967: 49 and 82) reported that, at Mopass, the Canadian testing and record-keeping policies were 'ignored'. He found that 'none of the prescribed diagnostic or achievement tests had been given to the children at any level'. They should have been tested every year for 12 years but the record cards were essentially blank. Even when a class teacher wrote a grade that should have led to the pupil's promotion to the next level, it was routinely ignored and the child was 'required to repeat the grade the following year'. Thus a major 'movement' that the majority of Canadian children make routinely each year – that is, upwards in the hierarchical structure from grade 6 to grade 7 and then to grade 8 – was not normal or routine for the First Canadians at Mopass. So, whereas Canadian

82

schools should be transfer places, in Urry's terms, Mopass was not. The children were immobilised in a non-transfer place. King was deeply disturbed, indeed angry about the institutional immobility.

Perhaps the most shocking passage about Mopass is the analogy King draws on page 55:

> The operation of the school at Mopass for Indian children bears a striking resemblance to a well-run stock ranch or dairy farm in which valued animals are carefully nurtured. The children are moved, fed, cared for and rested by a rotating crew of overseers who condition the herd to respond to sets of signals.

The only way in which Mopass is not like an efficient cattle ranch is its bureaucracy:

> The single exception is the manner of record-keeping. The system of records that have been kept at Mopass School up to 1962 would be unacceptable in any well-run stock farm.

King found one 16 year old girl in the fourth grade with a blank record (she should have been in the tenth grade) who had been at the school for eight years. Her file was empty except for one sheet bearing a single number for each of the eight years. This lack of mobility – the Mopass school as a non-transfer zone – was paralled by the findings of Wolcott (1967) at another First Canadian school on an island off Vancouver. Focusing on schools which are not zones of transfer for some, or all, of their students is an important use of Urry's proposals.

When more ordinary travel and in-school mobility is the focus, King's ethnography is equally depressing to read. The pupils at Mopass only travelled there once a year, in September, from up to 350 miles away. They went home once a year in late June or early July, both journeys by bus. The school was 50 miles from a town, so only staff ever went there. For ten months of the year:

> the children move, or do not move, at a signal from the supervisor – usually the police whistle, an indispensible part of each supervisor's equipment. (1967: 62)

There are five types of activity for the children: working at chores; religious services; lessons; meal times; and play. Of these, only the chores and the play allow pupil movement. Lessons are run by teachers, the other four activities by the supervisors with the whistles. King's ethnography was written in anger in the 1960s, and is a disturbing read today. Focusing on its mobilities clarifies why Mopass was such an inhuman experience for its pupils.

When we use the same framing device to look at the ethnographies of mainstream schools, it is an equally useful way to fight familiarity. The great irony of schooling is, of course, that pupils who do not wish to move, and especially to move outside, are required to do so in PE and at recess (break), while the same staff spend the rest of the school day repressing pupil movements they judge inappropriate, from running in corridors to fidgeting and wriggling in class.

If we are more concerned to analyse space than movement, or wish to focus on the two together, the *flâneur* is one useful concept to help us. As I described in Chapter 3, the *flâneur* was originally a male citizen in the urban spaces of Northern Europe in the 1800s; a man who walked, sauntered, loitered, lurked, promenaded, and observed in the public spaces where buildings and people could be watched. The *flâneur* had no occupation, except perhaps an artistic, creative one such as painter or essayist. He 'hung out' in cafés, went window-shopping, and observed the street life. As Wilson (2001) pointed out, when sociologists became interested in consumption, and in the post-industrial city with its reliance on tourism and culture rather than manufacturing, there was an academic interest in the idea of the *flâneur*. The sociological idea has its origins in the work of Walter Benjamin and Siegfried Kracauer in the 1920s and 1930s (see Wilson, 2001), but became useful for thinking about what Lash and Urry (1994) called *Economies of Signs and Space* in the late twentieth century.

84

Tester's (1994a) edited collection started a sociological discussion. The sociological debates on the *flâneur* rarely strayed beyond a few cities in nineteenth-century Europe, such as Paris and Vienna. In Brazil, the cities of the 1920s had a kind of *flâneur*, the *malandro* – a man usually portrayed as dark skinned (so mixed race, or African-Brazilian) who 'surfed' the city, snappily dressed in a white suit and hat, symbolising that he did not work and with no visible means of support. A snake-hipped seducer, skilled at dance and *capoeira*, he wove through the public spaces of the city detached from and unconstrained by the work relationships of the majority of men. He was, as one would expect, a popular figure in samba song and in novels.

When, as I argued in Delamont (2003), sociologists became immersed in debates about whether the city in 2000 was so unlike the city of 1800 that it was no longer possible to be a *flâneur*, the concept became embroiled in controversies that do not help us understand educational institutions. So without embarking on an account of those debates about types of city and their scope for *flâneurs*, we can consider whether formal educational institutions are firmly 'modern' in their framing of space, and therefore unlike the postmodern spaces of the city – or rather of the *not*-city: the shopping mall, Disneyworld, cyberspace, or Second Life (Boellstorff, 2008). We *can* use the concept to reflect on the ways pupils use space, on how ethnographers can and cannot use it, and on how it is framed, in any educational setting, formal or informal. The gendered nature of the concept, for as Wilson (2001) pointed out the historical *flâneur* was always a man, may be particularly helpful in thinking about how the ethnographer's movements are constrained or unrestricted, and how the work or 'occupation' of the ethnographer is understood by the actors in the setting.

In the next empirical example I have used the idea of a male *flâneur* to illuminate the early 'career' of a pupil in his first weeks of secondary school. In the first ORACLE project (Delamont and Galton, 1986) the complexity of the systems of organising hierarchical groups, called sets, for particular subjects provided pupils, and it was especially boys who exploited them, with opportunities for the avoidance of lessons. In the first weeks of their first term at their secondary schools, it was possible that some children were genuinely confused or lost when they arrived at the wrong classroom, or were found wandering the playground when lessons had begun. However, there were some pupils who seemed to the team of observers to be more interested in taking the role of *flâneur* than in undertaking any academic or physical activities. Two concrete examples of such boys from that ethnographic project at Kenilworth (11–14) Middle School in Bridgehampton and Melin Court (12–18) School in Coalthorpe will illustrate this.

At Kenilworth, which had streaming (tracking) and setting, the children from the two lowest ability classes, I Zeta and I Epsilon, were remixed into two maths sets. Three weeks after the term had started one observer recorded:

> Edmund came in looking very confused and asking if Mrs Lee knew where Mr Pompey's maths set was. Mrs Lee was brusque with him, telling him he had been in Kenilworth nearly three weeks now and this was the second or third time he had appeared in her lesson. Why didn't he write down on his timetable where Mr Pompey had maths each time?

It is possible that Edmund was confused about his maths lessons and there are not enough data from Kenilworth to label him an 'exploiter' of the complexities and perhaps even a *flâneur*. In another of the schools we saw other pupils who were clearly using the complexities to avoid being taught. The most noticeable 'user' of complexity to avoid lessons was a boy of 12 at Melin Court we called Wayne Patel to signal his mixed white British and South East Asian British identity. He was the most unsettled and difficult boy in the year, truanting a great deal and being disruptive when present. In his first year he avoided classes but stayed hidden in the school; after that he truanted more and more extensively.

85

In practice he had no proper secondary education at all as we discovered when we followed up his cohort five years later. We discovered that at 16 had absented himself from one of the two leaving exams he was scheduled for and failed the other, and was unemployed. The staff had been relieved when he truanted because his presence was so troublesome. We have detailed data on his first weeks, and I have labelled him a *flâneur* because it captures his role as a detached 'observer' of the school, strolling around watching the teachers and pupils working.

In the third week of their first term at Melin Court (12–18) a science teacher, Miss Fern, should have had 23 pupils from the mixed ability form IM in Group A. The rest were scheduled for a different science class. She began the lesson by calling a register, and giving out exercise books in which homework had been done.

> Miss Fern gives out the pupils' science notebooks one at a time, calling the children to the front so she can learn their names. When she finds she does not have his exercise book Miss Fern sends Wayne Patel to Mr Trelawny because she is sure he is not in Group A.

Wayne's name was not on her register, and she does not have his exercise book in the Group A batch, so Miss Fern sends him to see the Head of Science, who had organised the groups and had the master list. Wayne Patel left. When he returned:

> he tells Miss Fern that he is in Group B. She asks him where their lesson is, and he does not know. Miss Fern asks loudly why he did not ask while he was with Mr Trelawny. She sends him back to find out where the B group are.

As I commented at the time in the 'out of the field notes':

> I wonder if Wayne Patel *knew* he was in the wrong group but wanted to be with his friend Eamonn, or just got muddled, or wanted to waste his time.

If Wayne wanted to avoid science he had successfully wasted 20 minutes of an 80-minute lesson before he reached Group B. Given what we know about how new pupils in a school are concerned to discover what the teachers' 'limits' are – finding out how far they can go – Wayne may have been 'testing' his new school, and his new teachers to see how well organised and strict they were, as well as displaying himself as an uninvolved *non-worker*. Beynon and Atkinson (1984) showed a boy they called King starting at a South Wales school in the 1970s whose main preoccupation was to discover how far he could go before he got punished. Beynon watched King behaving badly, and heard teachers discussing how problematic King was for all of them. Beynon and the staff were concerned that King was 'leading other boys astray'. The metaphor of a possibly irreversible movement into an anti-school, bad pupil, career, is blatant. In fact, as Beynon later discovered, when the school sorted the boys into streams (tracks) after the first half term, King got poor marks in the selection tests and was placed in a low stream, while the boys he was supposed to have led astray were allocated to a top stream. It transpired that one clever and highly motivated boy, Morgan had used King to find out *for him* where the teachers' limits were. Once that 'research' had been done, he detached himself from King telling Beynon candidly that he did not want King for a friend, but had found him very useful. He had even allowed King to copy his homework, secure in the knowledge that King did no academic work and would therefore be consigned to a bottom stream, and be separated from him by the organisation of the school. Two other boys, Green and Levy, explained patiently to Beynon that King and a boy called O'Mally:

> were always messing, talking and acting a bit thick, testing teachers. (Beynon and Atkinson, 1984: 262)

Other boys watched, while King and O'Mally tested the staff. As Green explained:

> 'Someone had to do it' so that all the boys could 'find out about the school, the teachers, and see who your mates were. You've got to know where you stand'. (1984: 262)

It is likely that every other pupil in the first year at Melin Court was discovering what the limits were by observing Wayne Patel's 'wanderings'. Observing a *flâneur* watching the world is a great research strategy. As the early weeks of the school year unfolded at Melin Court, Wayne's behaviour, avoiding school lessons, continued. Nine days after the encounter with Miss Fern already described, the B science group to which Wayne had been assigned had a class with Miss Fern because Melin Court teachers shared teaching all the sets. So while Wayne did not have Miss Fern when Miss Fern taught Group A, he did have her when she taught Group B. It was possible in the first few weeks for the teachers to be confused about which pupils were in which of their classes, and for the adolescents to be muddled about which of their general science lessons were taught by each of the science team.

> The class arrived with a lot of noise and Mrs Fern warns them that although she is aware they may get lost there is no need to fuss when they arrive and shout as if they are in the yard. Wayne Patel is not present. Miss Fern starts to call the register which is divided by sex, with the boys first. She has just reached the girls

when Colin and Manji arrive. They are in Group C and have come to the wrong science lesson. Miss Fern says they are not in this group. Jim says Colin *is* in this group, as the boys near him say he is not. Jim shows by grimaces that he knows and is teasing Colin or testing Miss Fern. Miss Fern sends the two boys off to the C Group.

The observer could see Wayne Patel and two other boys in the yard wandering about. It had taken Miss Fern eight minutes of the lesson to call the register, and send Colin and Manji away. She then began the first educational activity.

> The books came out at 10.55 when the homework is returned. I can see, through the window, that Wayne and Glenn are now heading towards this laboratory. They have now missed 15 minutes of the class. Mrs Hallows comes in and she and Miss Fern leave together. Miss Fern returns with Glenn and Wayne. (Delamont and Galton, 1986)

These fieldnotes show how in his first month of secondary schooling, Wayne had already *either* demonstrated that the school's grouping system and timetabling were beyond his comprehension *or* become a creative *avoider* of lessons and tester of the Melin Court staff. Wayne Patel was a *flâneur* in his secondary school.

Leaving Urry's paradigm and the contested notion of the *flâneur*, the chapter now turns to what has been observed about the movements of pupils and students and teachers. School teachers face a series of paradoxes around pupils and movement in schools. Metz (1978: 148) pointed out that in the American junior high school, confining large numbers of active young people in small spaces causes many of the problems the schools have with order and control. Adolescents are physically active and sociable, she argues, yet in an American school day they can move and talk for 75 minutes while being required to sit still and not talk for 320 minutes. That stillness and confinement, or the teachers' attempts to attain them, is so common in schools for pupils over eight or so, that it is easy to overlook it in fieldwork. A good contrast, from an 'unusual' pair of schools, which helps to fight familiarity, is the study by Rose (1988). Hers is one of the few ethnographies of schools where American children were forced to sit still and silent, working alone on worksheets, in separate booths, summoning the teacher silently by placing a flag on the shelf above their heads. Such lack of movement is emblematic of the ferocious discipline of the Baptist sect she studied.

Teachers of classroom-based subjects frequently find pupils' physical restlessness, especially their 'inability' to sit still for 40–50 minutes, one of the most frustrating aspects of keeping order. In 1950 Wylie (1951) was struck by how French village children were expected to be able to sit still, and generally behave much more formally, than American children were 'able' to do, or were expected to do by adults. It was precisely this static, 'repressed' stillness, which Wylie reported from the early 1950s, which still characterised French infant and primary schools that the minority of parents in Brittany who opted for the *diwan* schools were trying to avoid for their children (MacDonald, 1989). At the same time there is a widespread belief in the UK that children are too fat, lack experience of 'proper' outdoor play and regular exercise because too many are reluctant to go outside for fresh air and vigorous movement, are driven to school, and lack stamina. This is paralleled by widespread teacher beliefs that children are 'mollycoddled', and allowed to wallow in small aches and pains (Prout, 1997). Yet at the same time, schools try to stop physical fights between pupils, even though these could be a good form of exercise.

In complete contrast, those teachers who are paid to teach subjects that are movement centred – physical education, dance, drama – struggle with achieving *enough* movement from many of their pupils. Researchers need to recognise that ideas about what movements, and more importantly, stillnesses and immobilities, are deemed to be appropriate for different age groups, and for males and females, are culturally specific and vary a great deal across time. The current lack of access to PE for girls and women in Saudi Arabia is seen as 'peculiar' and 'backward'. Yet in the USA and the UK in 1850, exactly the same views were widely held.

Many people in education today have no knowledge of the history of how girls' and women's education was a battle not only for access to academic subjects, but also for freedom of movement. It is hard to imagine in 2014 how shocked respectable people in Britain and the USA were by the first women who took up bicycling, field hockey, gymnastics, and lacrosse, and introduced those activities into schools and colleges (see Atkinson, 1978, 1987; Park, 1987). Today 'we' associate restrictions on women cycling or playing hockey with the strict Islamic regimes in countries like Saudi Arabia and Afghanistan, not with 'civilised' cities like Boston and Birmingham. The feminist pioneers of education for women were concerned that only healthy females could study, and wanted to prove that academic work would not destroy women's health as many 'experts' believed. So they introduced sport, which required the removal of the waist-constricting whaleboned corset, and involved bodily movement in the fresh air. Many commentators were shocked (see Delamont 1978a, 1978b, 1989, 1993). The feminist pioneers knew that corsets and tightly-laced waists impeded women's

89

movements, so introduced the gym slip which had no waist, so needed no corset, and therefore freed up women's bodies.

Movement may be encouraged or constrained by clothing. Patricia Jeffery (1979) writes with feeling about how hard it is to move in a *burqa* or *hijab*. She did fieldwork in 1975–1976 near Delhi in a village with a shrine, the site of pilgrimage, of a Muslim mystic. The women she studied were Muslims – the kin of the male custodians of the shrine – who lived in very strict segregation and wore the *burqa* (the body covering garment) when outside their homes. Her detailed account of the impact of *purdah* and the *burqa* on movement is a fantastic way to make the study of movement in any educational setting unfamiliar. Firstly the women rarely wore shoes. At home they worked barefoot, and occasionally wore loose sandals. Shoes for the streets were uncomfortable. Many so rarely left their houses that they found walking in the street exhausting. Additionally the *burqa* as an extra layer of clothing meant that for much of the year going out meant being unbearably hot. Worse, the informants complained, they had no local 'geography', so were terrified of getting lost unless escorted by a male relative. In the *burqa* women cannot see where they are going. As one said:

> You have to spend so much time peering out through the veil to watch your step that you do not have any time to look around. Why, only the other day when we going to that wedding in old Delhi, I tripped over some grating over a drain with hardly any practice going out. (Jeffery, 1979: 152)

These Muslim women believed that they were also taunted because of the *burqa* when outside. No wonder they described themselves as 'frogs at the bottom of a well', only able to glimpse a small 'slice' of the world. Jeffrey, as a woman, was able to live among these secluded women, and while she chose not to wear a *burqa* herself when outside, her description of their restricted movement – constrained by beliefs, by public ridicule, by physical discomfort, by lack of physical fitness, by ignorance of the locality – are vivid and compelling.

This research is an excellent example of how a scholar studying the movements of pupils or teachers should, literally, walk a mile in their shoes, to capture the immobility or mobility under scrutiny. Ethnographers who can live under the constraints of the conventions on movement, learn a great deal about those constraints. Abu-Lughod (1986) provides a parallel account to Jeffery's of how, by choosing to live in a Bedouin encampment, she found her movements restricted by the conventions of the culture, so she experienced the world of the women and their movements and mobilities. Studying such a strongly gendered culture by observation, or by reading the ethnographies about it, can sharpen the ethnographer's eye for parallel constraints and conventions much nearer 'home'.

It would be over-optimistic to assume that in 'modern', 'western' societies the physical education of adolescent girls is unconstrained by social conventions. An analysis of the first PE lessons for the new female pupils at Melin Court and Waverly (12–18) comprehensive schools revealed that a set of conventions were offered to the 12 year olds about the movements that were appropriate for them. The main reasons that were offered to the girls for the 'rules' on appropriate and inappropriate clothing in which to move, were biological, or an actual or potential male gaze.

In September 1978, a cohort of 12 year olds entered Melin Court School in Coalthorpe, a city in the north of England suffering from a post-industrial slump. I observed a double period (80 minutes) of girls' Physical Education with 40 pupils and two female teachers that took place entirely in the changing room; an entirely sedentary class. The data were partially published in Delamont and Galton (1986) and revisited for Delamont (1998). The latter account of the complete lesson revealed how circumscribed the girls' embodiment was to be – see also Chapter 7 below. In this double lesson the only movements that each girl experienced were to get up when her name was called, and walk to the teacher to show a specified garment (e.g. a short skirt to be won over a leotard for hockey). Each item of PE kit was inspected separately, so each girl was called up about six times. While that helped the staff learn the girls' names, it was hardly exercise. The paradox, an 80 minute PE class that involved sitting listening to homilies and lectures, while queues of girls were displaying name labels in garments, is not as rare as the outsider might think. Many PE lessons contain a great deal of watching, listening and queuing rather than actual movement.

Of course movement may be enforced – at worst for slaves, refugees, prisoners, etc. at gunpoint – it may be necessary for survival (hunter-gatherers, pastoralists when the flock need to move for grazing or water) – it may be a consequence of urbanisation (commuting to work) – part of a job (drill in the army, moving a bus or taxi for the driver) but a great deal of movement in wealthy cultures is voluntary – playing squash or golf, dancing for pleasure, and the martial arts which are widespread across North America, Western Europe, and Australasia. Some movement can be addictive. Some enthusiasts or addicts move from voluntary learning to become teachers, just as the commonest route to being a PE teacher is enjoyment and success in sports as a pupil. *Capoeira* teachers, especially much-revered masters, are often asked to tell their life-stories as public autobiographical narratives at festivals. The typical story emphasises how *capoeira* swept the teller off his or her feet so they gave up everything else to be 'totally *capoeira*'. Andre Luiz B Maciel Viera (2004: 21) writes of his first exposure:

> I was delighted, my body was shivering, and I fell in love with *capoeira*. That's when I started practicing. *Capoeira* came into my life and I couldn't get away from it!

A good ethnographer has notes on which movements produce bodies shivering with pleasure, which are loathed, and on which types of mobility do and do not take place at the fieldsite.

HOW TO... STUDY MOVEMENT AND MOBILITIES

Because my own research is on movement and mobilities, this section starts with a very brief vignette.

A Saturday Morning, April 2010

In the large, light-flooded hall of a Victorian building set in a suburb of a major British city, a large African-Brazilian man moves gracefully to the music of a drum, two tambourines and two bow-shaped instruments strung with wire. He demonstrates kicks and escapes to a class of over 60 people, who move in unison, copying him. At one end of the hall is a small stage, and standing on it is an old woman, scribbling in a notebook.

I am that woman, doing ethnographic fieldwork on the Brazilian dance and martial art, *capoeira*. For eight years I have been privileged to watch over 1000 hours of *capoeira* classes. That particular Saturday morning the teacher was one of the most famous *capoeira* masters (*mestres*) in the world; one of the greatest teachers I have ever been privileged to watch.

The Chicago boxing trainer, Dee Dee, rejected the idea that Wacquant (2004: 100–102) or anyone else, could learn anything useful about boxing from a book. The core of Dee Dee's objection was: 'You don't get no sense of *movement*. Boxin's movement, it's the movement that count'. Wacquant learnt about movement in boxing by learning to box, as Lewis (1992) and Downey (2005) learnt about movement in *capoeira* by taking *capoeira* classes. Neil Stephens and I (Stephens and Delamont, 2006a) learnt about movement in *capoeira* by two-handed ethnography. Neil Stephens took lessons, I watched them, then we compared our understandings.

Studying movement, especially highly skilled and technical forms of movement, such as dance, is currently fashionable not only among dance specialists, but in social science more widely. Fraleigh and Hanstein (1999) is an edited collection of papers on research methods for studying dance. The most famous recording system for dance is Labanotation, and there are software packages for analysing it (Frosch, 1999). A project on movement might justify the ethnographer learning Labanotation and investing in the software but it is important to remember that the readers of the eventual outputs (and they will be readers because print media still dominate) need a prose description of the movements, although multi-media materials via a link to a website with interactive capabilities are exciting. Recording movement with a system like Labanotation, or on film, may help the ethnographer's understanding but it may take a different skill to explain them to the audience for the thesis, books and articles.

It seems blindingly obvious that movement is best studied by audio-visual recording of it. However, there can be much greater difficulties in getting ethical approval, and informed consent, for using camcorders to 'film' people, especially if there are children present. More seriously, even if ethical approval and informed consent for filming is given, it is easy to forget, in the excitement of filming people, events, and activities, that making an audio-visual recording only *postpones* analysis, which will inevitably have to be selective in two ways. First, because of the need to write about what the film has captured, for those who have no access to the pictures; and second, because unanalysed film is in all important senses meaningless. The proposals made by Dicks, Mason, Coffey and Atkinson (2005) for deploying the resources of hypermedia in order to give 'readers' – or users – or fellow enthusiasts – access to multi-media materials via a link to a website with interactive capabilities are exciting. But there are so far no arrangements in place for the websites to be hosted and maintained in perpetuity; in the UK there are no legal requirements that they be 'deposited' in the copyright libraries, so they are likely to vanish. Print media are currently more durable.

93

A LOOK TO THE FUTURE

what research we need on movement and mobilities

The research we need on mobilities in formal educational settings can be defined by applying Urry's nine approaches to the school, or university, or any set of informants learning or teaching. Doing this will 'find' and highlight the known and the unknown mobilities and immobilities.

seven

bodies and performativity:
not pleasure dancing
but ceremonial

The teacher first called on a male student. He, as she had predicted to me, listed thin lips, light-to-brown skin, small (thin) nose, and long hair. One male identified the facial characteristics of the woman he wanted to marry as those belonging to a white woman; not one of the other males identified 'Black' features as ideal. (Fordham, 1996: 295)

Before I went to Wimblesham County School I was told by my sister that I should not pick pennys [sic] off the floor because that's why people get bullied and I would be labelled a 'sad loser'.

Fordham's ethnography of everday life for African-American teenagers in an ordinary high school is a bleak and depressing read. In the extract I have quoted, she is appalled by the way(s) in which the young African-American men entirely reject the bodies of their young African-American women contemporaries. In the urban legend, an 11 year old is warned that what might seem an ordinary behaviour (picking up a stray coin from the floor) would be interpreted by older pupils as a stigmatising, image-damaging act, leading to being bullied. In the subtitle, 'Not pleasure dancing but ceremonial', from Zora Neale Hurston (1935: 239) the interpretation of the dancing being done is crucial: in the specific case the body movements are ceremonial not for pleasure. What that highlights is that all movements have meaning(s) bits for the people performing them, and for anyone observing them, and that these meanings may be different. Hurston was clear that the dancing she was being told to do was magical or religious in its purpose, not pleasurable, social dancing. Throughout the chapter the focus is on the social meanings of movements for the informants and the researcher. Educational ethnography regularly reveals that socialisation and enculturation require new embodiments, new performativities; and, conversely, that familiar bodily features and embodiments can be stigmatising in new environments.

In the years since 1980, sociology and anthropology have refocused on classic themes of embodiment and performativity. Crossley (1995) separated the sociology of the body, which focused on 'what is done to the body', and carnal sociology, which 'addresses the active role of the body in social life'. He proposed that these 'twin aspects of a single problematic' needed to be fused into one 'carnal sociology of the body' (1995: 43). More recently Shilling (2007: 1) wrote that:

> the contemporary preoccupations with all things bodily might appear to represent the latest fad among sociologists.

but in fact

> embodiment was used to interrogate some of the longstanding nature/culture, action/structure, and subject/object dualisms that the discipline had wrestled with since its beginnings.

Educational ethnography has been re-enthused by these themes, and they have become prominent. The journal *Ethnography* had a special issue (9, 4, Dec 2008) on 'ethnography and physical culture' which included papers on ballet and boxing. Performativity was placed near the centre of the sociology of education by Ball (2003b) and extended in Ball (2007). This sense of performativity is a technology. The performance of either individual teachers, lecturers or instructors, or of schools, universities, or training organisations, is used to judge the quality, or the output, by managers or inspectors. So teachers or other instructors are judged by a spectacle that they can create for a specific audience.

This chapter has three main sections. It opens with a discussion of the core findings about bodies and performance in educational settings; it then addresses key research strategies for focusing upon those themes when gathering data; and highlights the gaps in the extant research.

Erving Goffman's 1959 book *The Presentation of Self in Everyday Life* set the sociological agenda for understanding how the body and performativity should be studied. There are some ways in which Goffman's insights have become outdated (e.g. when Goffman wrote that people who talked out loud in the street were 'peculiar': today they are assumed to be using a mobile phone) but the overall framework enables us to make sense of 50 years of ethnographic research in formal and informal education settings. When Erving Goffman wrote the first version of what became *The Presentation of Self in Everyday Life*, for an Edinburgh University monograph in 1956, he had only been awarded his PhD three years before for an ethnography of a crofting community on one of the Shetland Islands. The commercially published version

(Goffman, 1959) is not a core text in the sociology or anthropology of education today, although many writings on bodies, self-presentation and performativity are heirs to the book *Stigma* (Goffman, 1963). As many of Goffman's examples are drawn from American high school or college life, his ideas should be central to the study of education. Within the first 12 pages the reader has been told how female college students in the USA know that the number of incoming phone calls to the dorm is one indicator of popularity. As a result, they have strategies to max-imise the number of calls they get, and to ensure that when they are paged many people hear about it (1959: 4). Goffman also discusses how teachers 'start out tough' (p. 12) with new pupils. Susie Scott's (2009) contemporary 'take' on Goffman's core concerns enables education research to draw upon his ideas from a fresh angle. In this chapter the core ideas from Goffman are united with Crossley's carnal sociology in five sections: real and ideal bodies; changing the body: refusers and ethusiasts; clothes and clothing; the injured and wounded body; and the ethnographer's body and performance.

REAL AND IDEAL BODIES

96

Goffman set out the ideal body for an American man, which contains an 'educational' point:

> In an important sense there is only one complete unblushing male in America: a young, married, white, urban, northern, heterosexual, Protestant father of college education, fully employed, of good complexion, weight and height, and a recent record in sports. Any male who fails to qualify in any of these ways is likely to view himself – during moments at least – as unworthy, incomplete, and inferior. (1963: 153)

During schooling, stereotypes about bodies are a major factor in pupils' happiness or misery, especially because of peer pressures. It forms one of the themes in Crosnoe (2011) who draws on Goffman to explore how obesity is an important factor in American high school misery, drop-out, and failure to go on to college. Goffman distinguished discrediting stigma (those that are immediately obvious) from discreditable ones (those which if revealed would be damaging). Obesity is a discrediting stigma, and one that is much commoner in the USA among ethnic minor-ities and the poor. Among young women particularly, being obese was associated with feeling out of place in high school, especially in high schools where most young women were thin, with truanting, drug use, self-rejection, and not going on to college. His detailed fieldwork in

Lamar High School is the latest in a long line of investigations of the exclusionary power of the influential cliques in those schools. Those pressures are powerful long after the students leave school. In Ikeda's (1998) ethnography of American high school reunions, the body image of the informants at high school, and at the reunion (ten to 40 years later) frames their adult biographies. Betty, a key informant, starts her account of organising a reunion by saying that: 'I met a girl at Weight Watchers who was in my high school class' (Ikeda, 1998: 94). Betty had been fat in high school, but had lost a great deal of weight as an adult, and saw the potential of her impending school reunion as a place to perform her new, thin, identity. Ikeda explains that at the reunion, Betty:

> staged her new self-image through her interactions with high school classmates, she actually became what she staged, and confirmed and validated her new identity. (1998: 103)

Bodyweight is a key element for both sexes in that fat kids are ostracised in high school, and appearing thin at a reunion is a sweet revenge. For men, appearing either fat, or bald, at a reunion evokes pity. As a woman at a 40th anniversary explained, she had failed to recognise one of her male contemporaries, because:

> He used to be a good-looking guy with beautiful blond hair. He's absolutely bald now, not a stitch of hair. (1998: 113)

97

Teachers whose bodies are 'unusual' are also stigmatised in schools, because of their size, shape or dress.

One of the reasons Fordham (1996) was appalled by the young men at Capital High was their rejection of their own racial embodiment. Schools are places where bodies are harshly judged. One 'barrier' I found to the social integration of some of the adolescents with mild learning disabilities in Welsh comprehensives was the bodies of the pupils, rather than their 'mental' abilities. Several of the mildly learning impaired pupils were poorly integrated with peers because of other 'handicaps'. One target at Clipperstone, Elwyn, a second year boy, was unlikely to integrate in the dining hall because he ate alone, before the official lunch began.

> 1.08 Elwyn allowed to go early to lunch. This is because left to his own devices he has beans and chips every day. He has a bowel control problem and his mother complains that beans and chips don't help. Thus he has to collect his dinner from the canteen before the rush starts, partly so they can select a balanced meal for him. As he also has a walking disability this way he avoids the rush. Once served Elwyn sits down by himself to eat his lunch. At 1.10 the bells goes to release the rest of the class.

Elwyn therefore had a bowel problem, walked with some difficulty, and as he also had a speech impediment which made it hard for staff, observer and pupils to grasp what he said, his locational, social or educational integration was impeded by more than his intellectual impairment.

At Gorston Hall one boy in the second year had a tube permanently attached with a plaster to his face through which he had been fed while under treatment by a professor from the local University medical school because he had been anorexic. The boy was, by the time of our observation, eating school dinners, but his GP would not remove the tube until the professor authorised it. A boy who had not been eating, and had a tube permanently attached to his nose and mouth, was also likely to have problems integrating at meal times in school. It was not uncommon for all the 'remedial and learning disabled' pupils to have multiple problems (either physical, behavioural or both) as well as being slow learners. At Artinswell, Mrs Scudder told us that Stirling had fallen from a high bridge, suffered brain damage and had a metal plate in his head. This meant he had to be careful not to injure his head again. He had spells when he was unable to concentrate and went 'walkabout'. Alastair had been a premature baby and still had speech problems. Blake was receiving treatment for restricted growth and was tiny for his age. In all these cases the pupils' bodies, and their performances as pupils, were a barrier to their 'fitting in' when mainstreamed.

In all areas of learning and teaching, especially those where bodily skills are involved, there will be the actual bodies of the learners and teachers, and the ideal body that the learners aspire to. In any educational setting the research needs to pay attention to the body and its appropriate performances. Rose (1988) did a comparative ethnography of two different Christian schools in upstate New York. Lakehaven served a working-class fundamentalist Baptist community, Covenant served a middle-class charismatic fellowship. While both rejected many aspects of mainstream American life and its state schools, particularly equality for women, there was a class difference in how the parents expected the adolescent girls to embody and perform as females. The working-class Baptists were, Rose found, most concerned to suppress the flaunting of femininity. In contrast, the middle-class Covenant parents were more worried that girls might not be feminine enough, and might try to pursue jobs and power that are 'unnatural' and undermine male authority. An outsider could assume that all evangelical Christian schools would stress a similar 'modest' asexual female self-presentation, but in fact the class differences found by Rose between Lakehaven and Covenant mean we should all expect differences *between* evangelical schools in the appropriate performativity of students, and therefore to expect them anywhere.

CHANGING THE BODY: REFUSERS AND ENTHUSIASTS

In this section the focus is on teachers and instructors, working first with those who are reluctant to change their bodies, and then those who are keen to do so. For many learners the ideal body is presented as a goal that can be partially attained through hard, continuous, work. Salz (1998) from his Japanese theatre study, for example, explains that:

> 'Before the *kyogen* child can move or dance, he must learn to walk' (Salz, 1998: 93)

Not ordinary walking, of course, but the stylised walking done by actors in *no* and *kyogen* theatre.

> The particular glide is called *suriashi*. The tabs-sock clad foot is slid firmly along the stage floor in small steps, feet straddling an invisible pole, maintaining a low, steady center of gravity to create a serene but powerful glide, emanating suppressed energy. (Salz, 1998: 93)

Similar processes have been studied among ballet dancers and ballet students, and among sportsmen (Jennings, Brown and Sparkes, 2010). In such rhetoric and practice, the body is malleable: by diet, by repetitive exercise, and by learning to tolerate pain. These processes of dieting, exercising, and toleration, are often interrupted by injury (Wainwright and Turner, 2004; Aalten, 2007). In these contexts the respondents had all chosen to be serious body changers, and therefore were unlike many of the school pupils in the mainstream educational ethnographies, where many pupils who are anxious about changing their bodies, and reluctant to do so.

Anxieties about PE classes at secondary school have been reported regularly from studies of transfer. Woodruff and Curtner-Smith (2007) pull together the research, and present American data on fears about PE at high school. Many of the scary stories focused on bodies and performativity, such as:

> if you did bad in PE you wouldn't pass, and that if you were overweight you got a bad grade in PE

and

> I heard I was going to have to dance in PE. It was scary at the time because I couldn't dance and figured everyone would laugh. (Woodruff and Curtner-Smith, 2007: 420)

In schools the PE teachers are expected to change the pupils' bodies, or at least help the children maintain them, while developing their physical

99

skills. Children may resist this. When doing the ethnography of the integration of children with mild learning difficulties, we attended a good many PE classes because it was a subject in which all academic abilities could be taught together albeit in single sex groups. We found that avoiding PE was a regular practice both for the children we were targeting and for those they were supposed to be integrating with. Truancy and skipping lessons were an impediment to integration in all the nine schools studied. At Clipperstone, during a PE lesson, the teacher told us that, out of a class of 20, only four had been present the previous week and expressed surprise that as many as 16 boys were in the lesson on the observation day. The researcher knew that Adair, the target pupil that morning, was in school and should have been in the PE lesson, but he and some friends vanished before it began. Adair reappeared for his English lesson in a remedial class before lunch, but one opportunity for integration in the mixed-ability PE class had been missed. At Sharway Downs when we were following the second year girls from the special class to PE (for which they were integrated with the rest of 'B' band girls) we saw a similar event.

> 1.30 Bell, and the girls move off to the gym. While we wait for the PE teacher to arrive the girls from the three classes mingle. I am following Nerys, who talks to a girl from another form. As soon as the PE staff arrive, and the mistress says they are going into the gym, the girl slides away behind the gym, and is not seen again.

Nerys was fully integrated into this lesson, but at least one of the people she was supposed to interact with had 'mitched' and did no PE that day.

In the first PE lesson for new girls that I attended at Melin Court School in Coalthorpe, the two women set out for the pupils:

1) The sports they would learn: netball, hockey, gymnastics, trampolining, dance, badminton and swimming in winter.
2) The clothes they could wear for each activity.
3) The importance of the male gaze on their bodies.
4) Their future embodiments.

These are explored in detail in Delamont (1998) but the third and fourth points are recapitulated here briefly. In the double lesson the PE teachers explained that the girls needed to buy a leotard for dance, gymnastics and trampolining, and they would also wear it under a skirt for hockey, netball and badminton. Miss Sugnett warned them: 'if you don't wear a leotard you must buy decent knickers because of the boys in the top field' (1998: 10). They were told that they would not swim when they were 'on period', but they had to go to the baths, and tell the swimming teacher who would put 'P' on the register. They did not need to be embarrassed because 'he won't be embarrassed, he's a married man' (p. 10).

To get a research 'grasp' on the body issues facing school pupils, it is helpful to think contrastively about the ethnographies of boxers in training, male models, dancers and actors. Even when a person is an enthusiast for embodied change, wants to learn a new performativity, or can make a living from such 'improvements', they may find some of the rules and requirements irksome or even so unbearable that they become refusers. At the Chicago boxing gym, Wacquant learnt about the dietary regime that any serious fighter needs to follow and how some men could not cope with it:

> To reach his optional fight weight, every boxer must abide by a strict diet (avoid all sugar, starchy and fried foods, eat fish, white meats, and steamed vegetables, drink water or tea). (Wacquant, 2004: 67)

As one boxer, Jake, told Wacquant, the hard part is:

> layin' off the junk-food – the hamburger – the french fries (p. 67)

and no beer.

> You know what it's like to eat no junk food for a whole month, no cokes or ice-cream or chocolate cookies. It be hell. (p. 68)

As Woodward (2008: 540) points out, the 'punishing' regime in the gym is not only 'physically demanding', 'it also involves techniques of the self', especially regulating weight. Boxers compete in weight categories, so if you get too big for one category you have to compete in another where your chances of loss and injury are higher. There is a parallel literature on how female ballet learners and professionals are constantly forced to consider their diet, body shape, and performativity (Wulff, 1998; Aalten, 2007):

Entwistle's (2009) ethnography of the world of high fashion includes a study of male models. One feature of their lives is the large amount of time, effort, and money they have to invest in their bodies to keep a marketable look:

> dieting, exercising, styling one's hair frequently, and other such grooming techniques. (Entwistle, 2009: 64)

She found that the men needed to perform a 'slouchy', 'laddish' and 'casual demeanour' for the London market, while in New York a body honed by weight lifting was more important. These are both, of course, varieties of performance, of the kind that needs to be closely observed in educational settings.

101

Bodily performance is generally related to gender, class and ethnicity. As Herzfeld (1985) argued from Cretan fieldwork among shepherds, masculinity is performative in culturally specific ways. The varieties of male performativity that men who are not Argentinean can be faced with when learning tango are chronicled by Tobin (1998). He learnt tango in Buenos Aires, where most of the instructors are men, and keener, or richer, male students have private lessons. Some teachers hire a female to dance with the male learner, but many do not. In these classes men usually learn by dancing with the male instructor: or rather not 'dancing' but 'practising'. Tobin says

> Argentine men routinely teach one another how to dance in tango dance classes, and they often practice and even show-off dancing together in tango *practices*, but in the milongas of Buenos Aires and Montevideo men never dance together. (Tobin, 1998: 93)

Tobin had three teachers: a man in his 60s he calls Pedro Monteleone who asked his daughter to come to dance with Tobin in his private classes; and in contrast two younger male instructors in their 40s, Rivarola and Gomez, who taught Tobin by dancing with him themselves. The older man did not ask his daughter to attend classes for Argentine male students; the two younger teachers employed a female assistant when instructing North American men. The crucial issues here are definitional, locational, and performative. While tango danced in the public arena of the milonga is strongly heterosexual, and men dance with women, in other spaces, it is entirely acceptable for men to dance the women's steps for instructional and practice sessions. When Tobin was at a class where men outnumbered women:

> Monteleone assigned me and an Argentine man to practice the tango-walk with one another. The man, who was a physician, told me he was uncomfortable dancing with another man... Falling back on what I had learnt from other Argentines, I assured him we were not 'dancing', we were 'practicing' and he appeared to accept this distinction with genuine relief. (1998: 93)

Many aspects of embodied performance may need to be learnt, and teachers are expected to know how to enculturate the learners. That is as true of shooting instructors in the British army as it is of tango masters. Brian Lande (2007) has written about learning to shoot a rifle in the British army which depends on learning how and when to breathe to maximise the precision of the shot. The instructor wants the cadets to learn to shoot 'at the bottom of the exhale' (p. 103) when the lungs are empty. Lande watched a sergeant work with a cadet learning to shoot:

He gets down on the ground, lying on his belly at a slight angle away from the cadet and watches her shoot and gives her instruction. 'Ok, bring your elbows in more. Good, good. It hurts, I know, but you won't fatigue your muscles if you use your bones. Ok, now move your whole body around more so it is easier to have your natural point of aim pointing straight ahead at your target. Make sure that your ankles are splayed inward, yeah, that will keep you steady. Bring your right leg up and crook it. Ok. See, that's better, isn't it? (Lande, 2007: 103)

These are very precise instructions about many aspects of the body. As I argued in Chapter 4, what teachers expect a student to be able to do at a particular biological age is very different in different cultures. The adult expectations of the theatrical family in Kyoto are a good contrastive example for ethnographers in the UK or the USA. Salz (1998) shows how the traditional Japanese theatre *kyogen* family Sengoro Shigeyama – a lineage going back 600 years based in Kyoto – start the boys between the ages of three and six on stage playing a monkey. There is then a set of roles played for the next 16 or so years, up to a half-fox-half-priest played around the age of 20 which marks the transition to being a fully adult actor. In *kyogen* the child has to learn a special walk, a special posture, a special speech style, to memorise whole plays, to perform dances, before he appears as the monkey in *Utsubozaru*, a famous and powerful play about a Lord, his servant, an animal trainer and a monkey.

Inside any institution or subculture, teachers and learners will have clear ideas about bodily skills the learners have, and which are still beyond them. A good example of that comes from the *capoeira* research. In regional *capoeira* classes, if there is a *roda* at the end, it may climax with a very fast rhythm, set by the musicians, to which the '*alto ligeiro*' (the high fast game) is played by the best students. The *alto ligeiro* is only kicks, without escapes, so the players have to have skill, and trust each other's timing and use of space. When Neil Stephens and I first attended classes, the best students were Raksha and Phao, Portuguese brothers, who had done some *capoeira* before. They were the most likely to do the closing *alto ligeiro*, and initially other students let them, because they were the most self-confident, and, as brothers who played together a lot, they had the highest likelihood of being successful (i.e. not losing their balance, the rhythm, or kicking each other). As the months passed, other students got good enough, and confident enough to do the *alto ligeiro* at the end of the closing *roda*.

103

CLOTHES AND CLOTHING

Learning to decipher the meanings that informants in a field setting attribute to clothes and other bodily features such as hair styles, tattoos, jewellery, etc. is an important task in ethnography. The researcher's initial interpretation is often 'wrong', i.e. different from that of 'insiders'. Ho (2009: 117) provides a good example of this from her ethnography of top financial institutions in the USA. She reports how her assumptions about dress were challenged and overturned by two senior women at Lehman Brothers. Ho had assumed that 'most women who worked on Wall Street' (p. 117) travelled to work in socks and trainers, the socks over sheer tights, and changed into heeled shoes once at the office. When she heard two senior executives criticising that practice because the socks and trainers looked 'tacky', Ho expressed her assumption that all women commuted like that. Her informants were firm: travelling to the office like that is a marker of 'lower-class status'. High-ranking women live close to their offices, in expensive neighbourhoods. Routine office workers live much further away and have to commute on public transport. High-ranking employees have taxis paid for by their employees to take them home at night, so the women do not 'need' to wear trainers. Changing your shoes on arrival at the office is a sign of being in a low-grade routine job. High-ranking women carefully dressed to look like high-ranking women and avoided the 'socks and trainers' sign of low status. Only detailed attention to the views of actors in a setting enables the ethnographer to go beyond the stereotypes.

104

A parallel example can be found in Marion's (2008) ethnography of American professional ballroom dancing. He discovered how professional dancers of Latin and of 'Standard or smooth' styles learn the different conventions of dress, make up, hair styling and shoes, and how to perform in them. It transpired that dress and deportment 'off duty', for example, when watching others compete, are equally culturally specific. Marion also explored the performativity of gender in professional ballroom dance, where the crucial element is the performance of a gendered partnership of heteronormativity. A cultural model of leading and following has to be convincingly enacted. As Marion (2008: 149) summarises it: 'different understandings of how to dance as a couple are crafted within the couple'. The costuming is an integral part of the performance of the couple.

In educational settings we need to appreciate the interactionships between clothing conventions, bodies and performativity. The core ideas we can use to focus on clothes and clothing are set out by Entwistle (2009) in her book about the international scene in high fashion. She theorises about the aesthetic market place, and the cultural economy. Her data are illuminating about many aspects of taste, embodiment, identity, performance, tacit knowledge and the media. The fieldwork was carried out on two sets of actors: the first, male fashion models, model agencies and model bookers, in London and New York; the second, fashion buyers for Selfridges (a department store in Oxford Street, London).

Both sets of actors, the models, model agencies and bookers, and the buyers are all cultural intermediaries in the aesthetic marketplace. The framework Entwistle uses to explore the roles of cultural intermediaries in the high fashion aesthetic market place can usefully be deployed to analyse the aesthetic 'rules' of formal educational settings such as schools, or universities. In any such setting, key actors share an aesthetic perspective. In the high fashion world, Entwistle found that the model agents and bookers, like the buyers, have aesthetic knowledge. As a skilled ethnographer Entwistle studied both the 'world' of the models and the world of fashion buyers as ways into understanding the aesthetic marketplace of fashion. Given the relative lack of attention to the clothing and performativity of men in educational ethnography, the insights from Entwistle's work on male models are usefully contrastive.

The case study of models, and the people who get them bookings, is particularly focused on men, and starts from the economic base. As Entwistle (2009: 5) points out 'modelling is one of the few occupations where women earn significantly more than men'. One concrete example is an Australian man, who had been on the same shoot as Gisele Bündchen, the Brazilian super model who was earning three million dollars a year: Entwistle's informant got a few hundred dollars for the 'same' work on the shoot. The models, and those who advise them on what bookings to accept, operate in a world where prestige and earnings are, to an outsider, oddly divorced. A man who aims to be a *fashion* model needs to appear in the editorial pages and on the covers of periodicals like *Vogue*, which pay very little. A job modelling clothes for a catalogue might pay £2,000 per day, and a campaign for a global soft drink £35,000. Accepting these jobs, however, can damage the *fashion* career and significantly lower the man's cultural value at the *haute couture* end of the business. One head booker explained to Entwistle: 'All the better agencies try to protect the image of their models' (2009: 66).

105

These two findings, about a rare example of a male occupation that pays less even at the highest levels than its female equivalent, and about an inverse relationship between prestige and earnings in a male job, both help fight the familiar in educational settings. In their work on physics and art teachers in two English cities, Sikes, Measor and Woods (1982) found that the art teachers stressed their clothing and embodied self-presentation as a vital element in their aesthetic market place and their economic present and future. They chose to dress like artists and not like 'promotable' potential school managers. Educational ethnographers could focus more upon these relationships – aesthetic and financial – in schools or colleges. We can use Entwistle's work to search for areas where aesthetic market places may reveal *unfamiliar* economic and prestige hierarchies that are being taught and learnt.

THE INJURED AND WOUNDED BODY

One of the important areas for ethnographic attention is the injured, wounded, body. This has been central in research on sport, and dance, especially Wainwright and Turner (2004). Woodward (2008: 541) points out that 'The boxing body bleeds, sweats and is injured', partly because all contests are premised on one fighter injuring the other. All boxers train and fight 'though the threat of the damaged body'. Educational ethnographers have generally paid little attention to injured and wounded bodies in schools and colleges, but the lesson of the studies on ballet and sport is that it would be a good focusing strategy.

the ethnographer's body and performance

One key issue in the study of bodies and performativity is that of the ethnographer's own body: its posture, gestures, clothing and so on. A second is the extent to which core aspects of embodied learning can only be grasped by participating in that learning: in other words, to study learning ballet, the ethnographer has to learn ballet. The ethnographer's own body and performativity are always implicated in the data collection. The researchers' self-presentation, especially clothing, and the role(s) they play will enhance or impede the rapport with informants (Herzfeld, 2004, 2009).

106

HOW TO... STUDY BODIES AND PERFORMATIVITY

Dimitriadis (2008) drawing on Denzin (2003) writes engagingly about the performative turn both as an empirical topic and as a way to decentre the teacher (and therefore the ethnographer). His first research area was hip-hop, and the dialogic relationship between performer and audience which led him away from analysing the lyrics and towards a focus on the performance. Focusing on the linguistic distinction between *langue* and *parole* (between the formal structure of language and the way(s) in which it is spoken), he followed Dell Hymes's ideas about real language in real settings into studying rap music as 'emeshed in live activities' (Dimitriadis, 2008: 304) for the African-American adolescents he studied in a community centre in a small city in the Mid West of the USA. That research meant that 'the performative' helped Dimitriadis fight familiarity by requiring him to rethink what hip-hop songs 'meant'.

Gamradt (1998) observed workshops in which surgeons learnt a radically different way of doing gall bladder surgery at intensive two and three day weekend courses where they operated on animals. Gramradt contrasts the normal processes of fieldwork, especially the initial stages, when the researcher feels baffled by:

> Not knowing how to make sense of events taking place in a field setting is both troubling and troublesome. (1998: 76)

As the research proceeds, the ethnographer undergoes a shift from rudimentary comprehension to what Eisner (1997) termed connoisseurship. In her surgery research, Gamradt felt that her research was not going well, in ways she could not grasp, and whatever the problem was it had blown 'up suddenly' and was 'not soluble by hard work or rational action' (1998: 70). Her solution was to learn how to do the work of the scrub nurses, so that she could take over from them for brief spells and give them some respite during the intensive training sessions. Her new, active, embodied role, which she initially performed with great trepidation, reopened her fieldwork site so her data collection was possible.

Herzfeld (2009) has explored what he terms 'cultural intimacy' (p.133) and the need for us to understand our own postures and, particularly, gestures. He contrasts his own performances in Crete, Italy and Thailand. One amusing anecdote concerns Herzfeld realising that in a French committee he was performing as a Thai; for example flinching when offered a book with only one hand (rude in Thailand). Margaret Kenna (1992) discovered that in her early fieldwork on a tiny Greek island, far off the tourist map when she first worked there in the 1960s, when she was a young, single woman, she had, entirely in ignorance, conveyed very confusing messages to the women of the island. Kenna sat in a posture that was normal for respectable young American women, with her legs crossed above the knee. Years later she discovered that, in the local culture, the only woman who sat like that were prostitutes. It was believed on Nisos that the posture prevented pregnancies. Her posture sent baffling 'messages' to the people of Nisos. We should all be as acutely aware of our own embodied performativity.

107

A LOOK TO THE FUTURE

the gaps in research on bodies and performativity

What are the absences in our knowledge about bodies and performativity? Woodward (2008) argues that too much of the research on boxing is concentrated on the boxers' bodies, and not enough on the embodied researcher. In the educational ethnography, teachers' bodies have been largely ignored, although their performativity has been studied; and their clothes and clothing are a largely unstudied topic. Drawing on work like Marion or Entwistle would open up new vistas for educational research, especially in higher education. Among pupils and students, more contrastive work on expectations about embodiment drawing on 'other' cultures might fight the familiarity of what we have already.

eight

groups and identities: the profound silence of the initiated

They had not interacted with Black people at all... and you know me, I'm like, well you know I'm me. But it was weird because they listened to rap music. They listened to rap music. (Winkle-Wagner, 2009: 70–71)

I was told that you will get called a 'keeno' if you wear your tie normally (i.e. with the big fat bit out as opposed the small, thin bit). If you wear long socks (girls) you get called a virgin. (Chipping Langdon High School, 1996)

In the opening passage, Winkle-Wagner is quoting an African-American college student, Michelle, who chose to share a flat in her second year with white room-mates. These women had all grown up in small towns and had never met an African-American person before they came to College. They watched Black Entertainment Television (BET) because they liked rap music, but complained it had no white singers on it. They were entirely ignorant of the history of BET, which had been started when the MTV channel never showed any African-American performers. Michelle's point was that her room-mates had grown up in an entirely different America from hers and were marginalising her and her whole experience of American society through what she felt was their unimaginable ignorance. In the urban legend, the awful possibility of being excluded from desirable peer groups for being too 'academic' is held out before the incoming child. Being 'in' or 'out' of friendship groups is a core part of formal and informal education. The Zora Neale Hurston (*Mules and Men*, 1935: 185) quote in the title referred to the silence about magical and religious practices which is required of those initiated into their mysteries, but, as the chapter develops examples are given, particularly Jones (2004) on African-American fraternities, where initiation into mysteries can also be all too pertinently relevant to studies of some groups in education.

Groups and identities have been one of the major foci of educational ethnography for 60 years. Key findings are summarised, then the best ways to gather data on those themes are highlighted. Finally the chapter draws attention to what aspects of identity and groupings educational ethnographers have ignored or left undeveloped. The focus in this chapter is on school pupils and students in higher education, although there is some material on groups among school teachers (e.g. Datnow, 1997, 1998) and higher education staff. Peshkin (1997), drawing on research among First Americans in New Mexico, uses the powerful phrase 'communities of memory'. Such groups, whether in face-to-face contact, or in cyberspace, can be important: they can be what Shibutani (1955) called a reference group.

There are two main social science approaches to the study of pupils and students. One, like the educational institutions themselves, measures and classifies them, the other sets out to understand what education looks like to those who are the 'beneficiaries' of it. It is the latter that is explored in this chapter: the research that seeks answers to questions such as: Why would the way a tie is knotted, or the style of sock, produce such opportunities for fellow pupils to apply such apparently pejorative labels as 'keeno' and 'virgin'? What are the consequences of such labelling? One thing will be immediately clear to all readers: a peer culture that used 'keeno' as a negative term will *not* encourage academic success and is therefore potentially a culture teachers and parents will be unenthusiastic about. The role of peer groups in the 'under-achievement' of boys and young men, about which there has been a moral panic since the early 1990s across the Anglophone world, is captured in that scary story.

While most of the chapter is about the groups formed by school pupils and higher education students, it is important to recognise that the social science dynamics of such groups are by no means confined to formal educational institutions. Hence the first ethnography of small groups is not 'from' education at all.

Cottrell (2004) devotes a whole chapter to exploring how individual musicians are, or are not, integrated into musical ensembles. He had led a saxophone quartet for 18 years when he published his book, and three of the members of the quartet were the 'originals': Cottrell and two fellow students from music college. So his analysis of the relationships between the individual identity of the musician and the dynamics of ensemble formation and survival draws on his own biography as well as the field-work he conducted in London in the late 1990s. He argues that:

> The small group situation provides an ideal platform for expressing their sense of musical self within a social context. (Cottrell, 2004: 103–104)

In the ethnography, Cottrell shows how both the musical skills and the social competencies are equally important.

You get certain people and they're really soloistic and that doesn't work, and you get certain people who are timid and that doesn't work. (2004: 86)

Apart from the musicians' personal musical styles, Cottrell argues that:

social skills of a more general kind are needed to interact competently with other musicians in the intricate web of relationships that constitutes the community of London musicians. (2004: 80)

Allied to the social skills for playing in the *ensemble*, Cottrell found that adherence to the etiquettes and to practicalities of things like sharing small spaces for sleeping and playing are also important if a group is to survive.

Some of the most insightful research on students in higher education, and on different types of groups in childhood and adolescence has been done outside the sociology or anthropology of education, and been neglected by it. Fine's (1983, 1985, 1987, 1996, 1998, 2001, 2003) sociological research on fantasy games, Little League baseball, on catering students, on debating competitions in high school, is not drawn upon routinely. Similarly the research of Adler and Adler, on college athletes, on car pooling (an enforced, adult-led form of childhood grouping) and on cliques and peer pressures in American schools (1998) conducted by mainstream sociologists, is rarely cited in educational publications.

There are three categories that can frame the lives of learners. First are their ascribed characteristics: the class, gender, race, religion, and so on. Then there are the institutions they are put into and the sub-sections of those institutions (such as streams or tracks) to which they are assigned by adults. Finally there are the groups they form for themselves, which are often a consequence of the ascribed characteristics and the classificatory functions of the institutions they attend. The eventual identities of Winkle-Wagner's American college students, the 11 year old who had heard that warning, and the initiate in the secret society are all grounded in these three sorts of 'groupings'. When Katz argued that ethnographic

[d]ata are strategically well shaped to locate sociologically significant phenomena when they track how people move through an anxiously monitored transition from one state to another. Ethnographic data that vividly describe *how* people make such a transition are likely to find that the workings of a spiritual, magical or sentimental culture is a key contingency. (2001: 461)

He could have been describing the material in this chapter. It focuses on the extant literature on peer groups in educational settings and how they are affected by the ascribed characteristics of learners and by the educational institutes themselves, and then moves on to how pupils facing transitions evoke practical and 'magical' aspects of the involvement of the peer group in the transition. The peer groups of children and pupils and students provide the sentimental culture Katz evokes as the mediator between society and the individual. As Swain points out:

> Children are watched, judged, measured, described, compared, trained, corrected, examined and classified almost as soon as they step into the classroom on their first day. (Swain, 2003: 300)

Studying how pupils, or students, or other learners respond to the processes Swain describes, by developing small groups each with its own idioculture (Fine, 1987) has been a major preoccupation of educational ethnographers. There are several types of groups fundamental to education in formal institutions, which have received ethnographic attention. Separate schools create different groups of pupils and students. For example, Gordon (2009) reminds us that schooling in Japan is strongly segregated. The children of the outcaste group – the *Burakumin*, those of immigrants, even those who are second and third generation and those Japanese who were born overseas and have since returned – attend entirely different schools from the rest of the society. Mainstream Japanese children are also likely to attend *juku* (private crammers) after school, thus further segregating them.

112

Peshkin (1997), for example, is a study of four different subcultural, perhaps ethnic, perhaps linguistic, groups of Americans segregated into four different schools, and thus unlikely to meet. It is important to note that these four schools are all in one New Mexico area of America, and all the pupils are Americans. American researchers, at least the sensitive ones who want to pay attention to, and show respect for, the many different subcultures in the USA, sometimes forget that all the subgroups may share more American beliefs and dreams and inequalities than they, or the ethnographer, realise. Peshkin focused on an area of New Mexico with four different subcultures: first the Mexican–Americans; second the First Americans (who called themselves Indian, a term that social scientists have abandoned as derogatory); third the Hispano, who settled in Mexico when it was a Spanish colony; and fourth the Anglos (the first language English speakers who are 'white'). Peshkin, by separating the Mexican-American from the Hispano, is adding a complexity – disaggregating the wider category of 'Hispanic' or 'Latino' or 'Chicano' that is often used as a shorthand for residents in the USA (whether citizens, legal aliens, or illegal migrants) who are Spanish speaking and Roman Catholic.

The four sets of adolescents attended different schools: the Anglos in his research attend Edgewood Academy (a private, non-denominational school); the Mexican-Americans attended Haven High School (public);

the Hispano students went to Norteno High School (also public); and the Peublo Indians went to a non-public school he calls Indian High School. Indian High School is a weekly boarding school for Pueblo, Navaho and Apache teenagers, run by the Pueblo and the federal government's agency the Bureau of Indian Affairs (BIA). These adolescents had little opportunity to form friendship groups across ethnic divides, or, in the male case, to acquire other models of masculinity than those of their families and their own 'culture'. Peshkin himself did the research in the Indian and Anglo institutions, Shelley Roberts did the Hispano school and Marleen Pugach the Mexican.

Peshkin's work in Indian High School follows a tradition of such ethnographies which reads like a roll call of famous Canadian and American anthropologists of education: Spindler and Spindler, Wax and Wax, Wolcott, King, Phillips, Grobsmith, Kleinberg, Dehlye. Native or First Americans have the highest high school dropout rates of any ethnic, linguistic or cultural group measured in the USA. The First American students in these studies have not usually been disaggregated into subcultures or cliques by the ethnographers: rather their school performance is related to their common strong adherence to their tribal norms and values. If there are different cliques among students at schools like Indian High School, they have not been separately described by the researchers who have generally concentrated on explaining the pupils' ascribed ethnicity for the reader.

113

In institutions where students come from a range of different backgrounds, the main ethnographic focus has been on informal groups (cliques, gangs, etc.) and on the relationships between informal groups and individual identities. Both the sociology and the anthropology of education have reserved their more memorable efforts for the portrayal of anti-school pupils and those failing, or being failed by, formal education. The focus has been predominantly on boys and young men. Palonsky's (1975) account of the Hempies is much more vivid than that of the College Bound Boys at South High School, just as Willis's (1977) 'lads' are much more memorable than the 'ear'oles'. Anti-school, delinquent, rebellious, young working-class urban males have been lovingly chronicled, and even celebrated as heroes. Such young men epitomise everything no social scientist would actually want to live next door to in real life, and are the embodiment of the opposite of the social mobility grand narrative which produced the scholars themselves (see Delamont, 2000). Most of the male ethnographers who have vividly captured the rebellion and resistance of the hooligans to schooling are themselves the heroic products of the social mobility grand narrative of their sub-discipline. They worked hard at school, did their homework, passed exams, took the advice of teachers, went to university and became academics. They 'lived' the vision of the Fabians, embodied the grand narrative of Halsey, Heath and Ridge (1980). However, once middle-class, they have not only studied, but lionized, the very type of boys from whom they had to hide in the playground.

There are two 'classic' books, published seven years apart, which still epitomise the British research here. They are the (only) two that get cited in the USA. Lacey's (1970) *Hightown Grammar* and, even more spectacularly Willis's (1977) *Learning to Labour*, are ethnographies of boys in England, in a contrasting pair of schools. This laudatory narrative of anti-heroes is based mainly on the ethnographic work about adolescent white working-class and African-Caribbean boys in British schools such as Hargreaves (1967), Patrick (1973), Parker (1974), Willis (1977), Corrigan (1979), Beynon (1985), Abraham (1995), and Sewell (1997). In 1967, David Hargreaves published the pioneering ethnography of a boys' secondary modern school in Lancashire. It had a literary precursor in Blishen's (1948) fictionalised autobiography *The Roaring Boys* (see Whiteside and Mathieson, 1971). A decade later Paul Willis's *Learning to Labour* (1977) continued the tradition with his eulogy to 12 lads from a Black Country secondary modern. Corrigan's (1979) *Schooling the Smash Street Kids* took a similar celebratory view of the anti-school boy. Ethnographies by John Beynon (1985) in Wales and John Abraham (1989, 1995) in England followed. In these books, and many others like them, the working-class boy who hates school, truants, avoids his school work, copies and cheats when he does complete it, values fighting and toughness, despises his teachers and boys who do work as effeminate and weak, and gains status from boasting of sexual conquest, delinquent and criminal activities, and from the peer group, is the hero. Such boys make life hard for their teachers, reject the opportunities for credentials, and try to impose their definition of masculinity on other males in their schools (Haywood and Mac an Ghaill, 1996).

The research on the processes of schooling shows that British schools are outstandingly successful at polarising pupils, dividing the pupils into hostile camps, and creating anti-school pupil cultures. As long as the schools polarise pupils, any visions of increased educational participation will not be realised. The British literature on the lives of school pupils and students is much richer in its accounts of boys and men than girls and women. When ethnicity is considered, African-Caribbean and British-Asian pupils have received far more attention than the other ethnic groups in the UK, such as Italians, Maltese, Greek and Turkish Cypriot, or Chinese.

In other Anglophone countries there are parallel ethnographic traditions. In Australia, Walker (1988) is a well-known example. In the USA, because co-education is normal in state schools, there is less focus on boys rather than girls, and the vivid portrayals of the 'anti-school' pupils are normally contrasted with equally colourful accounts of the top cliques: usually focused on young men in the sports teams and young women who are cheerleaders from the wealthiest and socially prominent families. Palonsky's (1975) account had many precursors, and has had successors, such as Crosnoe (2011).

Given the aim of fighting familiarity, this chapter does not begin with or focus exclusively on a rehearsal of the peer group among Palonsky's 'Hempies' or Willis's 'lads'. Instead it deliberately rebalances the sociology by focusing first on the lives of British pupils from the middle classes who experience school success (even though some of them do not recognise that themselves), second on girls and young women, and then on young men who disturb teachers because they are neither classic anti-school 'lads' nor middle-class achievers. The chapter then moves back to the American material.

Ball (2003a), Power et al. (2003) and Reay, Crozier and James (2011), all used interviews to gather data. Taken together, there are data here on over 500 middle-class families in England and their educational decisions in the Thatcher and Major years (i.e. 1979–1997) and since. Their research can be seen to have continuities with ethnographic studies when compared to some of their predecessors (Delamont, 1984, 1989; Fox 1984; Aggleton, 1987; Walford 1984, 1986, 1991, 1994).

Reay, Crozier and James (2011) conducted their study between 2004 and 2007 in London, a city in the South West, and one in the North East of England, interviewing 125 families where a conscious decision was made to choose a 'normal' comprehensive secondary school rather than paying fees or seeking out a safe middle-class state school. Stephen Ball (2003a) reworked data from three completed projects on 'choice' and educational markets done between 1991 and 2001, all in Greater London. The first focused on how parents chose secondary schools and included interviews with 137 parents. The second explored choice at age 16 and included interviews with 64 adolescents and 46 relevant adults. The third was about higher education choices and included data on 502 adolescents and 40 parents. Sally Power and her colleagues report the results of a questionnaire and interview study of 347 young people, done between 1995 and 1999. These informants were, by then, in their mid-20s, and had been asked in the early 1980s about choice of secondary school (Edwards et al., 1989). They came from all over England, and parents were also interviewed.

In all these projects conducted since 1991, the young people show clearly that their educational careers were, and are, entangled with membership of, exclusion from, or rejection of, some peer groups inside school, and in home neighbourhoods. Parents too see friendships as a core factor in adolescent success and happiness, and are acutely aware of the dangers that association with the 'wrong' type of fellow pupils poses to their children. So Ball (2003a: 59) has parents seeking desirable peers for their children in schools where there was 'a likelihood of finding kindred spirits' who have specific 'social and cultural skills', and being pleased that '21 out of 24 mothers' of children in his daughter's class' have a degree. One parent (p. 67) specifically said he did not want his son mixing with people who 'find it just not cool to work'. A mother rejected a possible secondary school because her daughter 'would be too different from the majority of girls there' (p. 61). The Power et al. (2003) study includes poignant data from young men who had 'balanced' school work with a self-presentation that suited their peers:

> The thing to be seen to be was never to do any work and yet to do fairly well academically, but not too well so that you stand out

and

116

> People would appear to be better if they were seen to be doing less work... It was simply that the less you did, or were seen to do, the better you would look

and

> You were supposed to make it look easy and never get caught working. (2003: 67)

The young men could be successful with peers, in their elite schools, if they were known to be 'hard', to be quick-witted, or good at sport: anything to avoid being a 'boffin'. One young man recalled getting his father to tell friends he was out when he was actually at home doing his homework. All the research shows that the existence of groups that a pupil, student or teacher does *not* belong to is often more significant than any group they are part of.

The literature on young women's peer groups includes Lambart (1982) and Davies (1984) from the early years of school ethnography, and more recently Hey (1997) and Allan (2010). When I published *Knowledgeable Women* (Delamont, 1989) I included a table (p. 273) that showed how few of the ethnographic projects on young women's peer groups had been published in monographs compared to the work on young men. None of the British ethnographies of young women made an impact equivalent to Lacey (1970) or Willis (1977). In the research on working-class and on middle- and upper-middle-class girls, the importance of the peer group is equally striking in shaping the outcomes of the educational process. For many women, the friendships made and sustained produce a 'reputation': female friends share a reputation. Hence Hey's title *The Company She Keeps*. Her work in two schools – one with a mixed intake in class terms and the other a working-class one with an Asian minority, which includes close studies of friendships among working-class and middle-class girls – is exemplary. In the middle-class sample of Power et al. (2003) the importance of girls' friendship groups, and the dynamics of their formation, echo those I had found at St Lukes (Delamont, 1989) a generation earlier. One informant, 'Celia Fyfe', recalled 'clever ones' who were focused on academic work, wealthy ones who had 'horses and tennis courts', 'the anorexics' and the 'normal ones' (Power et al., 2003: 76). These map into the main groups I found at St Luke's: those who styled themselves 'the intellectuals' (and were called by the rest, 'the swots and weeds') who disliked sport but were the best academically; those who called themselves 'grown up' but were labelled 'debs and dollies' by the academic girls, who played sport; and 'the boarders' who hung out together because they lived in the boarding house.

In all these studies the importance of friendship groups for young women is revealed, and in adolescence the 'managing' of an appropriate appearance, deportment and sexuality is mediated through those groups. Where femininity and/or relationships with boys and men is construed as opposed to academic success in specific subjects (e.g. Physics) or in study altogether, the group membership is associated with poor achievement.

The Power et al. (2003) study includes the best UK data on how finding friends at university level is crucial to a positive experience of higher education. One perceptive young woman who read history of art told the interviewer 'we were the ones who lived in London and had the cars and it puts the other students off you' (p. 99). She and most of the people on her course had been to elite schools and she was clear that it was hard for others to 'belong', just as it was for Winkle-Wagner's (2009) African-American student Michelle to make friends with white girls who had lived in a different America.

Before leaving UK schools and higher education for the USA, it is important to remember the small number of studies that have revealed small groups of young men whose rejection of conventional masculinity made their school lives problematic. Aggleton (1987), Mac an Ghaill (1994) and Abraham (1995), are the best known, and each shows how teachers and fellow pupils feel 'safer' when 'boys are boys', than they do when boys choose to display other sorts of self-presentation, such as 'androgynous' or 'gay' dress or language.

When Power et al. (2003: 51) quote two of their sample sayings:

'I wish Milltown Boys' was still as good as when I was there'

and

'I wish Milltown Boys' had burned to the ground while I watched',

...readers 'know' that these two men had very different friends at the same school, (if the second informant had any friends at all) and therefore experienced Milltown Boys' in contrasting ways. The same polarization is common in the American research, and is captured well by Ortner. In the 1990s the anthropologist, Sherry Ortner (2002), whose academic reputation rested on her fieldwork among the Sherpas of Nepal, turned her investigative skills onto American secondary education. She traced all the living survivors of her graduating class of 1958 from Weequahic High School in Newark. Fourteen had died, but 290 were still alive, and Ortner traced 250 of them. Fifty of those refused to be part of her research, but Ortner interviewed around 100 in person, and another 100 by telephone. Her old school is thus unique and typical simultaneously. Newark in 1958 had several high schools, and Weequahic was in a middle-class neighbourhood. She classifies her graduating class as 27 per cent upper middle class, 45 per cent middle class and 28 per cent working class at that time. Males were 48 per cent of the graduating class, which was 82 per cent white or Jewish. The vast majority of her classmates had very strong feelings about their high school experience, which had not faded in 50 years. A large number remembered Weequahic as the best time in their lives: socially, intellectually and athletically. However, many others looked back in anger, reporting their high school years as the worst in their lives, because of the snobbish, exclusionary cliques. Those who had hated it were still eloquently bitter ('a horrible, horrible time'; 'the worst years of my life'). The people who had been in the top cliques in contrast were still thoroughly enthusiastic ('fantastic', 'really fun', 'the best thing that ever happened to me'). In her analysis of the social science research on US high schools from Hollingshead (1947) through Gordon (1957) and Coleman (1961) to Cusick (1973), Palonsky (1975), Peshkin (1982), Phillips (1983), Reed-Danahay (1987), Grant (1988) and Fordham (1996), Ortner shows how class and wealth inequalities have become increasingly unmentionable in American society, yet form the basis for the peer group hierarchies and belief systems which make so many adolescents so appallingly miserable.

118

The ethnographies published at the same period as Ortner, and since, such as Finders (1997), Lefkowitz (1998), Bettie (2003) and Crosnoe (2011) show the same patterns repeating themselves. The 'hidden injuries of class' in the American high school have been repeatedly revealed. However, these injuries are rarely at the forefront of research attention except when there is a public scandal (e.g. Bissinger, 1990) discussed below, or worse, an episode of violence. The massacre at Columbine High, in April 1999, is the best-known incident of its type. But most of the extensive literature on Columbine lacks historical depth, any understanding of the research on the peer group hierarchies in the junior high and high school, or any discourse about class and wealth inequalities. (Race was not a major cleavage in Columbine because of its catchment area.) Larkin (2007) provides a clear account of Columbine, its community and its consequences, drawn from published sources and interviews. He reports a chillingly familiar picture of the hierarchical cliques, the intolerance of diversity, and the relentless pressure exercised by the 'leading crowd' on everyone else in the school.

Richer adolescents, who have smart clothes and cars, are in the track where academic courses are taken (college prep), dominate the social agenda (yearbook, cheerleading, homecoming, the prom). This social agenda contains all the features of secondary education familiar in Britain from the film *Grease*, and TV comedies such as *Happy Days* and *Blossom* but totally alien to all those Europeans who expect to study algebra and Latin in school, not practise cheerleading or edit a yearbook in school time (Finders, 1997) and call it a lesson or course. The girls wear expensive clothes (in the 1950s, cashmere sweaters), the boys dominate the sports teams. They date each other and ruin everyone else's schooldays by their cruel exclusions and casual and/or systematically targeted ridicule of everyone else. The cruelty of the discussion of 'scheevos' in Canaan (1987) – pupils whose clothing was cheap, unfashionable and wrong – is typical of this hostility. Ortner shows how the basic student roles in high school are patterned, in an enduring way, which is class and wealth based, but it is simply not acceptable for Americans to talk about these roles in class or wealth terms. She tried to get her former schoolmates to reflect on class and wealth inequalities in 1958 Newark but failed totally. Her informants frequently denied that there were any class differences at Weequahic, answered her questions with material on race (Jewish v Gentile), or did not even 'understand' the question.

Male sporting teams are particularly important. In *Friday Night Lights*, Bissinger (1990) exposed the negative consequences for the American high school of the total lack of any local professional, semi-professional or good adult amateur sporting teams in most of the USA. Whereas in any other advanced nations people, especially men, in small towns would play sport themselves, and watch local teams of adult men who have lives outside sport, in the USA the high school teams become the obsessive focus of towns without colleges. Bissinger showed the negative consequences for the American football team at Permian High, who raped women, took steroids, cheated at their school work and later found life beyond Permian High too hard to cope with. As the very successful school team in an economically depressed small town, everyone had colluded to build them up into demi-gods with serious consequences for their morals, their long-term health, their education and their mental stability, as well as letting them endanger their school fellows mentally and physically.

Larkin's (2007) research shows the same happened at Columbine High. Star athletes were encouraged by staff to bully and harass other students, especially those thought to lack 'school spirit' or be anti-evangelical 'sinners'. Before the massacre at Columbine, one female pupil had taken out a restraining order to stop a footballer stalking her, and the school decided *she* should stay at home and the boy continue in the school. The boy, and some teachers, then labelled *her* as a devious liar. He was able, or enabled to go to a university on a lucrative sports scholarship and play football there because the school told the university the matter was trivial. The parents of a Jewish student had to go to the police before the school stopped Rocky Wayne Hoffschneider, who was state wrestling champion at the time, and his friends, physically attacking the Jewish boy while making comments about 'another Jew in the oven' (p. 106). Larkin is describing a 'jock-centred' culture that is almost unimaginable in any other industrialised country.

Larkin unearthed another aspect of the peer groups at Columbine that had not been highlighted in the previous research. There was a series of tensions between a peer group of powerful pupils who were all members of extremist evangelical protestant sects, and those other, lower status pupils who belonged to other Christian churches, or other religions or none, both inside Columbine before the shooting, and, much more publically after it. Everything Larkin has discovered about the tensions between evangelicals and others in Columbine suggests that amongst those who walked tall in the school, proclaiming and enforcing their particular brand of intolerant Protestantism, there was a good deal of hypocrisy. The evangelical in-crowd, Young Life, included 'heavy partiers, drinkers, dope-smokers and sexual players' (p. 105) as well as genuinely pious teenagers. Overall Larkin is convinced that by hijacking the massacre as an attack on themselves, the evangelicals impeded any serious attempts to understand what, at Columbine, had provoked it.

It is precisely because the experience of schooling is mediated, and made positive or negative by other pupils, and group inclusions and exclusions are so powerful that when children are about to transfer to secondary school (and many of their fears are focused on being bullied, or not having friends), they are raising issues that researchers have discovered to be real in their consequences. While much of published research on education in the UK for the past 60 years has been concerned with documenting and explaining the under-achievement and school failure of working-class pupils, especially boys, sociologists have never been reticent to discuss class as a structuring variable in school experience. Nor are our informants reticent about class themselves (Frazer, 1993). In the British research, social class and wealth inequalities are explicitly addressed by the 'school choice' literature (such as Ball, Power et al. and Reay, Crozier and James already discussed) and are implicit in the children's own discussion of friends and bullies in the 'big school'. The quote from Katz (2001) stresses the importance of ethnography on transition points, and, drawing on data from two projects in the UK on primary–secondary transfer where friendships loomed large for the children, Katz's point is illustrated.

In the first ORACLE (Observational Research and Classroom Learning Environment) project, the settings from which the pupils came, the groups to which the schools assigned them, and the importance the teenagers placed on their friendship groups and the 'othered' groups they feared, interacted (Delamont and Galton, 1986, 1987). The focus was on children's anxieties about transfer, their anticipations about their destination schools, and their experiences of the process. A team of ethnographers observed the children as they made their pre-transfer visits to their destination school, and then followed them in these schools for a month. The children were interviewed, with their parents. A year after the transfer, they wrote essays about their feelings and experiences. Meanwhile, Measor and Woods (1984) had conducted an ethnography of pupil transfer, in which Measor spent a year with the top class in their primary school and followed their transfer and first year in their secondary school. She had a much closer engagement with 'her' children's experiences and was entrusted with much more 'confidential' and 'conspiratorial' material than the ORACLE team were. Measor discovered the rich vein of contemporary folklore or urban legends that flourished alongside the more 'rational' anxieties about primary to secondary transfer (Brunvand, 1983, 1984). In 2003, Mellor conducted a study of children in their final year at primary school, focused on their friendships (see Mellor and Delamont, 2011). The similarities across ORACLE 1, and the later work by Ball (2003a),

Power et al. (2003), and Mellor (2003), around the importance of pupil friendships, are striking. There were expectations of new friendships, fears about losing friends, and being in danger from bullies – some rational, others classic urban legends.

Mellor and Delamont's (2003) data show how important the relationships among pupils were to them. For example, three boys were positive about expanding their network:

Henry: You'll have more friends 'cos you'll keep all the friends you've got here and you'll make loads of new ones at your new school.

Ollie: Only some of my primary school friends are coming to the Grammar School, so I'll have new friends and old friends together.

George: I think it will affect your friendships 'as I've got lots of friends who are going to be at different schools and you might not see them again.

In contrast the 'rational' anxieties were losing their friends from the current school, being isolated at the big school, and the fact that everyone would be bigger than they were. Eunice, an ORACLE pupil transferring to Maid Marion 11–14 School recalled (Delamont and Galton, 1986):

I was very nervous… everybody seemed to know their names and they all had loads of friends. I got settled in though, and made many friends.

Mellor's informants expressed exactly the same sentiments. His Jessica and Lilly could have been leaving a Bridgehampton first school in 1978:

Jessica: We're all best friends together, yeah.

Lilly: 'Cos we're going to high school soon we've become closer, 'cos we don't want to leave and be all broken up (Mellor and Delamont).

Mellor's sample included one group whose secondary school deliberately separated the incoming pupils from their existing friends during class allocation. His informants were outraged, and regarded it as a cruel and unnatural punishment, that they had done *nothing* to deserve. They had no concept of the school wanting everyone to have a fresh start, but only saw themselves as victims of adult unfairness.

The rational anxieties about the possible lack of friends in the new school is related to the rational fears about bullying and the myths about dangerous gangs. One reason why having friends of your own is important is that loyal, 'real' friends are a protection against being bullied. The lonely, friendless child is vulnerable to bullying much more than the child with a clique, gang or crowd of his or her own. The commonest school transfer myth, found in every generation, is that of the bullies who push boys' heads down the lavatory. Other less common stories also feature bullies. Bryan (1980: 72) was told about:

> my new school which is Seacombe High. I think there is no disciplin (*sic*) from what my friends have told me. They told me that groups of lads go around battering people up, they are supposed to be from the dreaded BEBB which stands for the Brightsea Estate Boot Boys.

The BEBB were clearly paralleled by Measor and Woods' (1984: 21) Old Town 'Terrorists': 'There's these boys, and if you have a fight, they wear punch gloves with spikes, and they hit you and leave punch marks in your face'. The social class subtext of this myth is clear: The feared gang, too powerful for any teachers to stop, come from an estate, and are from a class segment 'lower' than the informants'.

The ORACLE I children had similar fears of physical bullying. Bart, going to Melin Court (12–18) School said he:

> were bothered about coming here, Miss. Friends had told me it were bad. They said you got beat up a lot! (Delamont and Galton, 1986)

Dawn had been told that on the first day new pupils were endangered because: 'You got your head kicked in!' One of the ORACLE pupils asked Mr Southern, the head of Year 1, if boys at Kenilworth could carry knives. Mr Southern said 'of course not' in a shocked voice. He did not ask why any boy would feel the need to carry a knife at his school. The ORACLE researcher 'knew' that widespread myths about bullies had led to the frightened boy asking if he could protect himself.

123

GROUPS IN STUDENT LIFE

This is an area where British ethnographers have failed to do the type of innovative studies that characterise the work in schools. In the USA there are some excellent ethnographies of student life, from Becker, Geer, Hughes and Strauss (1961) on medical students, and Becker, Geer and Hughes (1968) on liberal arts undergraduates, through Moffat (1989) on undergraduates at Rutgers, and Holland and Eisenhart (1992) on the ways in which women students are caught up in the politics of gender regimes. Reading the ethnographies of college life in the USA provides a wide ranging set of challenges to the taken-for-granted familiarity of UK student life. As well as the Winkle-Wagner (2009) study of African-American College women that began the chapter, there is a strikingly 'unusual' student culture that makes great contrastive reading.

Ricky Jones's book (2004) about Black Greeks, that is African-American sororities and fraternities such as Alpha Kappa Alpha and Omega Psi Phi, serves well to help non-Americans fight the familiarity of higher education. He himself is a member of Kappa Alpha Psi, and has been Polemarch (Chairman) of its graduate chapter in Kentucky. For a non-American, the world of the fraternities and sororities – the Greek-letter organisations – is a bizarre and arcane one. The literature on these student societies is large, and does not normally cross the Atlantic or Pacific. Jones's bibliography is full of citations to other work on them, which are not part of the literature on higher education read and cited outside the USA. His focus is not, however, on the generality of American student life. Rather Jones focuses upon those fraternities and sororities which recruit only African-Americans: the Black Greek-Letter Organisations (BGLO).

Jones is particularly concerned to explain the fraternities (BGLF) and what he calls their 'unfortunate and abusive marriage' (2004: *xiv*) with 'hazing'. He focuses on BGLFs, and 'the landscapes littered with pledging and death' (p. *xiv*). People hoping to join a fraternity are pledges, and hazing is the violence perpetrated on them by older existing members. He states that 'hazing in BGLFs is all too real and its arm is long' (p. *xiv*). Hazing and pledging are part of the entry and initiation processes for fraternities, and Jones lists several instances where these processes have been so violent that would-be entrants have died. It is clear from his data that fraternities are extraordinarily important for their loyal enthusiasts. He does not report data from fraternity refuseniks or disloyal ex-members. The violent beatings and humiliations inflicted on new entrants to BGLFs are part of an initiation ritual, often a secret pact, done against written orders from head office. When beatings are too severe, chapters of the fraternity are suspended. However, brutalities go on.

Jones suggests that the initiation of candidates in most fraternities usually consists of the following stages: ceremonial robing and blindfolding, being led to another place by a guide after an exchange of signs, oath-taking, teaching the symbols and secrets of the fraternity, investiture with a badge, a ceremonial reading of the duties required of members, and then the symbolic journey, which is where hazing takes place. For men, especially African-American men, hazing can show how tough they are and how much they want to join the fraternity. The existing members of BLGFs regarded a tough hazing as the sign of a great fraternity which was worth belonging to. Jones quotes an Omega Psi Phi member:

You take wood [beating] to show your love for the frat. How else can you prove to brothers and yourself that you really want it? (Jones, 2004: 82)

He argues that:

Men seek rites of passage in many societies in attempts to develop a sense of manhood or reaffirm it and often feel they work. (p. 115)

In the case of BGLFs, Jones believes, the 'fraternal self' is constructed first, so that the brothers can then build 'the authentic black male self' (2004: 115). The world of BGLFs is a microcosm of 'the world of all black men' (p. 118).

HOW TO... STUDY GROUPS AND IDENTITIES

The classic way that groups of school pupils and students were studied was sociometry. In the pioneering ethnographies, groups were treated as relatively fixed and bounded on. Furlong's (1976) concept of the 'interaction set' was a self-conscious attempt to use a more fluid concept because the phenomenon he studied – African-Caribbean girls in a London school – *was* fluid. It is really important to be reflexive about all the groups in a setting. Very few researchers are able to hang out with all the different groups, and that is not a problem as long as the consequences of the various levels of acceptance and access are critically reflected upon. Falling into the trap(s) of taking male views of females, or white perspectives on ethnic minorities, or low ability anti-school views of high achievers, or the reverse of any of these, can produce fine ethnography, but the author needs to be constantly alert to the causes and consequences of such identifications, and to keep the reader aware of these.

125

A LOOK TO THE FUTURE

the research agenda on groups and identities

The UK has not yet produced rich ethnographic work on the lives of undergraduates, although Atkinson (1981) and Sinclair, (1996) are available on medical students. In recent years the main focus of research on UK students has been their mechanisms for coping with the shift from an era when grants were paid to one in which degree level study is financed by loans, by familial (parental) contribution, and by paid employment. The UK now has a mass higher education system in which the old pattern of sponsored mobility (Turner, 1960) has been replaced by the contest mobility normal in the USA and much of Continental Europe. In that climate there are debates about how far, if at all, working-class students acquire, or even have a chance to acquire, the tacit some-times called 'soft' social skills that many employers want from graduates (Brown, Green and Lauder, 2001). If working-class students are doing more paid work, living in the cheapest available housing, and 'choosing' different higher education institutions from middle-class ones, then their friendship groups will not be cross-class, and they will have less chance to acquire soft skills from their social interactions. There is an acute need for high quality ethnographies of student life in different sectors of the mass HE system. Among the topics that need sociological attention is the experience of those working-class people who reach higher education, and may not be getting the access to the tacit knowledge and behaviours they need to succeed either in higher education or thereafter.

Higher education can certainly be experienced as very unstructured, and it has been argued (e.g. Donohue, 2002) that one reason for the popularity of martial arts on American campuses is their highly classi-fied and framed visible pedagogy. There is certainly a contrast between student life in UK higher education and the culture of the *capoeira* classes. The *capoeira* teachers I have seen expect both instant obedience, and a high level of discipline and loyalty. Whether the order is to cart-wheel up the room, to wash, iron and wear the correct kit three times a week, to eschew the siren song of other teachers and other lineages for five years, or to drink nothing but water in a pub for six hours before a public display, students treat such orders very seriously and even obey them. No university student I have seen in 43 years would sit still for a lecturer either issuing such orders, or requiring such loyalty, and there is nothing in the ethnographies of British higher education to suggest my experience is unusual. Watching the combination of enormous gaiety, *axe*, and a visible hierarchy with explicit orders, is salutary.

A parallel argument can be made about the need to seek unfamiliar settings in which to explore 'successful' boys, in order to develop fore-shadowed problems for tackling the problem of failing boys inside schools. For the past two decades the Anglophone developed countries have had a moral panic about 'failing boys' (Delamont, 1999; Weaver-Hightower, 2003). This is a classic educators' problem, and ethno-graphic research relevant to it has not succeeded in 'fighting familiarity' or developing probing foreshadowed problems. One innovative approach would be to study settings or communities of practice in which boys and young men *are* fully engaged, discover what engages them, and then explore how schools and colleges could change to be more like those settings or communities. A thorough understanding of how boys learn to skateboard, fish, rap, breakdance or spray graffiti would be good starting points for such a research programme. I, (Delamont 2005b) developed this point using the example of martial arts, popular with many young men in the same countries that have a 'failing boys' problem. Specifically focused on *capoeira* (the Brazilian martial art) the paper highlights six features of *capoeira* (discipline, uniform, time, reading, the internet, and music) which, in addition to the martial art itself, appeal to young men in the UK. The argument is that understanding what *does* engage boys and young men is more likely to solve the 'failing boys' problem than endlessly claiming or demonstrating that it is an educational problem. When the success of teaching in martial arts (which attract male learners) is properly understood, then lessons can be drawn for transferring the model to schools and universities.

127

nine

narratives and other tales: 'ah come to collect some old stories'

Ana came from Mexico with her family. They came by covered wagon from Chihuahua, further down south. In Mexico her family owned a small carpenter shop and a grocery store. They decided to leave their beloved country... She taught Spanish forever in the schools. She taught Spanish from what I remember. She graduated in '26. I still wonder how she got into high school or college or whatever so she could become a teacher. (Pugach, 1998: 78)

Before I went to secondary school (Plash Meadow Girls Comprehensive) I was told by some students that I would be bullied, touched up by lesbian teachers and there was smoking in the toilets. It was all lies!

Many narratives gathered in educational settings are of that type: recounting links to the past, to traditions. The urban legends recounted are clearly labelled as 'lies' by the teller: the young woman was told three, scary, things about Plash Meadow, and none of them was true. These two types of narrative frame the material covered in this chapter. The subtitle from Zora Neale Hurston (1935: 8) is the explanation she gave the men talking on the store porch in Eatonville, Florida in 1928 about her folklore research, using 'the spy glass of anthropology'. Pugach is reporting a memory told to her by Lydia Siva, who graduated from Havens High School in New Mexico in 1935, one of the first Mexican students to do so. Lydia remembered Ana Herrera, the first teacher of Spanish in the school, whose career began in 1928. The point of the narrative is to highlight Ana's Mexican migration, and her unusual career at that date. Ana Herrera was doubly unusual because she was a woman, and an immigrant from Mexico, who got to university and into a profession.

The chapter deals with the collection of oral material, and its representations, especially those that use 'innovative' literary forms. Educational ethnographers have been gathering narratives and other types of story (life histories, curriculum histories, horror stories, contrastive rhetorics) for 60 years. Key conclusions that can be drawn from the research are outlined, before the chapter moves on to advocate practical research strategies for data-gathering, and to draw attention to the stories that have been relatively neglected.

ABSENCES AND LIES

What stories or accounts informants provide are often less interesting than their omissions, silences and blind spots. If you are interested in the career aspirations of 14 year olds, and all the girls mention that they expect to marry and have babies, while not one boy does, the absence is more interesting than the presence. Similarly if you study what sort of husband the young women want, and a majority say they want a partner who is not a heavy drinker and does not beat them or the children, but not one single young man says he wants a wife who does not drive him to drink or deserve to be beaten up, the absence is more exciting as a research finding than the presence. Similarly, lies and misrepresentations may be more academically 'useful' than truth. As Davidson (1997: *xxii*) says:

> Misrepresentations are just as interesting as representations, and even more useful, when you can identify them, are outrageous lies.

129

THE NATURE OF NARRATIVE

Davidson's work on ancient Greece might seem an unlikely source of insight into how we should understand the tale of Ana Herrera, or the legend about Plash Meadow. But in fact his comment on what we can learn from texts, or from oral data such as interviews, is highly pertinent. He goes on:

> Historians not only use texts as windows, sometimes they assume that is their purpose too. (Davidson, 1997: *xxii*)

He means by this that if we have a written record of a speech made in a trial, we must not assume that the orator wrote it for us, so *we* can 'see' what Ancient Athens, or Imperial Rome, or nineteenth century London was like. Of course that is nonsense. The orator wanted the 'jury' to decide the case for the side represented by the speaker, and the timing, content, rhetorical structure and 'facts' were all selected to achieve that result. The speech and the text we have of it were designed to change minds. 'The most obvious and unquestioned things, may never make it into texts at all' (1997: *xxiii*). In other words texts must not be used as windows but treated as artefacts.

All ethnographers gather narratives, stories, myths, reminiscences, jokes, horror stories, accounts and other oral materials. These can be individual, or from various types of group. Such data are a fundamental source for any ethnographer, whether produced on her request ('Are these pupils always so excited by…?') or spontaneously ('They aren't usually like this' or 'Mrs Williams hates me'). Central to this book, and therefore highlighted in this chapter, is the fact that what people say must not be understood by the researcher as a transparent, unvarnished description of 'reality' past or present. Stories and accounts are socially produced, in particular contexts, in standardised ways that fit the norms of any specific culture or subculture, and the researcher's job is to learn what those norms are, so she can situate the talk in its context. For example, Shirley Brice Heath (1983) on white American working-class stories, Cortazzi (1991) on teachers' stories, PhD supervisors' contrastive rhetoric (Delamont, Atkinson and Parry, 2000), school transfer stories (Delamont, 1981) and memories of influential teachers as in the Ana Herrera example that Pugach collected. The collection of narratives has become a major part of sociological and anthropological research in the past 30 years. It is particularly significant in health, illness and medicine, where it has been highly controversial. Thomas (2010) provides a thoughtful overview of the debate that followed Atkinson (1997) and Atkinson and Silverman (1997), which is revisited in Atkinson and Delamont (2006a, 2007b) and in Atkinson (2009, 2010).

130

The educational example I have chosen to explore is from the highest level of the education system: the oral examination that is the final stage of gaining a PhD or other doctorate. The academic research on this topic exemplifies the dangers of treating narratives as if they were windows, through which 'reality' can be glimpsed. The research on the doctoral viva is particularly blighted because there are only narratives (none of the other qualitative methods such as observation has been used), and the narratives have been gathered from only one of the parties in a multi-party session. In the rest of the formal education system, and in most informal and non-formal settings, there are many different types of study, so those narratives that are collected can be understood as one data source. There are researchers, who, drawing on interviews with volunteers who have come forward after their 'test', present the viva as an appalling ordeal (Tinkler and Jackson, 2004). There are several problems with these studies, because they draw on interviews with only one of the actors in the oral examination. There are problems in relying on interview data when the examination is a multi-party interaction that takes place in a specific location, with a timeframe, involving movement, focused on one large text (the thesis) and several small ones (reports by examiners, sets of regulations, expense claim forms, railway timetables, etc.).

A thorough study of an oral examination would need to be based on data triangulation, with observation, or even better, an audio recording or film of the multi-party interaction, and a social science scrutiny of the documents involved. A viva is attended by at least three and sometimes six or seven people. The smallest vivas consist of the candidate, and two examiners. In some vivas at some institutions there will also be a chair of the event, the candidate's supervisor or supervisors, and even a chaperone. If an interview-based project is to be done, all the parties need to be part of the research. The perspectives of all the actors are equally valuable in framing our understanding of the British oral examination.

Focusing only on the candidate, especially when the volunteers are generally recruited after the examination, produces problems even in its own terms. Those students who volunteer to be interviewed are a 'biased' subset of all the research students who submit a thesis for examination. First, they are nearly always British domiciled students with English as their native tongue. This is not because the investigators are insensitive to non-British students or are uninterested in their views. Rather their omission is because non-British students have returned 'home', and are not available for retrospective research. The students interviewed are normally full-time rather than part-time candidates who are less likely to be 'available' for researchers. In general these studies have been done with candidates in arts and social sciences, not science, engineering, and medical subjects (STEM). We lack research on the MD (an advanced research degree for medical doctors in the UK) viva and those getting professional doctorates, or doctorates by performance or creativity are also absent from the literature.

However, the most problematic aspect of the research for the purposes of this chapter is that the candidates who volunteer to participate in a study of vivas, and whose narratives actually appear in the books and papers published on that research, are very unlikely to be those who had entirely 'successful', or very 'routine' oral examinations. Given British academic culture, a person who wanted to tell a story of their success, even to boast, would not participate in research. Accounts that contained self-satisfied remarks like 'The questions were *easy*: I could answer all of them standing on my head', and statements such as 'I loved every minute of it', would probably not be volunteered to the researchers, and if they were, would not be incorporated into the reports. Equally a person whose viva was very dull and routine might volunteer, but their 'story' would be unlikely to provide any quotations or confessions for the eventual publication. A blow-by-blow factual account of how Examiner A focused on the access, the sample, the response rate, and the statistical tests would not make an interesting journal article.

'Good' data, i.e. those that make satisfying papers for the readers of journals such as *Studies in Higher Education* (e.g. Tight, 2002) are predominantly of the kind reported in Coffey and Atkinson (1996: 129–130). Dr Nancy Enright (a pseudonym) had done her PhD in social anthropology at Kingford University (a high status institution with a strong reputation in anthropology). When interviewed by Odette Parry as part of a project on the doctorate in social sciences we conducted in 1989–1991 which involved 24 graduate students and 25 academic staff, Dr Enright was 'in' the staff sample at Latchendon University but produced a classic 'horror story' about her own viva, some years before at Kingford.

Coffey and Atkinson (1996) wanted to find an interview extract that could be turned into a poem, to illustrate the use of poetic devices to convey emotions in a way that an extract from a transcribed interview can never capture. The extract is, however, exactly the sort that is used to criticise the British viva as an ordeal. As we work through the two texts, it is important to remember that Dr Enright passed her exam and got the PhD. The extract begins:

132

> I had the most horrible viva anybody could ever have, I think. I got upset and burst into tears, and that was awful, so I have a very bad memory of my viva.

Clearly Dr Enright has unpleasant memories: but she passed, so it cannot really have been more 'horrible' than those of people who fail. At the time of the interview she had only been an (internal) examiner once, so had only been present at two vivas. However, her interview continued:

> Looking back at the one I assisted with, I realised that with mine it was a question of human rights. It was appallingly badly examined.

Here the rhetoric becomes even more exaggerated. No one died, no one was tortured, no one was waterboarded, no one was detained without trial. Perhaps she had an inappropriate external examiner, but nothing she says makes his behaviour seem worthy of the label 'appalling'. He was not an anthropologist:

> I was examined by a historian from Reddingdale…

and

> the examiner missed the train, so I was waiting for two hours with the other examiner and the supervisor, so in terms of nervous stress it was awful.

That one mention of 'the other examiner' is very low key: he or she has no presence in the account. The complaints about the external examiner, the historian from Reddingdale, reported in the interview, apart from his lateness, are hardly the stuff of a trial for genocide at The Hague.

> There were things he didn't know like the conventions for the bibliography in anthropology – we have a convention where you don't capitalise every single word in a book title – and I had a 25 page bibliography and he went through it and put a circle through every letter he thought should have been capitalised.

Without seeing the regulations for the PhD thesis at Kingford, and the advice given to students by the Department of Anthropology, it is impossible to know if Dr Enright's 'we' is remotely 'accurate'. If her account were an accurate statement about British social anthropology or Kingford then her internal examiner and supervisor might have pointed that out to the examiner: but in any case most students would happily settle for changing letters from lower to upper case in order to get a PhD. Interestingly the speaker, although an anthropologist, does not compare the viva to an initiation ceremony, or any rite of passage. Degradations and humiliations, such as being made to correct a great many typing mistakes, could be understood as a 'normal' part of any significant rite of passage. Dr Enright went on:

133

> There were a lot of typing errors, but I got the cheapest typist I could, who typed a lot of things wrong, so that he (the external examiner) said things like 'This sentence hasn't got a verb in it.'

Here Dr Enright admits that she chose a poor typist, and failed to proofread her own work. Her final complaint was that:

> …they didn't say 'well done' or anything, it was just 'we want the typing mistakes corrected in three weeks'.

In other words, Dr Enright was given the doctorate, subject to correcting the typing mistakes. Treating the interview as if it is a 'factual' account of the event, rather than an account produced performatively, as part of a contrastive rhetoric in which Dr Enright described how, as a supervisor, she would never expose her students to such an unpleasant viva is to misunderstand the nature of accounts. Using such data as if they represent a valid and reliable account of any one examination is poor social science. A more 'rounded' project would have interviewed the man from Reddingdale, the supervisor and the 'other' examiner, to gain their perspectives on the thesis, and the viva.

This reading of Dr Enright's story is not intended to deny her sense of outrage, victimhood, and injury. Those are real, and that is why Coffey and Atkinson (1996) used it as an example of a narrative that worked well as an ethnographic poem. Treating what people say as data to be analysed is not a denial of the emotions their performance expresses. Dr Enright's story was a rehearsal of a still-live grievance, but it is also a perfect example of contrastive rhetoric: something said to make a clear distinction between what happens 'over there' or happened 'then', and what the speaker is going on to characterise as strikingly different, for better or worse. Hargreaves (1986) coined the term Contrastive Rhetoric to show how staff in middle schools distanced their practices from those in 'other' schools, as part of staffroom talk that 'consolidated' their viewpoints with those of their colleagues to create 'harmony' in the group. Hargreaves did not claim that the accounts of other schools were 'real' or that the teachers 'believed' their contrastive talk or practised what they described. The talk was rhetorical.

The collection of oral history, life history, and other narratives from school teachers is a well-established research strategy, but there are fewer projects in higher education or from informal and non-formal enculturation settings. Frequently oral history is the only way to investigate important educational phenomena, because no data collection was carried out when the events took place. The studies of women's scientific careers and of women who planned such careers but did not achieve them (sometimes called the leaky pipeline) are examples of oral histories being the only source available. Weiler (1988) for example includes four women school teachers who had initially gone to college to be scientists but 'decided' to change direction. Their interviews are full of 'I was going to' statements, such as 'I was going to major in biology' (Weiler, 1988: 883). She analyses these interviews and stresses that the accounts are intended to demonstrate to her that they were *not* 'passive creations of "fate" or social structures' (p. 89) but active agents in their own lives.

Exactly the same type of analysis needs to be done on the talk of school students, of course. Bettie's (2003) study of young women in the senior (final) year of a Californian high school, Waretown, shows how to capture the voices of different students, many of which are expressing injuries, and treat them analytically. For example, when Mary Beth, a girl who had resisted the school's values, says:

Teachers are always buggin' you about what you're gonna do with your life. I told one once I wanted to be a journalist, and she said I wasn't good enough at school. I told someone else I wanted to be a psychiatrist, and they said I needed one. (Bettie, 2003: 1090)

Bettie hears the anti-teacher rhetoric, but also recognises that this is a 'good story' to explain Mary Beth's position in the school. It is not important whether or not it is 'true', it is important that Mary Beth has been marginalised, and has self-excluded herself from the college prep track.

Some narrative research can embed one informant's story into a wider context. Heyl's (1979) study of a woman who ran the brothel in a small American town used life-history interviews with 'Anne', but also interviews with others in her social world, such as the police chief and Anne's lawyer. Ethnographers frequently embed narratives into other contextual data, such as observations or recordings of interaction. The educational work Anne did, training novice prostitutes to self-present appropriately, was analysed by Heyl (2012) using a tape-recorded 'class' as well as Anne's narratives. Riseborough's (1988) interview study of a cookery teacher in a Jewish school would have been much richer if her lessons had also been observed.

Thus far the chapter has focused on narrative data collected as the main focus of the research. However, there are as many narratives gathered by ethnographers, either embedded in their wider fieldwork because the scholar was in the field when they were collected from informants, or done on separate occasions but used for framing, deepening or widening the story they tell with their fieldnotes. Here the points (expanded in Chapter 10) made about listening by Forsey (2010) are particularly relevant because many ethnographers draw on interview material as well as observations. For example, Louis Weis's (1990, 2004) series of studies in Freeway, a de-industrialised American city, draws on observation in a school and interviews conducted initially with students and subsequent reinterviews conducted with the same informants as adults years later. Freeway at the time of the first ethnography in the 1980s was rapidly de-industrialising – taking away from the white working class not only the male jobs, but the men's pensions and health care plans as well. Weis then used reinterviews with the adults which are much richer because of the ethnographic study she had earlier conducted at Freeway. Her informants knew that Weis had seen, and smelt, and heard, their schooldays. The restudy includes recollections by adults of what their lives had been like when they were teenagers. For example, Suzanne, a schoolteacher herself at the time of Weis's follow up study, recalled:

Suzanne: Dad spent most of my growing up years either at work – he's a city firefighter and also worked at Macey Boiler Works – or at a bar for 70 to 80 per cent of my growing-up time. Mom went back to work when I was about eleven or twelve years old. There's a lot of family conflict because of Dad being so

135

> unavailable… I didn't have a male adult in my life to learn how adult men treated adult women. My father's the kind that would come home and yell and scream. (Weis, 2004: 124–125)

In 1985, as an adolescent, Suzanne participated in the ethnography of the high school serving a white working-class neighbourhood and told Weis that she did not want to be married; she did not want to be trapped, especially with a man who drank heavily, rather she wanted to earn her own living and make a good life for herself. Suzanne 'spoke for' many of her female contemporaries. When Weis originally studied Freeway High School, evocatively published as *Working Class Without Work* (1990), she found that the young women were much more determined to use post-school education to escape the city's dying economy than the young men were. The females were keen to go to college, get out of Freeway, and avoid the traditional marriages of their parents' generation. The young men were responding to the economic collapse by blaming ethnic minorities for destroying 'their' labour market. Fifteen years later, Weis (2004) traced 39 of the original participants. Of her core sample of Freeway students, all the women had undertaken some formal education after leaving high school, and 48 per cent of them had achieved a BA by 2001, while only 29 per cent of the men had. Suzanne had become a maths teacher in a Freeway middle school, was not married and had no children. However, her life lacked the financial and emotional autonomy she had aspired to – she has large debts, which prevent her completing a masters' degree that would entitle her to a salary rise. Her social life is spent with working-class men, and Weis concludes that:

> Suzanne's apparent 'freedom', then, is illusory, she carries a particular form of her class habitus in her soul, and on her back as she moves into adulthood. (Weis, 2004: 128)

Whether the interview data are life histories, narratives, or 'opinions' and perspectives, the core point is that they need to be analysed, not just celebrated as the true voice of anyone, or as an account of reality. Whether the voice is that of a researcher (as in autoethnography or autobiography), or a relatively powerful person such as a head teacher or tribal elder, or an 'underdog' such as an apprentice or a school cook, interview data have to be understood as accounts, which are produced as rhetorical performances.

The most coherent study that uses interview data in an appropriate way comes from the sociology of science (Gilbert and Mulkay, 1984). It was a study of bioscientists' responses to a controversial discovery, as they recounted them to the researchers. Gilbert and Mulkay analysed the talk as accounts, and showed the logics that underpinned them. Unfortunately the general points Gilbert and Mulkay established did not get adopted in educational research, to the detriment of the field. The best equivalent in mainstream educational research is the work of Cortazzi (1991, 1993) who collected and analysed the stories English primary teachers told about their work, and then produced a book on how narratives can be analysed. More recently Cortazzi and Jin (2012) and Watson (2012) have provided cogent arguments about the importance of analysing, rather than merely celebrating the rhetorical performances provided for investigation. Unfortunately few of those who have collected the stories of doctoral candidates, or of other educational actors, have absorbed that advice.

THE 'DANGERS' OF THE INTERVIEW SOCIETY

Atkinson and Silverman (1997) explored the growth of 'the interview society'. Their social science question was how the academic interview could and should be treated to separate it from the 'interview' as ubiquitous in contemporary media, cyber space and instant access. I do not repeat that argument here, except to alert researchers to the double problem that can arise from using narratives or other interview data. It is important to recognise that, partly because of the media strategy of illustrating all news coverage with one or two poignant or angry 'accounts', from or about colourful individuals, the narratives in social science texts may be the aspect picked up by the media or policy-makers or powerful groups, rather than any more nuanced material. The researcher may even be attacked by funding bodies, local managers or policy-makers, or even by informants because the narrative data *are* vivid and easy to read. Walsh (1998: 190–191), for example, reports a very hostile response to research he had conducted on American pre-school teachers. The US State of Virginia was piloting a pre-kindergarten programme for children of four who were thought to be 'at risk', i.e. not likely to be ready to benefit from formal schooling when they were due to start. Walsh had been hired to organise a study of the teachers who were being trained to implement the programme. When the research team managed to get the teachers to talk freely, they discovered discontent about the training, and the providers' lack of attention to teachers' views. When Walsh tried to convey the teachers' views, the bureaucrat (Mrs Jones) who had commissioned the training yelled at him 'Don't tell me we don't know what the teachers want! We know what the teachers

137

want!' (1998: 189). Mrs Jones then contrasted Walsh with a previous investigator who had produced 'the kind of research I want to hear!' (p. 190).

This official disliked the findings, and so blamed the messenger. Walsh reports that the research team were rejected because: 'Our group by going out listening [to teachers] was, in fact, creating the unhappiness. If we had not been there, asking the teachers questions, they would not be telling us that they were unhappy, and if they were not talking about being unhappy, they could not be unhappy' (1998: 190). The researchers had used the voice of the discontented teachers so effectively that the discontent could not be ignored. The managers, under political pressure from above, had to attack someone, and the researchers were available. A research report without the vivid narrative data might have been better received. Speaking truth to power, or being the conduit for the voices of the muted group, the powerless, the unheard, can be a risky business, and the 'catchy' quote from an interview can frequently be the one part of the whole study that is seized upon.

The next section moves on from data – such as the life-history interview with Lydia Silva that opened the chapter, or Dr Enright's outraged contrastive rhetoric, widely recognised as data – to an apparently more 'trivial' topic.

138

JOKES, HORROR STORIES AND CONTEMPORARY LEGENDS

As well as classic interview data and the collection of oral history and narratives, educational ethnographers do well to pay attention to the shared oral culture of the actors in the field setting. There are shared histories that live in the telling and retelling of stories and jokes, such as the affectionate memory of Mr Hogg and the consequences of his deafness. One ORACLE observer (Delamont and Galton, 1986: 131) recorded:

> When Miss Tweed comes back its mental arithmetic books. Hugh can't find his mental book. "I'll do it in my jotter" he says and everybody laughs. Miss Tweed turns to me and says "You won't understand this but the teacher who died last year was deaf and the children were always playing him up and coming up and saying "should I do it in my English book, maths book – etc.?" and he would always reply "Do it in your jotter". Then one day a boy came to his desk and said 'Can I go to the toilet?' and Mr Hogg replied 'Do it in your jotter'.

Past teachers can live on in jokes and anecdotes as Mr Hogg did. In the research on mainstreaming pupils with learning difficulties, we were told just such a story that was already a shared joke in the class for pupils with special needs. The teacher got a pupil to tell a story to the observer that parallels the Mr Hogg memory.

> At the close of the lesson, Mr Wymondham told Wynford to tell the observer 'the story about your reading book'. Wynford laughs and tells us that in his junior school, when he was told to bring the page he was reading out to the teacher, he had 'ripped it out of the book'. The whole class laughs and Mr Wymondham falls about because he thinks it is so funny.

This is a parallel to Walker and Adelman's (1976) strawberries story retold in Delamont (1983a: 31–32) and the 'Horace' joke from Gryll Grange (Delamont and Galton, 1986). In the Walker and Adelman joke, a master had once said that the children's writing was 'like strawberries: nice while it lasted but did not go on long enough', and ever after anything that was said to be too short got greeted by a shout of 'strawberries' and the whole class, including the teacher, laughed. Walker and Adelman used the joke to show how ethnographic research is more insightful about core aspects of classroom cultures than other data collection methods. In the ORACLE project the team saw such a joke begin at Gryll Grange (9–13) School:

> During the morning Miss Tweed has referred to 'Horace' on several occasions and each time the children have laughed. She says, for example. 'There's Horace at the window again'. One little girl's stuffed toy mouse is called Horace. Everyone giggles when it is mentioned. During the break Miss Tweed tells the girl to tell me why the mouse is called Horace. The girl laughs, and Miss Tweed then explains that when she was writing on the first day Yvette spelled 'horse' as 'Horace' and another child called out: 'Look! There's a Horace outside the window eating grass'. Then when she made a mouse in needlework Yvette called it Horace. There is much giggling from the listening children at this explanation of the joke.

139

The joke spread, so that all spelling mistakes became Horaces.

> For example Miss Tweed says 'It's like that Horace looking through the window' to another girl who has miss-spelt a word in her writing or 'take it away and alter it – we don't allow anyone else to have a Horace in here'.

For this class of nine year olds, the Horace joke was an audible signal that they were Miss Tweed's class with their own special joke. Neither the 'strawberries' nor the 'Horace' make any sense as triggers for legitimate laughter unless the researcher understands the culture in which the joke is embedded.

In his study of professional musicians in London, Cottrell (2004) devotes a chapter to myth and humour, in which he demonstrates how important these oral forms are in a culture, how vital it is to collect them, and how, when you can understand the jokes and appreciate the local stories you are beginning to grasp key aspects of the culture. As Cottrell (2004: 132) summarises it:

> Broadly speaking, if you get the joke you are potentially 'in'; if you don't you may well be 'out'.

Cottrell observed 'viola jokes' which illustrate the way in which humour conveys useful information to the researcher. Cottrell 'explains' that viola cases are similar to violin cases in appearance, that there is rivalry between violinists and viola players, and that violinists target viola players by telling jokes in which they are revealed to be 'worthless, stupid, or ignorant'.

He quotes a 'classic' viola joke, told *by violinists*:

> Q. How do you keep your violin from being stolen?
>
> A. Put in it in viola case. (2004: 136)

However, for an ethnographer to 'get' these jokes 'sociocultural decoding is required' (Cottrell, 2004: 130). Such sociocultural decoding is the key goal of any ethnography. Once the researcher has learnt to decode jokes, she knows many aspects of the field setting have been grasped.

140

ETHNOGRAPHERS' NARRATIVES

One increasingly common form of narrative found in the educational research literature is the researcher's account of how she got on in the field. These are often called 'confessional' tales, or less evaluatively, autobiographical pieces. There are collections of such papers, such as de Marrais (1998) and Barz and Cooley (2008). The novice reader can fall into the trap of reading these as factual accounts when, of course, they are constructed rhetorically, and need to be read in that way. Atkinson (1990, 1992) is a starting point for appreciating how that genre is 'constructed' to display the *real* success of the author behind an initial impression of incompetence. That is, the charming, disarming, apparently disingenuous researcher who made mistakes is a rhetorical façade, behind which are the skilled authors who are actually displaying how good their access, rapport, empathy and elicitation of data were. Delamont (2010) is an analysis of the published accounts of eight women who did ethnographies of neopagan witchcraft groups that reveals how the stories share a common narrative structure.

HOW TO... COLLECT, ANALYSE AND REPRESENT NARRATIVES

Collecting oral data is such a large part of qualitative research, and there are so many books of advice, and papers discussing interviewing that there is no need to rehearse the key things here. Gubrium and Holstein (2005) is a useful starting point for all types of interviewing; Spradley (1979) is the classic on ethnographic interviewing. The *analysis* of oral data often poses a problem for novices, and few follow the advice that analytic strategies should be fully grasped *before* data are collected. The inexperienced researcher who has untranscribed interviews, or piles of transcripts unanalysed, is an all too frequent feature of the 'visitors' outside our offices. Coffey and Atkinson (1996) was written for such people, and helpfully contrasts several classic analytic strategies using interviews with experienced social anthropologists. The main point that cannot be over-stressed is that interview data have to be recognised for what they are and, more vitally, what they are not. Atkinson and Delamont (2006a, 2006b) argue the case for proper analysis, rather than mere celebration of oral data.

Here I have concentrated on the presentation of interview data in novel ways. As well as proper analysis, interview data are particularly well-suited to exploring alternative forms of text – such as poems, plays, fictions, dialogues – to disseminate the findings. The narrative by Dr Enright about her viva became an ethnographic poem that I wrote for Coffey and Atkinson (1996: 129–130), and there is an example of such a poem later in this section. The bitter debates about oral data, particularly about illness narratives, explored by Thomas (2010), have been relatively absent from educational research. There is no group in education equivalent to patients, nor any scholars who are also cancer survivors like Frank (2010), and nothing in education is equivalent to death, cancer or chronic illness.

However, the feature of illness narratives that has been simultaneously present in the educational research of the past 20 years is the use of non-traditional textual forms to convey the 'voice' of the student or pupil, like the 'voice' of the patient. In educational research the narrative research has been particularly prominent in the publications that experiment with new textual forms. The representation of the informants, or of the researcher, and particularly the choice of textual form has changed over the past 20 years. The journal *Qualitative Studies in Education* regularly publishes poems, plays, and short bits of fiction. Delamont (2012b) contains chapters by distinguished educational researchers extolling a variety of new textual forms (Eisner, 1997) (and

141

also dance) for conveying results to audiences. Whatever your views about such representational innovations, it is necessary to understand why they are used, and how to construct them. Poetry is perhaps the most controversial form (Brady, 2005, 2009).

poetry

Delamont (2008) used two poetic forms to comment on debates about feminism and postmodernism in educational research. One is a strict metre piece, rare in ethnographic poems which are generally free verse like the lament of Nancy Enright. The general use of free verse to express emotions, particularly negative ones, is itself made problematic by the use of fixed metre forms with rhyme schemes such as the sonnet. For similar purposes, Neil Stephens and I took an incident from my fieldnotes of a class we both attended when we knew very little about *capoeira*, and turned it into both a *capoeira* song and an ethnographic free verse poem.

Poetry is probably the most frequently used of the 'new' textual forms. As Brady (2000: 963) wrote 'it is the poetic turf more anthropologists are traversing nowadays'. To illustrate the potential of poetic representation to convey emotion, in this case how much *capoeira* can mean to serious, committed *discipulos* (learners), poetic forms are used. I chose an incident involving one Tolnbridge student, who, in trying to behave more 'correctly', with much better adherence to the conventions of *capoeira* than any of his fellow students, got reprimanded by Perseus, his *mestre*.

There are two *capoeira* traditions: *angola* codified by Mestre Pastinha, and *regional* created by Mestre Bimba (see Lewis, 1992; Assunção, 2005; Downey, 2005). Early in the *capoeira* fieldwork, an episode occurred in a master class taught by two visiting teachers, Ulysses, an *angola* specialist, and Diomedes, a *regional* teacher. In the tradition of *angola capoeira*, ordinary clothing, or black and yellow, is worn. (Pastinha's students wore black and yellow because these were the colours of his football team.) *Regional* groups normally wear uniforms of white trousers and t-shirts with a coloured belt that shows how experienced the student is. Rashka, the most experienced and committed *discipulo* in the class, who is an African-Portuguese man, wore black trousers and a yellow t-shirt for the *angola* lesson and then changed to white trousers and t-shirt for the *regional* lesson. When he joined Diomedes's class he had not threaded his *corda* through the belt loops and tied it properly with the correct knot. The master in charge, Perseus, who had invited Ulysses and Diomedes, called to Raksha, prodded him with the *berimbau*, and told him sternly to thread and tie the *corda* properly. Rashka was behaving in an impeccably 'correct' way, in changing his clothes between the two classes, and his knowledge of the etiquette was so much greater than anyone else in the class including ours, that no one else 'understood' what he had done or why, until long afterwards. However, in his haste, his attempt at courtesy to Diomedes was marred by his 'failure' to thread and tie his belt 'properly'. Such an incident lends itself to a poetic treatment, and is the one chosen to represent the use of alternative forms of representation.

One way for the researchers to show mastery of the use of poetic representation, *and* the fact that *capoeira* has rules and etiquette, *and* demonstrate that as ethnographers we had understood the songs that accompany all *capoeira*, is to present the incident as a *capoeira* song. In the case of the Raksha incident, the poetic text should really be a *capoeira* song, in Portuguese, playing with the *capoeira* format, to celebrate the centrality of the call and response songs which accompany all *roda* play, in which the master sings the verses and everyone else responds with a short formulaic chorus, as in:

zum zum zum

Capoeira mata um (*capoeira* kills one)

A *capoeira* song which can be adapted to Rashka's reprimand in English includes a verse that goes:

Master: I hide the end of the knot

Chorus: Parana

Master: No one knows how to untie

Chorus: Parana

'Parana' is a state in Brazil and is often mentioned in choruses. The verse is metaphorical, about 'hiding', or secreting one's purpose in 'knots', that is, engaging in *malicia* (deception) in the *capoeira* game (Stephens and Delamont, 2009). However, it can be twisted to 'fit' the episode of Raksha's *corda*. In this *capoeira* song the word *camara*, friend or comrade, which features in many common choruses, is used to create a 'typical' refrain.

Raksha's Corda

Raksha: My master says

'Put on your cord'

Chorus: Corda on, camara

Raksha:	I thread my cord,
	I tie my cord
Chorus:	Corda on, camara
Raksha:	His cord is red
	He is my master
Chorus:	Corda on, camara
Raksha:	My cord is blue
	His cord is red
Chorus:	Corda on, camara
Raksha:	My cord is blue
	Perseus, I obey.

None of the ethnographers of *capoeira* has so far disseminated their research by writing real songs for real classes to sing. This song would, of course, have to scan in Portuguese, and fit one of the standard *capoeira* musical rhythms (see Lewis, 1992) if it were to be used in a *capoeira* class, but that would be dysfunctional for any reader of the ethnographic research who did not have a good comprehension of Brazilian Portuguese.

144 To do free verse, as most ethnographers do, is easier. Below is a piece of ethnographic poetry, intended to convey the emotion that Raksha felt when his attempt at courtesy and his display of enculturation was the cause of another breach of etiquette. It is in two verses, one for each lesson, each teacher, each outfit. Raksha's ethnicity, his commitment to the rules, conventions and etiquette of *capoeira*, and his inadvertent 'breach' of a convention are portrayed. The colours of the belts have symbolic significance: they represent the stages of capture, enslavement and emancipation of the African-Brazilian slaves; or the deities of the African-Brazilian religion *Candomblé*; or facets of Brazilian society (such as the colours of the flag). In the *Beribazu* group, to which Perseus and Rashka then belonged, the first *corda* is blue, for the Atlantic Ocean, across which the slaves were transported.

Raksha's Lament

I changed my trousers

Out of respect.

I wore black for Ulysses

To honour Angola, my father's land,

I am Angolan, I am Portuguese,

I am Capoeira.

Diomedes called.

He is Regional.

I changed my trousers

I wore white for the freed slaves

I ran, the corda round my waist

To join Diomedes.

Perseus spoke. He is my master

'Thread your corda'. 'Tie it properly'.

'Respect Diomedes'.

The blue corda is the sea.

The sea crossed by slaves from Angola

I earned my corda

In the roda.

Perseus is my master: I thread my corda.

This song is reasonably typical of the sorts of poetic representation that are now found in ethnographic texts: designed to emphasise the emotional aspects of the informants' experiences. It focuses on the disciplinary relationship between *mestre* and student, and the duty of the learner to obey the teacher.

A LOOK TO THE FUTURE

the research we need

There is not enough published material on folklore, jokes, atrocity stories and rumour in educational settings, either formal or informal. There are many interview studies, but few of them treat the data as performative and rhetorical. Good ethnographers of educational settings that mould observational work with informants' formal and informal talk to fight familiarity are always 'needed'.

ten

senses and multi-sensory matters: indescribable noises, sights, feelings

> I had been blowing glass for six months when I attempted to blow a rudimentary goblet. I had accrued through practice a basic set of glass blowing skills which utilised numerous hand tools. (O'Connor, 2007: 127)

> Before I went to Prior's End School in 1982 I was told by a friend already there that a teacher – Mr Paradine – had raped one pupil (girl) and hadn't been asked to leave because he owned the helicopter that boys took apart and put together again in metalwork.

I make no apology for quoting this urban legend here although I have used it before. I am pretty certain that the 18 year old woman who gave it to me in the late 1980s had made it up to fool me, to wind me up, but it is possible that she had 'really' been told that when she was ten. In 1979 the UK had elected a conservative government, led by Mrs Thatcher which, as Ball (1990) has chronicled, introduced to England in the 1988 Education Act a neo-conservative, privatising, marketising schools regime. Whether or not it was a 'real' scary story, it captured several features of such contemporary legends. It is relevant here because it reminds us all that schools are full of material objects (if not helicopters) that are central to the delivery of the curriculum. The focus of this chapter is material objects, such as clothes, musical instruments and scientific equipment, hence the opening quote from O'Connor on glass blowing. The ethnographer needs to deploy all five senses to study the material world. Although materials, and other sensory aspects of education, are the most neglected part of educational ethnography, we can draw some conclusions from the available literature. Once those have been explored, the chapter moves on to consider how data on them are best gathered, and then sets out an agenda that should receive attention.

Can you remember an ethnography from which you took away strong sensations that you had touched objects, tasted food and drink, or smelled the setting? This chapter deals with the five senses: both their importance for learners and teachers in formal and informal educational settings, and their centrality to the ethnographer's toolkit. The subtitle, from Hurston's *Mules and Men* (1935: 221) refers to her experiences, possibly in trance, when being initiated into hoodoo in New Orleans. Inside a magic circle she felt herself threatened by 'great, beast-like creatures' (p. 221) signifying Death, experienced through the senses of hearing, sight and touch.

This chapter works backwards, starting with taste, smell and touch, which are, or have been, the most neglected in the research and in the methods writing. Once the three neglected senses have been explored, the chapter moves on to sight and sound. Because these latter two are prioritised in other methods books (e.g. Lofland and Lofland, 2005; Hammersley and Atkinson, 2007) they receive less attention here. Educational ethnography has not been enthusiastically focused on using all five senses or exploring how actors in educational settings learn to use *their* five senses as they master skills; or discovering which senses 'matter' in which areas of education.

TASTE

Stoller (1989, 1997) began to focus mainstream anthropology on taste, and hence on the other senses. *The Taste of Ethnographic Things* called for anthropology to pay attention to that sense. The anthropology of education has not followed him, and the sociology of education has been just as impervious to calls for sensory ethnography. Taste, the English word, is used in both a literal sense (i.e. 'Is it sweet enough?') and in a metaphorical sense, meaning a sense of style. (Does he have 'good taste'? – meaning elite-approved style.) The two came together in Maryon McDonald's (1989) analysis of how gender and identity are related to food and drink choices in Brittany. In rural Brittany the peasant women ate and drank sweet things at celebratory events, while the men consumed sour, bitter, savoury things. A good woman drank sweet coffee and ate sugary cakes, while a proper man celebrated with beer or dry wine and coarse meat paté. Cowan (1991) reported similar norms from her fieldwork in northern Greece. The public display of appropriately gendered behaviour was marked by the taste of the food and drink consumed. Men drank ouzo or beer, with savoury snacks such as olives and cheese, while women drank sweet liquids and ate cake or ice cream. We lack such data on how teachers' consumption patterns signify and display to their colleagues such salient characteristics as class, femininity, refinement and adherence to a healthy lifestyle, although the data could be collected. There is a similar lack of data on how pupils and students relate taste to identity although we do know that food 'choices' are one way that gender is displayed. Eating salad, for example, is 'girly' and 'non-cool' in UK schools.

Taste rarely figures in educational ethnographies, and has been under-theorised. This is where Bourdieu's work reigns supreme (1984). His work on taste, *Distinction*, is less used in the sociology and anthropology of education than it is in the sociology of culture, but can be used to theorise all the sensory aspects of educational institutions. Fine's (1985) work on catering students in the USA addresses both meanings of taste: Bourdieu's class-related sense of taste as a cultural marker and the actual sensations of food in the mouth. The working-class American teenagers had had little or no exposure to the foods they were being trained to cook for a gourmet clientele. For example, the students did not know what different types of, and especially good, well kept olives, were meant to taste of because they had never eaten olives, or had tried them once and disliked them. The instructors explained that, in order to cook with such ingredients, which were vital to *haute cuisine*, they needed to learn to be able to judge quality, freshness, and recognise varieties as well as appreciate those items. They did not need to become enthusiastic about eating them themselves, but they did have to know what the 'right' taste was for key ingredients and dishes.

148

Wacquant (2004) who conducted an ethnography of boxers learning to fight in a gym in an African-American neighbourhood in Chicago, reports that taste was one of the main barriers to successful enculturation. Fighters in training were expected, even required, to eschew 'junk' food such as hamburgers, pizza and hot dogs high in saturated fats, salt and sugars. Some men found that simply unpalatable and gave up their potential careers as boxers because, they told Wacquant, they could not bear to stay on the prescribed 'healthy' diet. The healthy foods, like steamed vegetables, did not have the 'right' taste for these men.

The absence of familiar tastes, and especially of specific flavours, is frequently reported by anthropologists describing culture shock (either their own, or that facing their informants). Hagedorn (2001: 156) reports that when the dancers and drummers of the National Cuban Folklore Touring Company were abroad, for example, in Paris, they found the food available to them was inedible. It was not only unfamiliar but also *tasteless*. The carbohydrate was not rice, the meat was too lean, and there were no familiar 'hot' spices. When taste does figure in ethnographies, the researcher often focuses on the absence of specific foods or flavourings. In Carolyn Ellis's (2009) autoethnography about the ethical issues that might arise if she were to study the year round residents of the mountain community where she has a vacation home, the tastelessness of the food in Mapleton is a significant feature. Ellis contrasts the variety and the piquancy of the food available in a multi-cultural university city compared to that in a mono-cultural mountain village. Such culture shock can be fundamental to educational encounters, but rarely figures in the research. One exception is Wee Loon Yeo (2010) who recalls his first experience of an Australian buffet with cold meat: he had never seen cold meat before, far less eaten it. In his experience meat was always served and eaten hot.

Oddly, ethnographies of cooking classes are silent about the actual taste of the food prepared by the students they were watching. Fine (1985) who observed trainee chefs in the USA discusses their food tastes but does not report on eating what they cooked himself. He does describe eating what was prepared by professional chefs in his ethnography of restaurant kitchens (Fine, 1996) and others have produced qualitative research on classes in which food is being prepared – Coxon (1983) on a cookery class for adult men in the UK; the work on the 'cream team' apprentice bakers (Riseborough, 1992) and Riseborough (1988) on a cookery teacher in a Jewish school – but the authors never mention the taste of the food. Coxon writes of the 'classed' nature of the food the men wanted to prepare, but not its taste. Riseborough and the gentile cookery teacher in the Jewish school do not seem to have eaten the Kosher food she taught the pupils to prepare. If either ate the food, nothing of its taste survives into the published text. We do not learn if the teacher *liked* the kosher food she was cooking, nor if Riseborough did.

If we turn to smell, the literature becomes richer, although it is fiction authors rather than researchers who have used smell to evoke education.

149

SMELL

Fictional evocations of schools routinely began with the smell of the place. For example, British and American novelists often use the characteristic smells that pervade school buildings to create the background for the action, and it is clear that they expect their readers to recognise the typical educational atmosphere from the smells. The thriller writer Anthony Price wrote a book about a Russian 'sleeper': an adult with a false identity placed as a student at Oxford to be activated when in a top job. The secret service man, Colonel Butler, sent to check the 'sleeper's' supposed history goes to a small private boarding school in the South East England of the 1960s for boys aged 7–13 (a 'prep' school in

Britain) to consult its archives. Price's evocation of the school starts with its smell. Butler breaks into the building and:

> The changing room contained an encyclopaedia of smells: sweet feet and dirty clothes, dubbined leather and linseed oil and linament – the natured smell of compulsory games. ...
>
> Through the changing room into the passage the smell was subtly altering now, from athletic boy to scholastic boy: chalk and ink and books and God only knew what – floor polish maybe, and feet still... It was a combined odour Butler remembered well. (Price, 1973: 23)

Reading this passage it is clear that Price expects his readers to recognise everything they need to 'know' about the place because the whole institution has been encapsulated in the smells. We walk with Colonel Butler through Eden Hall, so skilfully does Price conjure it up. In the USA, the same device is used by Robert Parker, who set several of his Spenser stories in educational institutions. *School Days* (2006) is a crime story that reflects on the Columbine School massacre, but it is set on the East Coast, rather than in Colorado. Like Price, a crime fiction writer is wanting his readers, who may never have been inside a fee-paying school, to identify it *as a school*. So when Parker wanted to evoke Dowling – an elite private high school, set in the 'deepest dark center of exurbia' (p. 12), a fictional equivalent of Edgewood Academy studied by Peshkin (2001) – he too begins with its smell:

150

> Inside, it smelled like a school. It was air-conditioned and clean, but the smell of school was adamant. I never knew what the smell was. Youth? Chalk dust? Industrial cleaner? Boredom? (Parker, 2006: 18)

Greenwood (1994) contrasts two schools in a detective story set in London using the same literary device of smell. One is a South-West London Secondary Comprehensive School, the other St Veep's Girls School – a single sex elite day school in London's affluent district of Kensington founded in the 1880s. The comprehensive's ethos is partially captured by smells: 'cigarette smoke', 'coke fumes', 'commercial cleaner'. The coke fumes appear repeatedly in the five pages (pp. 13–20) in which the reader 'enters' the school. In contrast, St Veep's smells only of the wax used to polish the oak panelling in every room.

Those writing autobiographical memoirs frequently deploy the same device. The novelist Andrew O'Hagan was born in 1968, and his family moved out of inner city Glasgow to Irvine New Town in 1970. He recalls starting school at St Winnin's Roman Catholic infant and primary:

We were led inside. I'd never smelt a room like it before. The classroom was high windowed and cold, and it had the roving odour of pee and plasticine. The teacher seemed old... and she smelt like a maternity nurse. In other words, she smelt of sick. (1995: 81)

All researchers who have studied educational settings for young children will be able to imagine themselves in St Winnin's from that brief passage. Reading the ethnographic research on educational settings, however, does not usually remind us how characteristic and evocative smell is. Too often we do not record smells properly.

Leaving smell, the next sensory topic discussed is that of 'touch and feel', again drawing on Andrew O'Hagan's memory of Scotland.

TOUCH AND FEEL

O'Hagan (1995: 81) recalls the feel of his first book in his infant school:

She handed out books. I feel funny describing it – books would become the most important thing of all. But it didn't feel like it on the day; the one she gave me felt slimy.

Many kinds of formal and informal education involve becoming familiar with the feel of 'new' objects, and being enculturated is, *de facto* mastering and manipulating material objects from pencils to violins or electron microscopes appropriately (Appadurai, 1986). As educational ethnographers we need to observe closely the apprentice and the skilled manipulations, and, whenever possible it is also important for the researcher to touch things; to pick them up, hold them, use them.

As far as touch is concerned, one good data collection principle is to record all objects in a setting, and who does and does not touch them. Detailed observation in school science laboratories, for example, can reveal that some pupils never touch any equipment, because all the things available are seized by other pupils, or due to fear of it, or because the small groups operate with a division of labour in which some 'do' the physical tasks and others record them.

There is often a strongly gendered division of labour in object use in science classes (See Measor, 1984; Solomon, 1991) and in educational settings for young children. The ethnographic research on the object use of young children conducted from the 1970s onwards in Anglophone countries (see Delamont, 1990 for a review) showed that sex-segregation in object use was 'normal', and a child who violated that normality was regarded with suspicion by adults and other children. Commentators on

151

those data were concerned both about the stereotyping, and children's failure to develop all the skills that a well-rounded person ought to have: that is, spatial reasoning, literary readiness, nurturing, number awareness and interactional capabilities. Observation (e.g. Serbin, 1978) showed that teachers only used some of the objects and only spent time in some of the space. Girls tended to cluster round the teacher, and if she did not, for example, spend time setting up rail tracks and running trains on them, then no girls handled those objects. Unless the teachers actively intervene, girls do not use the toy cars, trains and other vehicles (which help children develop spatial reasoning) and boys do not use the Wendy house or doll corner (where nurturing skills are developed). If teachers have strategies, such as using all the objects themselves, they can break down the gender barriers, but most teachers did not and do not have such strategies.

There have been discussions about how much active manipulation of objects should be required in formal education for at least 200 years, and changing technologies can be controversial. In 2010 concern was voiced about the lack of object and tool manipulation in the English schools. The serious slightly left of centre UK newspaper, the *Guardian*, printed a letter on 19 July 2010 written by a set of leading engineers arguing that schools in England were not giving pupils any experience of handling tools.

152

> It is an unfortunate truth that an increasingly large proportion of young people are leaving school without any basic hand skills in woodwork, metalwork or detailed drawing, or an understanding of the interrelationship of materials in engineering or construction. We believe an early introduction (i.e. at primary school) to such training, by teachers who are themselves skilled, provides interest for young people, leading to enthusiasm to achieve skills, which can later be applied to engineering, architecture, design and construction at all practical and management levels and, more widely, for the benefit of all of us in business, sport or home life. If these skills are not introduced at an early age, they may never be learned. Hand skills stay with you for life.

There are some interesting points here. The engineers wrote about 'people', but in fact for most of the history of formal education in the UK, only boys were given opportunities in school to learn woodwork, metalwork, or technical drawing. For most girls these three practical subjects were not available: they were only for boys. Girls got sewing, cooking and laundry work instead. From the nineteenth century up until the Sex Discrimination Act of 1974, craft subjects were one of the most sexually segregated areas of the curriculum. Girls' schools were built with cookery kitchens, needlework rooms and laundry suites, plus rooms equipped with typewriters to learn office work (Valli, 1986); boys' schools had rooms for woodwork, metalwork, technical drawing and sometimes motor mechanics areas. So these engineers are calling for something that boys did have for many years, but most girls never had, and the letter is not clear about whether both sexes 'should' have these tactile experiences (re)instated in their education. The authors of the letter do not seem to think that learning to handle the implements and tools that are used to work with food and textiles are as important as those that manipulate wood and metal.

There may have been a time when all boys did get exposed to what the engineers call 'hand skills' and materials in English schools. Many young men, such as, memorably David Hargreaves (1982) never acquired those 'hand skills' and were relieved when they could stop trying to. However, there was only a brief period when those subjects, and their associated material objects, were meant to be offered to young women. The Act passed in 1974 made it illegal to segregate the curriculum in the traditional way, though many schools were slow to comply. When the first ORACLE project fieldwork on the first year of secondary school in three English cities was being conducted in 1977 and 1978 (Delamont and Galton, 1986) it was found that the schools were working to provide all the practical subjects for all the pupils of both sexes, although there were some difficulties (discussed in Chapter 8) but when doing fieldwork in comprehensives in four local authorities in South Wales in 1985 I was shocked to find that no attempt had been made to comply with the 1974 Act in one of them. At Sharway Downs only the boys did woodwork and metalwork, and only the girls did cookery and needlework. The brief period when English secondary schools possibly gave girls those 'hand skills' lauded in the engineers' letter ended when in 1988 the 'national' curriculum for England and Wales *de facto* 'abolished' all those practical subjects, as Paechter (2000) showed.

Whether or not any particular formal or informal setting is offering pupils or learners 'hand skills' or not, the duty of the ethnographer is very clear. Objects, and anything involving the touch and feel of things, are important. Precision in the note-taking is particularly useful here. When an excited boy said to me at Sharway Downs when the boys and girls were reunited after sex-segregated woodwork and needlework:

Oh miss, you should have come to woodwork. Mental Trefor stabbed me with a chisel.

It clearly mattered to the boy that it was a *chisel* – and had I been present, I should have recorded the tool used by 'Mental Trefor', as well as

153

the attack. That incident is a good reminder that the researcher needs to pay attention not only to who touches what, and who does not, but also whether the touch is legitimate (i.e. using a chisel as the woodwork master has instructed) or not (i.e. stabbing a classmate with it).

Perhaps because the objects, and the touch and feel of them, in *capoeira* were all unfamiliar, that fieldwork included more precise notes on touch and feel than some educational research I have done. Newcomers to *capoeira* quickly realise that a variety of material objects are regularly used. *Capoeira* is done to music, and novices quickly learn that in addition to the drum(s) and tambourines (*atabaques* and *pandeiros*) there are cowbells (*agogos*), a hollow scraper (*reco reco*), and the *berimbau* – an African origin instrument, which is a large (5 foot) bow, strung with a wire, struck with a small stick. Additionally, *capoeira* groups often do *maculele*, a dance with sticks that are clashed together, and a fisherman's dance where straw hats are worn and a large fishing net manipulated. The *berimbau* is a powerful symbol of *capoeira*, not only its unusual sound, but its exotic shape. Women wear tiny *berimbau* earrings; indeed, I do fieldwork with a silver model *berimbau* on a chain round my neck. Its picture appears on CD covers, t-shirts, posters and websites. To anyone 'in' *capoeira* the sight of a stranger carrying one, even shrouded in a carrying case, means that a class, festival, street *roda* or performance is near by. The *berimbau* is an object, but also a symbol (see Stephens and Delamont, 2006a).

Just as the ethnographer needs to focus on what objects are touched and which are not, and on legitimate and forbidden touch, it can be particularly insightful to explore what objects are regarded as perishable and which are designated, or designed to be permanent, to be heirlooms, and by whom. In educational institutions, such as libraries, who can touch which books, with or without gloves, and the handling of books is a 'marker' of many things about the organisation. In *capoeira* the difference between *berimbaus* and drums is a good example of how understanding the way(s) objects are and are not handled can give ethnographic insight into a whole culture. *Berimbaus* perish – they break. Drums are more long-lasting, and because drums are also used for dancing, in carnival, and in the African-Brazilian religions, they link current *capoeiristas* to other Brazilian, African, and African-American and Caribbean beliefs and practices. *Capoeira* drums stand waist high, made of planks of wood held (vertically) in place either by metal bands or rope. There have been fashions in drums, with claims that roped drums are more 'authentic' (i.e. African) and traditional (i.e. what the old *mestres* used).

In *capoeira* classes everyone is encouraged to learn to play the drum and to share playing it for *rodas*, so *capoeira* drumming is not esoteric

154

or gendered. In contrast in the African-Caribbean and African Brazilian religions drums are sacred. Women were not traditionally allowed to learn the sacred drums, or to be drummers. Today some teachers will allow female students to pay for drumming lessons, but ceremonial performance is still a male activity. Hagedorn (2001) was taught to drum by a Cuban master so she could play but even when she was initiated into Santeria she was still barred from performing in Santeria ceremonies. Similarly in the Pueblo Indian High School, Peshkin (1997: 41–2) observed a class in traditional drumming: attended by six boys and two girls. Both sexes sing, but only boys drum, because the girls' parents believe it is 'improper' for females to play drums.

Every educational setting has its equivalent objects. Novices taking up the French martial art *savate* need to become familiar with boxing gloves, and mouthguards. The instructor brings a suitcase of gloves for novices to use, until they are committed enough to buy their own. Serious learners of *savate* know that the colour of the gloves worn indicates the level of proficiency: the gloves in the instructor's suitcase are all red signalling beginners, while the more advanced students wear gloves that are blue or yellow, and the instructor has silver gloves. No one can borrow mouthguards, however, and novices initially learn without them. If serious about learning *savate*, students have to buy a guard that fits them, and come to class with it in a small case.

155

Objects like drums, or boxing gloves, are portable, and their presence may be enough to transform a setting. In a gym, for example, one class may be marked as artistic gymnastics by the presence of ribbons, hoops and Indian clubs. The next class is marked as *savate* by the boxing gloves and mouthguards, and the third as *kendo* by the face masks and staves. In schools some rooms change function in this way: the hall is 'for' music when sheet music is handed out, 'for' eating when tables are laid with cutlery and lunch is served, and then 'for' exams when the desks and question papers are set out.

Other objects only occur in specific settings and 'live' there permanently in fixed assemblages. A kiln is essential to 'do' pottery, and defines a studio; sinks, benches and Bunsen burners define a laboratory; and the chisel is one element in the assemblage that defined a 'woodwork' room in the 1970s, and a Craft, Design and Technology room in a current English school (Paechter, 2000). Ethnographies of learning skills, such as glass blowing, frequently start from the objects in the assemblage that defines the setting.

A glassblowing studio consists of a furnace, which 'cooks' and holds molten glass at approximately 1800 degrees Fahrenheit, the glory hole (a small cylindrical furnace located in front of the workbench of the glassblowers in which the glass is continuously reheated while being worked upon), and an annealer. (O'Connor, 2007: 127)

One way in which the skilled ethnographer introduces the unfamiliar setting to the reader is by describing their own shift from an ill-informed observer of the unfamiliar assemblage of strange objects whose significance is unknown, to a sense of knowing familiarity. There is a reflexive analysis of this process in Karen McCarthy Brown (1991: 7). Mama Lola, a Haitian Vodou Priestess in New York, lives and runs a temple, in a small flat. As Brown reports, as she learnt more about vodou, when she enters the little room used to venerate the spirits it 'feels bigger' than it did when she first visited because 'its contents' are 'no longer confusing'. Later in the book she uses her knowledge to describe and explain a Vodou assemblage, on an altar for Azaka, one of the deities. She says that 'Vodou altars are texts, ready for the reading' (1991: 41). For Azaka's feast day celebrations, Mama Lola has sourced and laid out bottles of Haitian cola; rum, gin, tequila, scotch; 'plates of cookies and candy'; 'bananas, grapes, apples and cherries [which] formed a mound around a plump pineapple'; three commercially baked cakes from a bakery; raw sugar cane; and cassava bread (p. 42). In the kitchen large pans of rice and black beans, cornmeal and black beans, and *chaka*, a pork stew, were bubbling. All these items, plus the colours in which the altars were dressed, tell an experienced observer which deity is being honoured.

What had seemed to Brown as a novice observer to be a disorganised and baffling 'heap of stuff', became, as she learnt about Vodou, a text she could recognise, read, and relate to a set of cosmological beliefs about the various deities. A Vodou altar in Haiti or New York may seem ridiculously 'far' from anything related to touch in an educational setting but in fact schools and universities have 'magical' objects in them that the researcher needs to understand. When Albas and Albas (1984, 2009) were studying how American college students dealt with assessment, especially exams, they discovered that like athletes, soldiers, and actors, in student culture magical rituals and magic charms were employed. On investigation they found between one quarter and one third of American students reported magical beliefs and practices, such as: e.g. 'Don't sit near anyone wearing pink', or 'Don't let anyone wish you "good luck"', or the use of material items such as lucky sweaters (2009: 109).

Appropriately, reflexive ethnographers also draw on their own use of objects, and in some cases, disastrous mis-use of objects. Deyhle (1998) was at the beginning of her research on Navaho education when she was embarrassed by her incompetence with a jar of mustard. She was in a large communal diner, and as a stranger and a non-Navaho, she was already an object of suspicion.

> As I got to the end of the table, I picked up the industrial-sized jar of mustard and turned it over to squirt out a little on my hot dog. The lid was loose and its entire contents burst out and completely filled my plate, the table, and my chest. The room fell silent. (Deyhle, 1998: 41)

Much later, when more embedded in the Navaho community, Dehyle was inadvertently implicated in a series of events around sacred objects that 'was a cultural disaster'. The incident took place before an Enemy Way ceremony: a very expensive and important curing ritual. Dehyle was invited to attend, perhaps because she had a robust vehicle that could be used to take things to the ceremony. So 'the water drum and prayer sticks were put into the back of my Honda station wagon'. The family for whom the ceremony was important travelled with Deyhle in her car, and only they actually handled the sacred objects, but she recalls still feeling uncomfortable around the drum and prayer sticks, even though she did not touch them. Indeed at the ceremony she felt so intrusive that she left early on the last night. Later she learned that, in violation of all the rules and tradition of Navaho ceremonies, there had been a fight on the evening she left and she was told that even worse: 'the water drum broke, the one that was in your car' (1998: 41). Her gatekeepers, Joe and Sally, told her that she should not be anxious about the drum, but later still she learned that:

> Joe and Sally had to have a medicine man perform a one night ceremony to avoid bad luck because of the broken drum and to allay the suspicion that the breaking was connected to my presence. (Deyhle, 1998: 42)

In this 'confession' the importance of objects and of who cannot touch them is crystal clear, *and* informative about the Navaho.

Closer to 'home', the ownership or display of certain objects can be an important indicator of status. Cottrell (2004: 13) makes this point about mobile phones:

> Mobile phones, particularly, quickly became *de rigueur*, implying that you were a busy musician, often on the move, who needed to be easily available to deal with offers of work.

That meant, Cottrell argues, that before mobile phones became normal for all musicians, those who did not have one were seen to be 'not serious' about their careers.

157

I have myself experienced this on several occasions. Having been a late arrival to the mobile phone party I occasionally felt that I detected a degree of surprise when people who were dealing with me as a musician discovered I did not have one: an implied subtext which says 'How can you be a musician and not have a mobile? You can't be much good'. (Cottrell, 2004: 13)

A theoretical concept that helps ethnographers make sense of things is the *Boundary Object*. Star and Griesemer's (1989) work on the 'boundary object' is useful. Where different subcultures, occupations, or social worlds meet, or collide, or abut each other in mutual incomprehension, boundary objects can be constructed, or reconstructed, to meet the demands of more than one subculture, occupation or social world. This concept was first used to illuminate the work of scientists when a museum of natural history in the USA was being developed, a project that involved many actors other than scientists such as sponsors, curators, volunteers, etc. It is an idea that has mileage in most educational settings. Star and Griesemer (1989: 393) originally defined boundary objects as things which:

> [b]oth inhabit several intersecting worlds and satisfy the informational requirements of each of them...

An important element of boundary objects is that they are

> [b]oth plastic enough to adapt to local needs and the constraints of several parties employing them, yet robust enough to maintain a common identity across sites. They are weakly structured in common use, and become strongly structured in individual site use.

For Star and Griesemer (1989: 393), boundary objects were a 'means of translation': helping groups to work together. In a paper published shortly before her death, Star (2010: 604) reiterated that her initial framing of the concept was motivated by a desire to analyse the 'nature of cooperative work in the absence of consensus'. In science and technology studies the concept went fast from being analytically useful to being deployed so widely that it was a cliché and retained little meaning (Clarke and Star, 2008. The power of the concept is enhanced if it is only used in its original sense. It is useful to be precise about the boundary objects in the fieldsite (Star, 1989, 2010; Suchman, 1994). In many settings where formal or informal teaching and learning take place, searching to see if any material goods are boundary objects is a useful lens through which to make the familiar strange.

158

SOUND

Listening is a central theme in the methodological writing of Forsey (2010). He starts from an important question posed by Fabian (1983: 107–108):

> What makes a reported sight more objective than a reported sound, smell or taste? Our bias for one and against the other is a matter of cultural choice rather than universal validity.

Forsey recalls that he had been somewhat uncomfortable as a doctoral student, studying an Australian government high school, because many of his data were dialogue from casual conversations and formal interviews rather than observations. In summary 'the data presented reflect more of what I heard in the field than what I saw' (2010: 560). Forsey's focus is on *engaged listening* (p. 560, emphasis Forsey's) and he argues that 'listening is as significant as observation to ethnographers' (p. 561). Forsey (2010: 562) makes it clear that his fieldwork is committed to 'a democracy of the senses', adding that much of what is 'reported as the "seen"' in ethnography texts was in practice 'observations of people conversing, singing, listening, speech making'(p. 563).

Taking sound seriously has two aspects: what sound means to the actors in the setting, and what strikes the researcher. Recording carefully what can be heard (and that there are other things that cannot) is important in school and other educational settings. Hall, Lashua and Coffey (2008) argue forcefully both for a greater research attention to noise, and for using noise as part of gaining access to important aspects of the lives of young people by interviewing them as they moved through 'their' soundscapes. One set of ethnographic projects which paid careful attention to the soundscapes of a variety of locations and social contexts, and made the use of music 'strange' rather than familiar, is De Nora (2000), *Music in Everyday Life*. She foregrounds music in several settings where it had not previously been researched (including aerobics classes where informal learning is taking place).

When the noise is music there is much to learn from ethnomusicologists. Anthony Seeger is an expert on the music (and the cosmology and social organisation) of the Suyá Indians of the Matto Grosso of Brazil – a very small and very isolated community. Seeger and his wife Judith have worked with the Suyá for 37 years. In 1976, he was 'for at least the 300th time' sitting in the village plaza in the dark with the

159

men of a Suyá community 'listening companionably'. There were no lights available, nothing else to do and:

> I learned a lot listening to men talk among themselves about things that I would never have thought to ask or did not know how to ask – including the terms for musical structures. (Seeger, 2008: 274)

In British schools it is a feature of many ethnographies that the level of noise coming out of a classroom or other space is the most powerful evidence of the subject being taught and of the teacher's competence and style. Voices singing in harmony 'mean' that the music lesson is orderly; shrieks and yells and thumps 'mean' that the teacher has 'lost control'. Denscombe's (1984a, 1984b) work on how a teacher's status among colleagues was crucially dependent on the noise 'leaking' from the closed room, explores this element of teacher performativity and how it is judged by colleagues and pupils. Beynon's (1987) classic paper 'Miss Floral mends her ways' chronicles a young female drama teacher in a boys' school learning this 'reality', and altering her classroom regime accordingly (Fordham, 1993).

In 1971 I worked in a research unit that was developing Computer Assisted Instruction (CAI). One programme was intended to provide a computer assisted drill and practice in number facts, to encourage children to become thoroughly familiar with them. A child logged on and was presented with a series of simple problems that tried to help him or her build on what they 'knew' to appreciate other ways of 'seeing'. So the child got a sequence such as 3+2 = ?, 2+3 = ?, and once those were 'correct', moved on to 5–2 = ?, 5–3 = ? If these were done wrong, the student was shown that he or she had already got two earlier sums 3+2 = 5 and 2+3 = 5 correct, was praised for that and then 5–2 = ? was presented again. It the child still got that wrong the positive results were represented and so on. Once the second type of problem was mastered, ?+3 = 5 and ?+2 = 5 were presented in the same pedagogical style. The idea was that such drill was not a sensible use of an expensive teacher's time, but pupils would learn better if they had constant feedback and position reinforcement of an individualised sort from a computer terminal.

At these early stages of CAI (it later became Computer Assisted Learning – CAL) the costs were far too high to make it feasible in mainstream schools, but it could have been financially viable in schools for those with special needs where there were many fewer pupils per teacher. The unit ran a demonstration for special needs teachers. To the surprise of the CAI research team they were very hostile. Part of their hostility was unfamiliarity and associated technophobia: the terminals were connected to a mainframe that occupied a huge air-conditioned room on the floor below the 'lab', and none of them had ever touched a terminal before. However, there were two other reasons. These special needs teachers were approaching the end of their careers and were hostile because they 'remembered' the teacher unemployment of the Great Depression of the 1930s, and were scared that these machines might replace them. What is more relevant here, however, was their terrified reaction to the noise. When six terminals were running the lab was not silent, but no one who worked in computing then 'noticed' the 'clatter'. For these teachers the noise was *unbearable*: they shuddered and said they could not tolerate such a racket in their classrooms. The development team were amazed: the noise was so normal they no longer heard it, and for them it was no barrier to implementing an innovation.

In our research we need to think seriously about our own 'needs' for enjoyment of, and tolerance about quiet or silence, or music or talk when we read, write, dance and so on. Do we take our own noise into our fieldsites? Do we make noise when we *ask* things? Are we unhappy with silence(s)?

SIGHT

It seems absurd to have a section on sight in a book about ethnography. However, I am frequently amazed that doctoral students I meet have no notes on what they *saw*. They only record speech and conversation. The development of cheap disposable cameras and lightweight ways to make 'film' have changed the recording of 'sights', but there is no substitute for the sketch maps of every space, every time it is visited, with every actor's location recorded. In buildings the layout of furniture and its use, the contents of noticeboards (and their currency), pictures (if any) and the state of the decor are all important. Anything the observer *can* see should be in the notes. In old fashioned medical education the senior doctor taught the students to examine a patient in the following order 'eyes first', 'hands next', 'tongue last'. The same principle is a good one for ethnography – watch and record what you see, then what you hear and smell and taste and can touch. Talking and questioning should come last.

HOW TO... RESEARCH MATERIAL AND SENSORY FEATURES

In anthropological fieldwork there is a stronger tradition of recording smell, taste and touch which sociologists working in more familiar settings are less attuned to recording and reporting, unless they are offended by the smell. Ethnographies of prisons, hospitals and residential settings for old people focus on smell much more frequently and explicitly than those of education settings. Taste may be harder to include in fieldwork: researchers in schools rarely seem to eat school dinners, and if they do they rarely write about them. In contrast, anthropologists do dwell on the tastes of the foodstuffs they encounter. These omissions can be remedied.

One of the lessons that can be drawn from the literature discussed above is the importance of using all the senses in the field, and ensuring that the fieldnotes record all the sensory data. My advice is to keep good notes on what you are wearing, and how you smell, as well as what the actors are wearing and how they smell. Do different spaces have different smells? Does the smell vary across the 24 hours, the week, the seasons?

In school ethnographies there has been a tendency to focus more on noisy pupils rather than quiet ones, on disrupted lessons rather than silently productive ones, and on disastrously incompetent or showily flamboyant staff rather than those of quiet competence because silence is hard to write about. There are, for example, very few ethnographies of school or college libraries rather than playgrounds, corridors or cafeterias. Noise is related to time, e.g. the library may be quiet when exams are imminent. Paying careful attention to noises and to silences can be insightful. This is as true for reflecting on one's own working habits as it is when observing others. If you reflect on whether you like to read/analyse data/write, to music, to whale sounds, to sports commentary, or to silence, that will help you learn to notice and then to record what accompanies the lives of your informants, and how they respond to the various sounds. It is worth forcing oneself to write good notes about the quiet pupil, the quiet classroom, and the quiet spaces. In any setting there will be social constructions of the 'silent' student. Foley (1996) has analysed the social construction by 'anglos' of the 'silent Indian', and Heath's (1982) work on the 'silenced' African-Americans in Trackton who so frustrated their teachers, is a classic. Such analyses could be done in all formal and informal settings.

In the field we might want to consider that as well as asking the 'Tell me' questions, we should ask the 'Show me', 'Touch me', 'Can I taste?' and 'Can I smell?' questions.

162

A LOOK TO THE FUTURE

what we need to know about materials and other sensory features

The short answer here is 'nearly everything'. Ethnographers need to work in multi-sensory ways: and actually use all five senses. This is particularly true of research in higher education, and on non-formal learning and teaching in 'familiar' contexts such as driving lessons or apprenticeships.

eleven

knowledge and its transmission: 'taught me all that he could'

Mr Chang, you do not really believe these things about 'cancer' do you?... I mean, you are Hmong. You know that a person gets sick because they have lost their *pleng*, and that you must get the shaman to do the proper rituals if you are to be reunited with your *pleng*. (Rosiek, 2006: 262)

Before I went to Martle Quay Comp in 1993 I was told by my sister who was already there that there were dead babies in jars in the science labs.

This chapter focuses on curricula and knowledge. The urban legend focuses on a specialist subject, science, which is taught in an esoteric space (a laboratory). Because the knowledge and the specialist classroom are both absent from the British primary school, the fear of the unknown 'science' is a focus for many of the school transfer stories. Some knowledge is esoteric, like the magic referred to by Hurston in *Mules and Men* (1935: 205), who decided to change her instructor in hoodoo when her first teacher had passed on all his transferable knowledge. Most is mundane. Some is both at once, and which is mundane, which esoteric depends on who you are. In the first extract, Rosiek is reporting an interaction between Paokong John Chang, an Hmong American biology teacher, and Lia, a Hmong student in his class. Rosiek thought that this was a story of 'a poor little immigrant girl trying to find a way to integrate her beliefs into a new culture' (2006: 272–273). Chang knew better. He politely, but firmly told Rosiek that the professor of science education had the story backwards. Lia was not 'confused or worried' about herself and her identity; rather she was focused on Chang:

she knew she was correct in her belief about the *pleng*. She was concerned about how far I had strayed from being Hmong. She was concerned that I had become lost. (Rosiek, 2006: 272)

Paokong John Chang is an American life science teacher, who has collaborated with Jerry Rosiek to work towards 'anti-colonialist' science teaching for cultural minority students. Chang is of Hmong descent, and he is not only a graduate biologist teaching in California, his mother had survived a cancer which had gone undiagnosed and untreated by American medicine for longer than a cancer attacking an educated American woman with health insurance would have been. Chang taught biological science to S.E. Asian students, mostly Hmong, and wanted them to understand Western bioscience (see Chang and Rosiek, 2003; Rosiek, 2006). However, he also values Hmong traditional beliefs, a system of values that have sustained the Hmong through 2000 years of persecution, and pressures to assimilate (to Chinese culture, to Laotian and Vietnamese culture, and now, for those in the USA, to 'American' culture).

It may seem perverse to leave knowledge and its transmission to the end of a book on educational ethnography but something had to come last. Core concepts here are manifest and hidden curricula, and tacit or indeterminate versus explicit or codified knowledge. This topic was, for the first generation of sociologists and anthropologists of education, taken for granted, 'invisible', masked, implicit, unspoken. Then in the 1970s it became the focus of a 'new wave' of educational researchers. As an area where the British scholars set the agenda, so a section on the UK contribution opens the chapter.

165

CURRICULA

The sociology of curricula is an area where British sociologists were pioneers, and in the UK it became high profile after 1970 when the BSA conference, held in Durham, was focused on Sociology of Education (Brown, 1973). There was a group of 'Young Turks', centred on the Institute of Education at London University, who produced a paradigm change in sociology of education. Their manifesto (Young, 1971) appeared a year after they had been the radical success of the 1970 conference. The New Sociology of Education offers 'coherent and related theories of knowledge, control, value and action which present a radical alternative to traditional views' (Bates, 1980: 77). There have been many secondary analyses of their manifesto, and accounts of its successes and failures (e.g. Bernbaum, 1977; Davies, 1995). The group were all associated with Basil Bernstein, who gave the closing address at the conference, an early version of one of his most influential papers 'On the Classification and Framing of Educational Knowledge' (Bernstein, 1971). Young's introduction is especially famous, including the quote on 'making' rather than 'taking' problems that is central to Chapter 2 (p. 12). As Young pointed out, knowledge, curricula and assessment had been taken for granted, when instead they should be subjected to sociological scrutiny:

> It is suggested that in this way, certain fundamental features of educators' worlds which are taken for granted, such as what counts as educational knowledge, and how it is made available, become objects of enquiry. (Young, 1971: 2)

That core argument is as valid in 2014 as it was in 1972.

Some American commentators (Heap, 1985 and Karabel in his introduction to Karabel and Halsey, 1977) confused and conflated the proponents of the 'new' sociology of education centred in London and at the Open University, with another network of researchers of the same academic generation who pioneered school and classroom ethnography whose work also got published around 1970. In fact the two networks were intellectually, socially and geographically distinct: the ethnographers were outwith London (in Sussex, Manchester, Edinburgh and Birmingham), inspired by symbolic interactionism or anthropology, and not in social or intellectual contact with the Young Turks before 1971. Intellectually the school and classroom ethnographers were more driven to use observation and ethnographic interviews and to draw their perspectives from symbolic interactionism and anthropology, while the 'new' sociology of education drew on documentary analysis, was not focused on ethnography as an intellectual commitment though they used it as a method, and drew on Marx and phenomenology. The main focus of this book has been on the ethnographic traditions, and it now turns to knowledge where those scholars set an important aspect of the research agenda for everyone (Levinson et al., 1996).

The tripartite structure of the chapter is, by now, familiar. After the 'results' of the ethnographic research enterprise have been explored, the chapter then focuses on 'How to…' use ethnographic methods to study knowledge transmission, and finally, as it looks to the future, it sets out the known unknowns.

TAKING AND 'MAKING' PROBLEMS

Central to the manifesto of the 'new' sociology of education was the distinction between 'taking' educational problems as opposed to 'making' sociological ones. The manifesto is a difficult one to deliver, and therefore it is not surprising that in several areas we have fallen short of it in the past 35 years. Sociologists need to be their own toughest critics, and in the sociology of education it is always easy to slip into taking educators' problems. Drawing inspiration from this basic premise the proponents of the 'new' sociology of education focused attention on the curriculum: what was specified in written documents, what was delivered by teachers, and how it was received and responded to by pupils and students. Before exploring the sociological research on knowledge in the formal educational settings of schools and universities, the major focus of the chapter, the difficulties of 'taking' not 'making', and the types of issues that arise when knowledge is the researcher's focus are illustrated from my own current project, on how *capoeira* is taught and learnt in the UK. This is education in a non-formal setting but it shows the problems of 'taking' not 'making', and the complexities of studying knowledge.

Central to the Young Turks' manifesto was the accusation that the dominant scholars in the sociology of education had focused on structures (families, schools, employment, universities) and on trajectories in, out, and between these structures while neglecting to analyse the educational content offered, taught and learnt in those institutions. So, they argued, we knew who was likely to pass the 11+ exam and go to a grammar School, but nothing about what they learnt when they got there, compared to the syllabuses offered at other types of school. It was time, they argued that the sociological gaze was turned to the content of education, and how it was planned by curricula designers and exam boards, selected from in schools, delivered in classrooms, assessed in exams, and made sense of by pupils. In the words of M.F.D. Young (1971: 19) which have been used as an exam and essay question in innumerable sociology of education assessments for the past 30 years:

> The almost total neglect by sociologists of how knowledge is selected, organised and assessed in educational institutions (or in any other institutions for that matter) hardly needs documenting.

The collection he edited set out to rectify that neglect. Bernstein's (1971: 47) opening formulation of the research agenda is equally famous:

> How a society selects, classifies, distributes, transmits and evaluates the educational knowledge it considers to be public, reflects both the distribution of power and the principles of social control. From this point of view, differences within and change in the organisation, transmission and evaluation of educational knowledge should be a major area of sociological interest.

The timing of this revolution was not coincidental or accidental. In England and Wales a Labour government, under Harold Wilson, had come to power in 1963 and been re-elected in 1964 with a majority large enough to legislate. Committed to abolishing the 11+ exam and the tripartite system of secondary schooling brought in under Rab Butler by the 1944 Education Act, in its time revolutionary and progressive, the

167

Labour Government issued circular 10/65. Unusually, there was not an Act of Parliament. The circular effectively brought in comprehensive secondary education across England and Wales, because Local Education Authorities could not obtain Treasury funding for school buildings – needed because there were increasing numbers of secondary school pupils – unless those buildings were suitable for comprehensive schools. Few local authorities could raise money to build new schools without funds from London, so they were 'forced' to go comprehensive by the carrot of building funds.

As the majority of 11 year olds began to enter comprehensive secondary schools, the big issue became not 'what type of school does X type of pupil get in to?' but 'what is the internal organisation of the school X type of pupil attends, and what is he (or very rarely she) taught there?'. When the 11+ existed, the school type determined the knowledge offered, and was synonymous with it. If you passed the 11+ and went to a grammar school in England and Wales or a Scottish senior secondary school, you were offered Physics and Chemistry, Latin, Greek, French or German, and had teachers who were university graduates in those subjects. If you failed and went to a secondary modern (England and Wales) or junior secondary school (Scotland) you did vocational subjects and low status things like 'general' science and were not offered modern or classical languages, or serious science subjects. Northern Ireland did not have any reform in the 1960s, and still has not 50 years later. As Connolly (1998, 2004) has reminded us, the type of secondary school attended still determines the curricula content there. There were also massive gender differences in the curricula, but no one writing in the 1971 (Young) or 1973 (Brown) volumes from the landmark BSA conference mentioned them. Byrne (1975) was the first to investigate the desperately impoverished curricula and facilities in girls' secondary modern schools in England, and make them problematic.

Until Circular 10/65 therefore it was easy for sociologists of education to ignore the content of the curriculum, because it went with the structures: if a boy did not go to a grammar school and do Latin up to the exams (GCE) taken at 16, he would not be able to go to University at 18 to study any humanities discipline. If he did not do Physics, higher education in science was only possible via a long alternative vocational route. Harold Wilson, the Labour Prime Minister in the 1960s, had characterised the reform as 'grammar school education for all', and that clearly meant access to grammar school *subjects*, such as Latin and Physics. So sociologists had focused on social class and how it correlated with entry to, and exit from, specific institutional types. The 'new' sociologists of education opened up the issue of what was taught inside those institutions, and who was able to try and learn it, just as *that* curricula distinction became the crucial determinant of life chances. As Circular 10/65 gradually turned England and Wales comprehensive, the research focus became streaming and banding inside those schools (Ford, 1969; Bellaby, 1977; Ball, 1981) and the curricula consequences of that internal organisation.

There was, from the outset, a tension in the work of the new sociology of education. Many of the papers in Young (1971) were based on an unstable mixture of ideas from Marxism and from phenomenology. The scholars subsequently followed different intellectual paths. For the sociologists who were interested in the sociology of knowledge, the research focus was on topics such as what counted as school music (Vulliamy, 1976); how science curricula were constructed (Young, 1976); and the debates over English language and literature (Mathieson, 1973). Another faction ceased to write about educational processes or use ethnographic methods and are not discussed any further in this book.

The questions they raised were, and continue to be, central to any anthropological or sociological study of education. Bourdieu's (1998, 1999) work on the hierarchies of disciplines in French higher education are in that important sociological field. In higher education in Britain there is scope for an imaginative analysis of the status and social power of different disciplines and fields as set out in the frameworks imposed on UK higher education since 1985 which served to bureaucratise, and allow audit of, the previously more autonomous institutions. Among these frameworks are the criteria set out to evaluate the research done in higher education: the six successive Research Assessment Exercises of 1985, 1989, 1992, 1996, 2001 and 2008, and the 2014 Research Excellence Framework. In these frameworks disciplines are codified, and peer judgements of the quality of publications exert power over what research gets funded, carried out, and how it is published for the next six to ten year period. In a parallel set of exercises, greater codification and public scrutiny of the contents of teaching, and of its delivery and subsequent assessment, developed in the 1990s under the auspices of a body called the Quality Assurance Agency (QAA) in the programme of Teaching Quality Assessments that took place between 1994 and 2002, and in the QAA's Benchmark Statements. The latter are standardised documents, for 60 disciplines, of what a graduate should know and be able to do. It is an indication of the lack of a thorough going sociology of higher education that no ethnographic analyses of the practical, everyday consequences stemming from the ideologies of these activities have been published. In fact, each is ripe for a classic 'new' sociology of education analysis not only of the documents, but more urgently, ethnographic studies of how these frameworks are (or are not) manifest and latent in lecture halls, seminar rooms, staff meetings and exam boards.

When the 'new' sociology of education movement lost its initial impetus, ceased to be a coherent group of scholars and failed to become a grand narrative in the sociology of education, it was too easy to lose sight of the importance of making our own problems and scrutinising our own practice(s). One of the terrible, generally unrecognised, consequences of the school 'reforms' in England since 1988 has been the resurgence of precisely the same kind of curricula segregation in a masked and unnamed form that had previously existed in grammar and secondary modern schools, via the tiering of the exams at 16 (Gillborn and Youdell, 2000). But where it had been 'visible' by its existence in two different types of school, it is now 'masked' inside one type, and needs (re)investigation.

The part of the 'new' sociology of education that lasted, and made the real impact in and on the sociology of education, was the work of Basil Bernstein. After the years of publishing opaque and easily stigmatised work on language and child-rearing, he developed, after the 1970 BSA conference, a sociological approach to the study of curriculum and assessment which provided a conceptual framework for analysing knowledge and power. (See Atkinson, 1985 for an exegesis of Bernstein's work.)

170

KNOWLEDGES, CURRICULA AND PEDAGOGIES

Bernstein (1971) argued that educational content needed to be analysed in a two-dimensional space. First there was the axis of framing. In strongly framed curricula, students have no control over the pacing of the teaching and assessment or the sequence of material. Learning tasks are presented in a set sequence. In weakly framed curricula, the learner has autonomy to choose the sequence and pace of learning. A PhD student, for example, could decide to research and write the review of the literature chapter in Year One, or leave it until Year Three; or could decide to draft all the chapters before revising any of them. Many professions in the UK are shifting from a requirement for continuing education towards a requirement for continuing professional development, and this, because the onus in CPD is on the learner to diagnose her own needs and seek out ways to meet them at her own pace and scheduling, is a shift from strong to weaker framing.

The orthogonal dimension is classification, which can also be strong or weak. In a strongly framed curriculum, subjects are kept separate, with very tough barriers between them. So in the medical schools of the

UK before 1993 (when the GMC produced *Tomorrow's Doctors*: a totally new curriculum and pedagogy for medical schools) there was a strong classification. Anatomy was quite distinct from Physiology, from Biochemistry, from Psychology, from Sociology, and all the pre-clinical subjects (done in labs and lecture halls) were clearly separated from the clinical subjects (taught in hospitals at the bedside of the patient) such as Surgery, Dermatology and Psychiatry. Today medical schools have a weak classification curriculum, where the pre-clinical versus clinical divide has gone, and so have the old 'subjects'. Students learn, for example, about the cardiovascular system, and do its anatomy, physiology, biochemistry and clinical management and surgical interventions all mixed up. These changes can be appreciated by reading, and contrasting, the ethnography of a medical school in the 1968–1972 era (Atkinson, 1981, 1996) with Donetto (2012).

These powerful concepts were, and are, enduringly useful for making sense of ethnographic data on the processes of education. Observational material can be usefully 'organised' to illustrate and develop these powerful concepts. Bernstein (1973) went on to elaborate his initial thinking when he contrasted two opposed ideal types of curriculum and two types of pedagogy. A collection code is strongly framed and strongly classified, and that is the core part of a visible pedagogy. An integrated code is weakly framed and weakly classified, and that is the core of the invisible pedagogy. For a school or university to be described as embodying a visible pedagogy, the disciplinary regime, the roles of adults and students or pupils, and the patterns of interaction need to be explicit, hierarchical, and formal, as well as having a collection code curriculum. For a school or university to be described as having an invisible pedagogy there needs to be not only an integrated code curriculum, but also an implicit, tacit, apparently negotiable disciplinary regime, ill-defined and fluid adult and student or pupil roles, and interaction patterns that are individualised and apparently malleable.

Bernstein subsequently coined the terms positional and personal to characterise two opposed ideal types of family: and argued that the 'new' middle class, who worked with symbolic property, preferred to live in personal families and send their children to schools with an invisible pedagogy until the age of 11 or 12. In contrast, the old middle class, who work with real, material property, prefer the security of the positional family and choose the visible pedagogy from the age of 5 (or even 3).

The English education system from the time of the Plowden Report (1967) until the 1988 Reform Act, could be said to have been designed for the 'new' middle class, so that primary schooling was intended to be based on the invisible pedagogy, and these ideas were strong in secondary schooling up to the age of 14 or so. The evidence from the classroom observation studies is that this never actually happened (see Galton and Simon, 1980; Galton, Simon and Croll, 1980; Delamont, 1987), but it was widely believed to be happening, and was very unpopular with the old middle class and the working classes, partly because no one ever systematically explained how the invisible pedagogy was supposed to work (see Sharp and Green, 1976 for a UK example; Sussman, 1977 for an American study; and Berlak and Berlak, 1981 for an account by two Americans of the English system). The 1988 Act, drawing on the work of New Right thinkers, who were the old middle class baying for blood, was an imposition or (re)imposition of the visible pedagogy.

The visible pedagogy is designed to equip people to work in the material world with real objects. The invisible is designed to equip people to work in a post-industrial world with symbolic property; and the failure of England and Wales to adopt and sustain an invisible pedagogy may be the most damaging blow to the nation's economic prospects ever struck.

Of course, Bernstein was acutely conscious that in schools or colleges that claimed to be bastions of the invisible pedagogy and in the personal family, the *real* power still lay with teachers or lecturers in education, and with the adults in the family – only an idiot was 'fooled' by the appearance of unstructured personal negotiations. In a classroom run as a visible pedagogy, the teacher would say 'When we have maths we use the green books with squared paper to get our work neat, and we have silence. Recite your 8 times table, once 8 is…'. In a classroom run as an invisible pedagogy the teacher would say 'What sort of exercise book do you think is good for maths?' 'Why is squared paper good for maths?' 'Why don't you think how to find out how many fish there are if each of eight cats gets six fish?' and 'Justin, if you yell like that it is hard to for me to hear Sunita read me her story'. In both classrooms it is very clear where the power actually lies, if the regimes are examined sociologically or anthropologically, but the latter can look anarchic, subversive and dangerous to parents, who do not run their homes and especially their child-rearing that way. The ethnographic research also reveals that children reared in positional homes with clear hierarchies can find the invisible pedagogy so invisible that they violate its rules before they have 'spotted' them.

172

BEYOND BERNSTEIN

Beyond all these issues so far discussed, educational ethnographers also need to focus on the knowledge that is widely available 'out there', but is 'unwanted', and therefore is not acquired by the group being studied, or by some other set of people whose knowledges govern their interaction with the informants being researched. All cultures have conscious or unconscious 'blind spots' or 'tabooed' areas of knowledge or unknown unknowns. One example of either unwanted, or 'blind spot' research in the life of a famous American university was the Harvard 'scandal' of 2005.

That year American higher education experienced an unusual event: the President of Harvard was removed from office, and one reason was apparently a piece of sexism, which can best be understood as a perfect example of a blind spot about a body of knowledge. Lawrence Summers had spoken at a conference focused on how America could diversify the workforce in engineering and the sciences. He suggested that the shortage of women in the higher ranks of these fields could be explained in three broad ways: women might be choosing not to aim for the higher level jobs in those disciplines; or fewer American women had the right aptitudes at a high enough level to do those jobs; or there might be biases in those fields that systematically thinned out women from the ranks of job seekers in them. These were categorised as an economic (rational choice) explanation; a biological, genetic, psychometric explanation; and a sociological explanation. Summers, drawing *not* on scholarly meta-analyses of the large bodies of peer-reviewed research in any of these disciplines, but on an anecdote about his pre-school twin daughters, announced that he felt the 'choice' and the 'aptitudes' explanations were convincing. By using only an anecdote, Summers had revealed his total ignorance (or his unexplained repudiation) of a large body of scholarship. During the ensuing public furore in the USA, Harvard not only removed Summers, they replaced him with a woman – an inconceivable act 30 years ago.

May (2008) edited a collection of essays which are responses to the 'Summersgate' scandal. Many of the authors report evidence that challenges the 'choice' and the 'aptitude' explanations. Central to many of the essays is the question: how could Summers have been ignorant of (or possibly, but less likely, been unconvinced by) so much research that undermines the 'choice' and the 'aptitudes' arguments? Summers claimed his view was 'evidence based', but never subsequently produced any of that evidence. His failure to address any of the peer-reviewed public evidence was egregious, especially when some of the relevant data had recently been collected in his own city. One of the published investigations, which Summers conveniently did not know about, had revealed that women scientists at MIT were allocated far less lab space than men at the same professorial grade even when they held more grants and had more publications. Many contributors to the May collection were angry that Summers failed to disaggregate the effects of gender and of parenthood on careers in science and engineering in the USA. Several of the contributors also show that Summers's ideas were those of equivalent men in 1873 and 1904 and wonder why a man at Harvard in 2005 was content to advance such ancient views about women when he would not have done so about atoms, molecular structures, evolution, mental illness, space travel, catalysis or bridge building.

Carla Fehr's (2008) essay on the history of research to measure the intellectual abilities of men and women is, in itself, a useful account of many such attempts from the 1820s onwards. The sheer amount of material, all ignored by Summers, makes his preference for a personal anecdote which in fact reflected on his own sexist child-rearing practices, a useful reminder of how many scholars have tackled that issue. More interesting, however, is her concurrent discussion of the epistemology of ignorance. This is research on:

> the creation and persistence of ignorance, or in other words the study of how we do not know things and how ignorance can be systematically generated and maintained. (Fehr, 2008: 103)

174 False knowledge can prevent research, policy change and social action – and this is the most important lesson for ethnographers. Ethnographic research on learning and teaching needs to be focused on what 'false' knowledge people in any setting have, and how it can prevent social action. Fehr uses the example of American understandings of heart disease in women. Although heart disease is the biggest killer of American women, the false 'knowledge' that its symptons were the same in women and men prevented systematic research on women and heart disease for many years, needed because, in fact, the symptoms are different. Fehr chronicles how the evidence on male and female aptitude, enthusiasm for and performance in maths, science and engineering, which has repeatedly shown there is *no* male superiority, has been ignored, forgotten, overlooked, neglected and discounted for 150 years.

Her example of a parallel epistemology of ignorance is the Federal Government Agencies' response to Hurricane Katrina. The then director of the Federal Emergency Management Agency said, on the record, that 'we are seeing people we did not know existed' (Fehr, 2008: 103). In other words the 'responsible' authority had no knowledge of the size of the population, and no knowledge of the high percentage of residents who had no access to a car in which to evacuate the area. Fehr points out that these data had repeatedly been collected, but still that 'knowledge' was not 'known' in the agency. The material on Katrina and its aftermath collected by Vollen and Ying (2008) consisting of *testimonios* of victims, reveals how devastating the 'ignorance' of the high level bureaucrats was for the poor of the city.

In the same way, Fehr argues there is an epistemology of ignorance among those, like Summers, who claim 'the evidence' supports their deep instincts about women's abilities. In the USA, for example, female engineers have higher scores on maths tests than male engineers, an 'aptitude' Summers ignored. Fehr concludes that Summers's 'free market' argument 'assumes that administrators make decisions based on accurate knowledge of the quality of women scientists – knowledge that research shows 'they likely *think* they have, but don't' (Fehr, 2008: 111) (emphasis mine).

In any setting, whether a formal educational context or a process of non-formal, or informal enculturation, the ethnographer needs to focus upon the 'knowledge' people think they have, and the actions that they take because of it, to discover whether it is actually 'knowledge' and actually 'rational'. The most famous example here is Heath's (1982, 1983) original research in Piedmont Carolina. Teachers in elementary schools were convinced that the incoming African-American children had no language that could be used in the classroom as a basis for reading. Heath's work in the homes of these children showed there was a vivid, vibrant, imaginative, oral culture there. However, the language use patterns in the school were so alien that the children became mute there. The teachers 'knew' from experience that African-American children were monosyllabic in the classroom, but did *not* know that if they changed the language regime of their lesson the children could be fluent, creative and funny.

175

Less relevant to this book, but worth a brief mention, is an ethnocentric blindness in May's compilation. May (2008) points out that in 2002 more American women than American men achieved PhDs, while the percentage of women working, with tenure, in American higher education has not changed for 20 years. Much of the book addresses reasons why those figures are as they are. There is less attention to the fact that, because the USA compared to, for example Sweden, France or the Netherlands, has no statutory maternity leave and benefits, no state provided high quality preschool childcare system, and no public health service, it is *parenthood* that really causes the inequalities they map. If these scholars had read, for example Susan Rogers' (1991) ethnography of a French farming community where the agriculture flourished because the educated women hold down professional jobs, or Crompton's (1995) studies of women in pharmacies in France, they would not have been so confused about the lack of gender equality in American higher education. Being culture bound, the authors in May (2008) fail to criticise the tenure system in American higher education itself from the perspective of other countries.

HOW TO… RESEARCH KNOWLEDGE AND ITS TRANSMISSION

Wacquant (2004: 100–102) reports how the inspirational African-American boxing trainer, Dee Dee, virtually rejects the utility of books on boxing. When Wacquant said he had found a text (called *The Complete Workout for the Boxer*) in the campus library and asks: 'Is it worth reading it to learn the fundamentals?', Dee Dee is adamant that: 'You don' learn to box from books. You learn to box in d'gym'. This opened up, as naïve questions when one is at the beginning of fieldwork often do, a range of big issues: about book learning versus practical, physical learning; about places; about time; about theory versus practice; explicit versus tacit knowledge; and about monadic versus dyadic movement, public versus private.

Here the most important questions for the ethnographer of any learning context are what are the teachers trying to impart? What do learners think they are supposed to know? And in both areas, what is explicit and technical, versus what is implicit and tacit? The official curriculum in formal education settings, such as schools, and the written texts that embody it needs to be recorded; but the hidden curriculum needs to be explored too. Best (1983) has a good example of explicit or manifest and hidden curricula. In her study of 7 year olds in an American school she found three different levels of gender regime: one explicit, one tacit, and one deeply hidden.

Jamous and Peloille (1970) argued, in an unjustly neglected paper, that all occupations have some knowledge and skills that are explicit, technical and probably written down and thus codified, and other knowledge and skills that are tacit, implicit, indeterminate and are nowhere written or codified. The same is true of all educational settings, and successful learners have to acquire both the technical (T) and the indeterminate (I) knowledge and skills. Jamous and Peloille suggested that one way in which occupations could be differentiated was the balance between the two realms: they called it the I:T ratio. To give a concrete example, successful barristers have to know the law (technical) but if they are to appear in court (rather than write opinions) they also have to persuade by their oral arguments judges and juries of their 'case' (indeterminate). So too a successful worker in any occupation will have both the technical skills and a set of indeterminate skills that enable him or her to get along with customers, workmates, etc., for example, Spradley and Mann's (1975) cocktail waitress, Heyl's (1979) brothel owner or Desmond's (2006) fire fighter. In the *capoeira* research (Stephens and Delamont, 2009) we explored how students acquire the technical skills (the physical movements, the rhythms, the words of songs, how to get noise out of the instruments) and the equally, or even more vital, indeterminate skills, such as playing with style and beauty, and even more important, the tricksy, deceitful ways to outwit an opponent that are glossed as *malicia* (deceit).

Generally one of the benefits of ethnographic work is that it enables us to separate the explicit knowledge from the tacit, but it is sometimes important to recognise that there may also be secret knowledge. Many cultures have subgroups who are initiated into mysteries, and once the researcher is initiated he or she is then bound by the initiation vows and promises to *keep* the secrets they learn secret. As Zora Neale Hurston (1935: 185) put it 'the profound silence of the initiated' has to be recognised by the ethnographer, but cannot be 'breached'. Between the religious secrets of the initiates of voudou or Neopagan witchcraft and the tacit knowledge shared by an occupational group, lie many things that a researcher may need to learn.

A LOOK TO THE FUTURE

what we do not know about knowledge transmission

The biggest 'topic' across all formal educational settings that ethnographers could, and should address, is the epistemologies of ignorance (Fehr, 2008) in that setting, focusing on all the various actors. Close attention to how knowledge is communicated and understood in any setting is always valuable but what is *not* 'known' is the biggest gap.

twelve
conclusions: through the roiling smoke

The chapter subtitle comes from James Lee Burke's conclusion to his novel *In the Electric Mist with the Confederate Dead* (1995: 344). Burke's hero, who has been troubled by ghosts of Confederate soldiers from the American civil war era throughout the story, sees, through 'the roiling smoke' the 'weary' yet still gallant combatants for whom 'the contest is never quite over', because 'the field [is] never quite ours'. I write this conclusion with a strong sense that the contest is not over, the field is not mine, and roiling smoke obscures important fundamental issues. Writing from the UK, but paying attention to the much larger landscape of ethnographic educational research in North America, I often share the sense of (un)reality that disturbs Burke's hero when he, apparently, sees the Confederate dead: the battles in the USA and Canada are not the same as mine, never have been, and never will be.

However, from a distance, I am confident that qualitative researchers need to think hard about whether their investigations are the best social science they could be. Looking at American qualitative education research I see some deeply embedded weaknesses and argue that dealing with these would be a good way to ensure the long-term health of qualitative studies in education. A small number of my reservations are expressed in what follows. First, I have argued that educational researchers have been too concerned to study schools, rather than widening their gaze to include higher and professional education, and even more important, all the learning and teaching that goes on in other settings (Atkinson, 1975; Delamont, 2006, Delamont, Atkinson and Pugsley, 2010).

Of course, I am appalled by the absurd proposal that educational research should be forced onto the Procrustean bed of inappropriate definitions of scientific research, and that qualitative research should not be funded if it fails to match up. However, given the political context in which American educational research operates (Berliner and Biddle, 1995; Dimitriadis, 2011) I am not surprised. The research community needs to articulate resistance against such external threats to the collective research endeavour. However, qualitative research has been attacked before, and the good scholarship survives and flourishes regardless. I am confident that, when the current roiling smoke clears, there will be excellent scholarship apparent on the battlefield, including, I hope, mine. The best way to defend qualitative research is to go out and do some exemplary data collection and transform those data into robust social theory.

I believe that overall, the conduct of qualitative research has become compromised by a set of preoccupations that – while valid in their own right – too easily divert attention from the conduct of major empirical research. Too often, I believe the claims for postmodernism, postcolonialism and similar research form clouds of mystificatory argument that divert scholars from doing any data collection or rigorous analysis (cf Atkinson and Delamont, 2006a). The debate between Adler and Adler (2008), Hammersley (2008, 2010), Denzin (2009) and Delamont and Atkinson (2010) addresses this point. There has been a tendency for 'qualitative research' to be treated as if it were a quasi-discipline in its own right, and for the intellectual work of developing sociological, anthropological and similar disciplinary knowledge to be forgotten. The hard intellectual work of developing and extending the empirical generalisations and theoretical frameworks that are characteristic of 'disciplined' research needs to be done. Vague appeals to 'grounded' theory do not substitute for theoretical development in the wider sense – as if 'grounded theory' were a theoretical or epistemological approach in its own right rather than a general strategy for the development of theoretical ideas. The rationales for qualitative research in the social sciences need to be regularly reaffirmed. There are too many appeals to the documentation of 'experience' or to describing a life from the informant's 'point of view'.

179

THE FALSE TRAIL: AGAINST AUTOETHNOGRAPHY

The last 20 years have seen a rise in autoethnography, in which the focus is not a fieldsite and its participants, but the ethnographer's own body, self and social network. By contrasting a couple of incidents from my own research I set out what I see as valuable and not valuable in ethnograpic reflexivity and not valuable in autoethnography. Peshkin (1997: 22) contrasted the autoethnographer who wrote about him or herself to say to the reader 'Look at *me*!' and the scholar who said to the reader 'look at who it is that has come here' to conduct this study. The latter helps the reader contextualise the data. In the examples that follow I have illustrated the difference from my own research.

Many of the most difficult moments in fieldwork burst suddenly out of a clear blue sky (Lareau, 1996; Gupta and Ferguson, 1997; Faubion and Marcus, 2009). The data collection is apparently proceeding smoothly when something suddenly places the ethnographer in a dilemma or even at the centre of a small crisis. Two such incidents that occurred in the autumn of 2007, during an on-going project, are used to contrast autoethnographic writing with autobiographical reflexivity. These two currently fashionable forms of writing for publication (as opposed to writing for the private records of the scholar) are contrasted to argue that the latter is central to the progress of ethnography while the former is an intellectual *cul de sac*. The two small crises in the *capoeira* project are outlined, and then the lessons for ethnography are explored. Before exploring the dilemmas, I need to explain briefly how I record my fieldwork. Three different sets of written records are kept. In the field, abbreviated immediate notes are recorded in a 'reporter's' or 'shorthand' notebook. At home in tranquillity these are written up into a full narrative account, with as much amplification about events, interactions, comments and the setting as I can recall, and choose to add. My personal reflections on the research are kept separate, in a different set of notebooks that I call my 'out of the field' diary. The distinction between the fieldwork, and the personal engagement, is thus physical as well as intellectual and emotional.

The material which follows is drawn from the 'out of the field' diary. It is also important that the research and its outputs are not mine alone. The fieldwork is, in part, a joint enterprise with another social scientist who is himself a *capoeirista* (Stephens and Delamont, 2006a, 2006b, 2007; Delamont and Stephens, 2008). For publication purposes we have adopted the pseudonymous *capoeira* nicknames of *Trovao* (Thunder) for the player and *Bruxa* (witch) for me.

SMALL CRISIS ONE: 'HONESTY' AND 'POLITICS'

In 2007 I was told by a master that the research Neil Stephens and I had presented at a public meeting had been 'the only honest thing' at the event. This comment, made to me at Hercules's festival in Burminster in the autumn of 2007, was a minor 'crisis'. A little background is necessary to understand why. *Capoeira* teachers and groups are frequently in competition, to recruit and retain paying customers; to maintain their autonomy as practitioners, and as representatives of an *authentic*, historically located line of descent from original African-Brazilian *mestres*. Disputes between groups or individual teachers can be fierce. Attempts either by sections of the Brazilian government, or by particular *mestres* or groups, to codify or regulate *capoeira*, or to certify or register its teachers are highly controversial (Assunção, 2005). Students in the UK use the phrase '*capoeira* politics' to summarise such controversies, feuds, acts of resistance, etc. Most *discipulos* (students) try to avoid any entanglement in '*capoeira* politics', regarding them as a matter for Brazilians, and for teachers.

In 2007 a Brazilian government ministry was engaged in an attempt to 'map' *capoeira*, record legendary performers on film and find a way to pay pensions to elderly teachers, as part of a wider project to make *capoeira* a 'National Cultural Treasure': the living equivalent of Stonehenge or Angkor Wat. Making DVDs of legendary musicians and singers, and getting pensions for elderly, poor, African-Brazilian *mestres* were *not* energetically resisted. Other aspects of the government initiative, such as codifying who could and could not be certified and called a *mestre*, were and are controversial, and there was dispute about which groups were, and were not, being consulted and involved in the project. Recognising that there is a large amount of diasporic *capoeira* in the UK, the Brazilian Embassy in London had invited a speaker for the project to come to London to showcase it. *Trovao* and I had been invited to speak about our ongoing research at the opening session of a series of events and had done so. We focused on the perspectives of *discipulos* (students) in the UK, and raised an academic question, namely whether *capoeira* would, by 2025, have become globalised (Robertson and Whyte, 2005). As we watched the rest of the event unfold (it lasted over a month), it became clearer and clearer to us that the majority of *capoeira* teachers in London were boycotting it.

Trovao and I would probably have given our paper anyway, but if we had realised that the embassy involvement was going to plunge us into '*capoeira* politics' we might both have declined the invitation, or thought more strategically about *Trovao*'s involvement. He is bound by the ethics of loyalty to one teacher (Achilles) so trains only with him or, if away from Tolnbridge, with other groups and explicitly labelled as a visiting student from Achilles's group. As a researcher, I have more licence to watch anyone from any group, and am explicitly told that I *should* watch other teachers to see how different they are from Achilles. However, neither of us could afford to be labelled as 'tools' of the Brazilian Embassy, or puppets of the ministry's controversial project without risking our ongoing research access. Between September 2007 and Hercules's festival

181

in late November, I had not been aware of any negative consequences of our involvement. I went to Burminster feeling falsely relaxed about our, unwitting, incorporation into '*capoeira* politics'.

I had never been to any of *Mestre* Hercules's festivals before, although I had met him at Achilles's and Perseus's festivals several times and one of his students, Shere Khan, had been training with Achilles while working in Tolnbridge. I arrived in Burminster in time for the two Friday night classes in the University sports hall. On the Saturday the festival was scheduled to last from 10 a.m. to 8 p.m., and I had set off for fieldwork with food, drink, sticking plaster, aspirin, notebooks and pens.

When the big *roda* that concluded the morning's classes began, I was feeling satisfied, it had been worthwhile coming. Hercules's festival had introduced me to another group's normality, and given me a chance to see two distinguished Brazilian *mestres* new to me teach. I stationed myself behind the musicians (*bateria*) where I could see the play:

> As usual I have odd items of personal property that I am keeping safe for those who expect to enter the *roda*: I am wearing three watches, two belonging to students, and I have a student's mobile phone in one pocket, a girl's bangle and some earrings in another. As people learn I have plasters a few come to ask me for some to patch blistered and/or bleeding feet or hands. I clap and sing, smile at people as they come to play the instruments, or leave the *bateria*.

Two things happened during that *roda*: one was a nice surprise – Leontis, a teacher from London, arrived. I had not seen him for several months, and was not expecting to see him at that festival. Then a fieldwork 'crisis' blew up.

> It is about 2.15, and I am hungry. Students are beginning to slide away to eat, and it is clear that the *roda* will soon end so the *mestres* can eat before the *Batizado* at 3.30. A master gives his *berimbau* to another teacher, steps out of the *bateria*, and stands next to me, blowing his nose and coughing. He looks ill – and I realise that I haven't seen him do any *capoeira* himself. I offer him the aspirin I have in my bag, but he replies he has already taken lots of pain-killers. Then he introduces himself, as *Mestre* Belisarius, and says 'I heard your talk with *Trovao* at the Embassy festival in September – I enjoyed it'. I felt a surge of shock. I felt 'ambushed'. I blushed and said I was glad (I had not realised any UK *mestres* were in the audience). Belisarius went on 'I agreed with what you said – and you were the only honest thing about it'. My heart sank. I flannelled and said that *Trovao* and I had tried 'to ignore *capoeira* politics' and just do what we were asked. 'How wise' he said, and explained how the project in Brazil was deeply political, and the Embassy was complicit in those political affairs, adding some scathing remarks about individuals in Brazil and London. It was clear that the powerful opinion formers among the Brazilian *mestres* in London and the south of England had no faith in the

project, and had all decided to boycott it. *Trovao* and I had thought that was happening at the time, but had no confirmation of it. *Mestre* Belisarius and I established that we had mutual friends, including *Ferao*, one of his students who had done a PhD in Tolnbridge and trained with Achilles and Perseus, then to my relief Belisarius went off to talk to Perseus.

When *Trovao* and I attended the Embassy event there were no *mestres* we recognised in the audience, and only one, visiting from Australia without clear affiliations to any of the London groups, explicitly lauded as present. We had not been concerned that by co-operating with the Embassy we might jeopardise our fieldwork. Only afterwards did I worry that perhaps we too should have refused to participate. However, I comforted myself that so few activists in UK *capoeira* were present that our involvement would probably not be noticed by anyone who could, or would, deny *Trovao* access to train, or me the right to observe. I comforted myself with the thought that if either of us were confronted, we could plead ignorance of '*capoeira* politics' and would probably be 'forgiven' because we are not Brazilian or masters and therefore would be assumed to lack intuitive understanding of them. I had not prepared any script to use if confronted, and as *Mestre* Belisarius spoke I realised that had he chosen to 'expose' me, he could have arranged for Hercules to turn me away, or labelled me as an Embassy 'stooge' in front of 15 or 20 teachers whose classes I had, or might want, to watch. Such was the *potential* crisis.

183

SMALL CRISIS TWO: FIELDWORK VERSUS HOME LIFE

The *capoeira* project normally occupies only a few hours each week. I attend class for 90 minutes on two evenings, so am out of the house for about two and a half hours for each class at most, and it takes about another five hours to write the notes up into the A4 book, plus perhaps a further hour keeping the 'diary'. That time commitment is manageable, and is not an unreasonable imposition on my home life. My cohabitee (called here Criollo because he prefers tango to *capoeira*) has been happy to see me doing that much regular data collection, and it has been manageable physically, domestically and emotionally. In the autumn of 2007 I was facing an 'overload'. There were events I wanted to attend, indeed felt I *should* attend, four weekends in a row. The winter festival of Hercules's Burminster group, the joint meeting of Achilles's three clubs in Cloisterham, and Perseus's *Batizado* in Longhampston, had been arranged for successive weekends, each necessitating an overnight absence. Not only were three weekends full of *capoeira*, there was also a Sunday when Achilles had planned a special celebration in Cloisterham to honour his *mestre*, Chronus, who was being given an award for a lifetime's service to *capoeira* at a festival in Brazil. Achilles had decided he could not afford the time or money to go to Brazil himself, and so he would organise an afternoon of *rodas* in Cloisterham, film them, and give *Mestre* Chronus the DVD.

One evening, organising overnight stays in Burminster, Cloisterham and Longhampston, and consulting rail schedules, I was overwhelmed by a surge of guilt. I wrote in my diary:

> I feel really, really mean: four weekends 'away' in a row. Criollo is bound to feel neglected – he'll be left doing all the housework, and he'll point out I'll be exhausted. He won't say anything about himself but he's bound to think I'm self-ish and be worried that I'm overworking.

I fretted about this for some hours over several days, and wrote about ten pages of introspection in my 'diary' – and then was swept away by a tsunami of positive emotions and a brainwave. If Criollo came to the celebration for *Mestre* Chronus *with* me then the position would change. The celebration would be short (3–4 hours), slightly interesting (all performance, no practice moves), joyful, and was, therefore some-thing a newcomer might not find deadly dull. Criollo is a serious ama-teur photographer, devoted to black and white, who enjoys doing his own printing, and I had been proposing for four years that he should take some pictures of Achilles's classes. If we went together, instead of me vanishing for hours 'doing fieldwork', that Sunday could be rebadged as 'a day out together'. In my diary I wrote:

> I really want Criollo to come with me. Achilles would love it, it should be a really warm event with loads of *axe* (energy) and if Criollo took photographs I'd have pictures that weren't anyone else's copyright and he'd have a role – something to *do* – he can learn all about the technicalities and practicalities of photographing *capoeira* as I've been begging him to do – and he'll meet some of the people I talk about…

I laid a plan. I checked the Sunday train schedule to Cloisterham (no engineering work necessitating long bus journeys), found two art exhibi-tions we could go to before the *capoeira* event, and then offered Criollo a day out. Criollo agreed, and came with me. Achilles was delighted, Criollo shot three rolls of black and white pictures he could then work on printing in the darkroom, and learnt a lot about photographing *capoeira*. Some of the pictures have since been used in a publication, so the investment of Criollo's time has paid off.

184

LESSONS FOR ETHNOGRAPHY

What lessons can be learnt from these 'crises'? I contrast them, to exemplify productive and unproductive uses of reflection versus autoethnography. The example of my guilty feelings before the celebration for *Mestre* Chronus is an example of autoethnography. It is *about* me and my introspective emotions and my personal life. In contrast the interaction with *Mestre* Belisarius does open up academic issues which are a legitimate focus for social science. Of course, any enthusiastic advocate of autoethnography can object that I have trivialised the genre by deliberately choosing a dull episode as my example. My guilt is not 'a big issue' such as racism, life-threatening illness or 9/11. However, it is not different from many published examples (Myers, 2008; Richardson, 2008) which focus on the minutiae of the everyday life of people no more interesting than Criollo and me. I chose these two small 'crises' on the basis that they occupied the most space in my reflexive diary for 2007, and would therefore defend my choice of autoethnographic 'crisis' as something that loomed very large in *my* life. That has, by anyone's criteria, to be one legitimate reason for focusing upon it. Autoethnography is, whatever else it may or not be, about things that matter a great deal to the autoethnographer.

185

This section defines autoethnography, separates it analytically from critical autobiographical reflection upon fieldwork, and develops a series of arguments against autoethnography. Central to the distinction drawn here is a more conceptual discussion of what is productively classifiable as social science *research*. As Leon Anderson (2006) has written, the last 20 years have seen the growth of autoethnography as a genre. Anderson defines autoethnography as texts which claim to be *research* but in which the *only* topic or focus is the author herself or himself. This trend is particularly associated with Ellis and Bochner (1996), and includes 'studies' like Tillmann-Healy's (1996) reflections on *her* bulimia, or the piece by Ellis (2002) on *her* response to the events on 11 September 2001. Since *Composing Ethnography* (Ellis and Bochner, 1996) there has been an explosion in autoethnography. Journals such as *Qualitative Inquiry* and *Qualitative Studies in Education* regularly feature autoethnographic papers. Denzin and Lincoln's *Handbook of Qualitative Methods* (1994) had one index entry for autoethnography; in the second edition (2000), 13 entries and a chapter by Ellis and Bochner (2000), while in the third (2005) edition there were 37 index entries, with a dedicated chapter by Jones (2005).

Anderson (2006) starts to draw fine distinctions between evocative and analytic autoethnography, between those and autobiographical ethnography, and contrasts all three with traditional realist ethnography. However, there is no agreed set of definitions of autoethnography or indeed of allied genres. For example, Heewon Chang's (2008) defence of 'autoethnography' is actually a reflexive account of doing research in a subculture to which one has previous links of ethnicity, language or biography. That is *not* what is meant by 'autoethnography' here. Such distinctions can always be drawn. Here the contrast is between reflexive ethnography, where the scholar is studying a setting, a subculture, an activity or some actors *other than* herself, and is acutely sensitive to the interrelationship(s) between herself and the focus of the research; and autoethnography where there is *no* object except the author herself to study. Reflexive writing, and the judicious use of the autobiographical in such writing about research, is an entirely different matter from autoethnography (Coffey, 1999). The distinction drawn here is, of course, in the eye and the judgement of the reader of either autoethnography or analytic reflection.

Autoethnographic self-obsession, such as my personal crises about my fieldwork as a greedy institution, intruding too much into my personal life, have *no* analytic mileage, and tell the readers *nothing* about fieldwork, or *capoeira* or embodiment or habitus or anything of social scientific, pedagogic or educational interest. The following 'manifesto' of six objections to autoethnography summarises objections to it as a genre. They are deliberately phrased in a confrontational or polemical or provocative style to promote debate. The six points in the manifesto, which *de facto* contrasts autoethnography with what is called in this paper 'traditional' or 'peopled' ethnography, are a distillation of arguments spelled out at length in Atkinson, Coffey and Delamont (2003) and Atkinson, Delamont and Housley (2008). Essentially the argument is that autoethnography cannot meet core social science objectives. In the list of six points, the first three are primarily about the nature of social science, the second three are primarily ethical.

1. Ethnographic research should, however hard it is for the scholar, make the familiar anthropologically strange (or make the anthropologically strange familiar). The task of the educational research is to fight familiarity, but autoethnography cannot fight familiarity. Studying ourselves can never make anything anthropologically strange.
2. Autoethnography is almost impossible to write and publish ethically. There are many examples of ethically problematic publications from core exponents of autoethnography. It is hard to believe that when Clough (1992, 2002) published poems about a lover's genitalia, he had agreed to the poems and the genitalia being made public. When

186

Ronai (1996) published 'My mother is mentally retarded' it becomes increasingly clear that her mother could not have given 'informed consent'. These ethical issues are compounded because of the conventions surrounding the reception of ethnographic texts (Atkinson and Delamont, 2008). It is normally impossible for other actors to be disguised or protected in autoethnography. Readers will always wish to read autoethnography as an authentic, and consequently 'true' account of the writer's life, and therefore the other actors will be, whatever disclaimers, or statements about fictions are included, identifiable and identified.

3. Research is supposed to be analytic not merely experiential. Atkinson (2006) has argued at some length that autoethnography is all experience, and is noticeably lacking in *analytic* outcome. These points are made at great length in Atkinson (2006) and Atkinson and Delamont (2006a and 2008) and so are not elaborated here.

4. In 1967 Becker posed a classic question to ethnographers 'Whose side are we on?' That is, should they illuminate the worldview of those at the top of organisations such as schools and prisons, or capture and record the ways such organisations were experienced by the powerless and unvoiced such as pupils and prisoners. The answers to that question are not simple or straightforward, as Hammersley (2001) and Atkinson, Coffey and Delamont (2003) have argued in recent years, but the question is no less valid in 2014 than it was in 1967. Autoethnography focuses on people on the wrong side of Becker's (1967) classic question, on those easy to access, abrogating the question.

5. Ethnographers have powerful methods available to them so that *unknown* social worlds can be studied. The social worlds of pupils, of prisoners, of jazz musicians and of *capoeira* teachers are interesting and worth researching. Autoethnography focuses on social scientists who are not usually interesting or worth researching. The *minutiae* of the bodies, families or households of social scientists are not likely to provide analytic insights for social science.

6. Academics in the developed world who get salaries that allow them to do research have a moral obligation to gather data, analyse them and publish the results. Scholars are paid from public funds to get out of the university to do research in the world. Sitting in offices inside the university contemplating ourselves and our bodies is ethically a problematic interpretation of that obligation. Introspection is not an appropriate substitute for data collection.

In these six ways, autoethnography is antithetical to the progress of social science, because it violates the two basic tasks of the social sciences, which are: to study the social world, and to move the discipline forward. These are six aspects of autoethnography, as defined above, which render it problematic as social science *research*. Drawing a line, or lines around research, is 'unfashionable' among ethnographers who have embraced a postmodern standpoint, for whom a distinction between the researcher's self and the investigation appears old-fashioned. It is precisely the argument of this paper that there *should* be demarcation between the ethnographer's reflexive self when there *is* a research topic, and the academic who focuses on themselves *rather than* having a research topic. The two dilemmas outlined above illustrate this distinction, using the six principles already outlined.

My guilt does not make anything strange: all academics feel guilty about time and their families. Anderson (2006: 389), whose research is on sky-diving, comments that he finds himself 'worrying about unmet familial commitments while driving to the drop zone on a Saturday morning'. The account is not publishable without exposing Criollo's 'real' identity. Even if I had invented a fictional Criollo that would not protect my 'real' cohabitee, because he would be *thought to be* Criollo. The guilt I felt and my solution do not provide a standpoint for social science analysis. The focus on Criollo, whose 'side' I am unreflexively 'on', is intellectually lazy, and his interests (art, photography, tango) his concern about me or our housework are not academically interesting if seen via my introspection. Of course tango, photography and art are all appropriate topics for research but such projects could not start from my diary. Nor, by any stretch of the imagination, could it be argued that our salaries should be spent on writing about each other.

In contrast, the interaction with *Mestre* Belisarius has important academic lessons for research. They are familiar lessons, to be sure, but it is salutary to be reminded of them. These include the fact that access is a *process* not an event, and must always be treated as a precarious accomplishment not a stable state. I had become rather over-confident about access: I turned up in Burminster in time for the Friday night classes, paid my £60 fee to the student on the door, and greeted Hercules with a big smile, a hug, and a message from Achilles. I had taken it for granted that Hercules would be pleased to see me (if only to get my £60) and that I did not need to 'negotiate' access to his festival at all. Equally, the encounter with *Mestre* Belisarius was a sharp reminder that breaking the core values of the group being studied, should either not be done at all, or, should only be done with reflexive sensitivity. In this case collaborating with the Brazilian Embassy, and talking about my research informants (albeit carefully anonymised) without a much more cautious 'investigation' of exactly who was (and was not) in the audience, were potentially careless mistakes. It is always desirable to exercise extreme care when speaking or writing about a group who routinely read academic research about their pastime or livelihood.

All crises in 'access', or in fieldwork generally, provide a new set of research questions. While mine are specific to this project, they have parallels for any researcher studying any subculture or setting. Any curious person might want to follow up why the *mestres* boycotted the events; what the project workers in Brazil thought about that; whether any old *mestre* in Brazil will ever get a pension; and even whether embassies in other European cities will try to run similar publicity events for the Brazilian project, and if they do whether those will be similarly resisted by local teachers. The encounter with *Mestre* Belisarius *is* informative about the UK *capoeira*, and can be used as a cautionary tale by other fieldworkers.

Reflexive autobiographical writing about *Mestre* Belisarius and the Burminster festival could, I have argued, be used to improve not only my project, but also the empirical research of others. It has analytic and pedagogic power. In contrast, the domestic guilt episode does not have potential to improve the research, nor does it offer analytic or pedagogic power.

Ethnographic research is hard. It is physically tiring, intellectually taxing, demands a high level of engagement, and at every stage crises can arise. Precisely for those reasons it is worth persevering, capitalising on all the insights that can be drawn from reflexive writing about ethnography. Retreat into autoethnography is an abrogation of the honourable trade of the scholar.

189

references

Aalten, A. (2007) Listening to the dancer's body. In C. Shilling (ed.) *Embodying Sociology: Retrospect, Progress and Prospects*. Oxford: Blackwell, pp. 109–125.

Abraham, J. (1989) Gender differences and anti-school boys. *Sociological Review*, 37, 1, 65–68. Reprinted in S. Delamont (ed.) (2012) *Ethnographic Methods in Education*. London: Sage. Four volumes, Volume IV, pp. 63–82.

Abraham, J. (1995) *Divide and School*. London: Falmer.

Abu-Lughod, L. (1986) *Veiled Sentiments*. Berkeley: University of California Press.

Adam, B. (1990) *Time and Social Theory*. Cambridge: Polity Press.

Adler, P.A. and Adler, P. (1991) *Backboards and Blackboards*. New York: Columbia University Press.

Adler, P.A. and Adler, P. (1998) *Peer Power*. New Brunswick, NJ: Rutgers University Press.

Adler, P.A. and Adler, P. (2008) Of rhetoric and representation: the four faces of ethnography. *The Sociological Quarterly*, 49, 1, 1–30.

Aggleton, P. (1987) *Rebels Without a Cause*. London: Falmer Press.

Albas, D. and Albas, C. (1984) *Student Life and Exams*. Dubuque, IN: Kendall/Hunt.

Albas, D. and Albas, C. (2009) Behind the conceptual scene of *Student Life and Exams*. In A.J. Puddephatt, W. Shaffir, and S.W. Kleinknecht (eds) *Ethnographies Revisited*. London: Routledge, pp. 105–120.

Allan, A.J. (2010) Picturing success. *International Studies in the Sociology of Education*, 20, 1, 39–54.

Anderson, L. (2006) Analytic autoethnography, *Journal of Contemporary Ethnography*, 35, 4, 373–395.

Anderson-Levitt, K. (1987) Cultural knowledge for teaching first grade. In G. Spindler and L. Spindler (eds) *Interpretive Ethnography of Education at Home and Abroad*. Hillsdale, NJ: Laurence Erlbaum, pp. 171–194.

Anderson-Levitt, K. (1989) Degrees of distance between teachers and parents in urban France. *Anthropology and Education Quarterly*, 20, 2, 97–117. Reprinted in S. Delamont (ed.) (2012) *Ethnographic Methods in Education*. London: Sage. Four volumes, Volume IV, pp. 297–316.

Anderson-Levitt, K.A. (1996) Behind Schedule: Batch-produced children in French and US classrooms. In B. Levinson et al. (eds) *The Social Production of the Educated Person*. Albany, NY: SUNY Press, pp. 57–78.

Appadurai, A. (ed.) (1986) *The Social Life of Things*. Cambridge: Cambridge University Press.

Assunção, M.R. (2005) *Capoeira*. London: Routledge.

Atkins, Ace (1998) *Crossroad Blues*. London: Constable.

Atkinson, P.A. (1975) In cold blood. In G. Chanan and S. Delamont (eds) *Frontiers of Classroom Research*, Slough: NFER, pp. 163–182. Reprinted in S. Delamont (ed.) (2012) *Ethnographic Methods in Education*. London: Sage. Four volumes, Volume II, pp. 229–244.

Atkinson, P.A. (1978) Fitness, Feminism and Schooling. In S. Delamont and L. Duffin (eds) (1978) *The Nineteenth Century Woman*. London: Croom Helm, pp. 92–133. Reprinted by Routledge (2012), pp. 92–133.

Atkinson, P.A. (1981) *The Clinical Experience*. Aldershot: Avebury. 2nd edition (1997), Aldershot: Ashgate.

Atkinson, P.A. (1983) The reproduction of professional community. In R. Dingwall and P. Lewis (eds) *The Sociology of the Professions*. London: Macmillan, pp. 224–241.

Atkinson, P.A. (1985) *Language, Structure and Reproduction*. London: Routledge.

Atkinson, P.A. (1987) The Feminist Physique: Physical Education and the Medicalisation of Women's Education. In J. Mangan and R. Park (eds) *From 'Fair Sex' to Feminism*, London: Frank Cass, pp. 38–57.

Atkinson, P.A. (1990) *The Ethnographic Imagination*. London: Routledge.

Atkinson, P.A. (1992) *Understanding Ethnographic Texts*. Thousand Oaks, CA: Sage.

Atkinson, P.A. (1996) *Sociological Readings and Rereadings*. Aldershot: Ashgate.

Atkinson, P.A. (1997) Narrative turn or blind alley? *Qualitative Health Research*, 7, 3, 325–344.

Atkinson, P.A. (2006) Rescuing autoethnography. *Journal of Contemporary Ethnography*, 35, 4, 400–404.

Atkinson, P.A. (2009) Illness narratives revisited: The failure of narrative reductionism. Sociological Research Online, 14, 5, 16, http://www.socresonline.org.uk/14/5/16.html, doi: 10.5153/sro.2030.

Atkinson, P.A. (2010) Negotiating the contested terrain of illness narratives. *Sociology of Health and Illness*, 32, 4, 661–62.

Atkinson, P.A. (2012) The literary and rhetorical turn. In S. Delamont (ed.) *Handbook of Qualitative Research*, Cheltenham: Edward Elgar, pp. 512–520.

Atkinson, P.A. and Delamont, S. (1980) The Two Traditions in Educational Ethnography. *British Journal of Sociology of Education*, 1, 2, 139–152. Reprinted in S. Delamont (ed.) (2012) *Ethnographic Methods in Education*. London: Sage. Four volumes, volume I, pp. 39–54.

Atkinson, P.A. and Delamont, S. (2006a) Editors' introduction. Narratives, lives, performances. In P.A. Atkinson and S. Delamont (eds) *Narrative Methods*. London: Sage. Four volumes, Volume I, pp. *xix–ljii*.

Atkinson, P.A. and Delamont, S. (eds) (2006b) *Narrative Methods*. London: Sage. Four volumes.

Atkinson, P.A. and Delamont, S. (2007a) Rescuing narrative from qualitative research. In M. Bamberg (ed.) *Narrative – State of the Art*. Amsterdam: John Benjamins Press, pp. 195–205.

Atkinson, P.A. and Delamont, S. (2007b) In the roiling smoke. *Qualitative Studies in Education*, 19, 6, 747–755.

Atkinson, P.A. and Delamont, S. (2008) Introduction. In P.A. Atkinson, and S. Delamont (eds) *Representing Ethnography*. London: Sage. Four volumes, pp. *xix–l*.

Atkinson, P.A. and Delamont, S. (2010) Can the silenced speak? *International Review of Qualitative Research*, 3, 1, 11–16.

Atkinson, P.A., Coffey, A. and Delamont, S. (2003) *Key Themes in Qualitative Research*. Walnut Creek, CA: Alta Mira Press.

Atkinson, P.A., Delamont, S. and Housley, W. (2008) *Contours of Culture*. Walnut Creek, CA: Alta Mira Press.

Atkinson, P.A., Delamont, S. and Hammersley, M. (1988) Qualitative research traditions. *Review of Educational Research*, 58, 2, 231–50.

Atkinson, P.A. and Silverman, D. (1997) Kundera's *Immortality*. *Qualitative Inquiry*, 3, 3, 304–323.

Bagley, C. and Castro-Salazar, R. (2012) Dance. In S. Delamont (ed.) *Handbook of Qualitative Research*. Cheltenham: Edward Elgar, pp. 577–590.

Ball, A. (2002) Three decades of research on classroom life. *Review of Research in Education*, 26. Washington, DC: AERA, pp. 71–112.

Ball, S. 1981. *Beachside Comprehensive*. Cambridge: Cambridge University Press.

Ball, S. (1990) *Politics and Policy Making in Education*. London: Routledge and Kegan Paul.

Ball, S. (1994) *Educational Reform*. Buckingham: Open University Press.

Ball, S. (2000) Performativities and fabrications in the education economy. *Australian Educational Researcher* 27, 2, 1–24.

Ball, S. (2003a) *Class Strategies and the Educational Market*. London: Routledge Falmer.

Ball, S. (2003b) The teacher's soul and the terrors of performativity. *Journal of Education Policy*, 18, 2, 215–228.

Ball, S. (2007) *Education plc*. London: Routledge Falmer.

Ball, S.J., Maguire, M. and Macrae, S. (2000) *Choices, Pathways and Transitions Post-16*. London: Routledge Falmer.

Ball, S., Hull, R., Skelton, M. and Tudor, R. (1984) The tyranny of the 'devil's mill'. In S. Delamont (ed.) *Readings on Interaction in the Classroom*. London: Methuen, pp. 41–57.

Barker, D.L. (1972) Keeping close and spoiling. *Sociological Review*, 20, 4, 569–90.

Barz, G. and Cooley, T.J. (eds) (2008) *Shadows in the Field*, 2nd edition. Oxford: Oxford University Press.

Bates, R.J. (1980) New developments in the sociology of education. *British Journal of Sociology of Education*, 1, 1, 67–80.

Bauman, R. (1982) Ethnography of children's folklore. In P. Gilmore and A. Glatthorn (eds) *Children in and out of School*. Washington, DC: Center for Applied Linguistics, pp. 172–186.

Beale, D. (1904) *History of Cheltenham Ladies College 1853–1904*. Cheltenham: 'Looker-On' Printing Works.

Becker, H.S. (1952a) The career of the Chicago public school-teacher, *American Journal of Sociology*, 57, 470–477.

Becker, H.S. (1952b) Social-class variations in the teacher–pupil relationship, *Journal of Educational Sociology*, 25, 451–465.

Becker, H.S. (1967) Whose side are we on? *Social Problems*, 14, 239–247. Reprinted in H.S. Becker (1970) *Sociological Work*. London: Allen Lane.

Becker, H.S. (1971) Footnote added to the paper by M. Wax and R. Wax (1971) Great tradition, little tradition and formal education. In M. Wax, S. Diamond and F. Gearing (eds) *Anthropological Perspectives on Education*. New York: Basic Books, pp 3–27.

Becker, H., Geer, B., Hughes, E.C. and Strauss, A. (1961) *Boys in Whit*. Chicago: The University of Chicago Press.

Becker, H., Geer, B., and Hughes, E.C. (1968) *Making the Grade*. Chicago: The University of Chicago Press.

Behar, R. and Gordon, D. (eds) (1995) *Women Writing Culture*. Los Angeles: University of California Press.

Bellaby, P. (1977) *The Sociology of Comprehensive Schooling*. London: Methuen.

Berlack, A.C. and Berlack, H. (1981) *Dilemmas of Schooling*. London: Methuen.

Berliner, D. and Biddle, B.J. (1995) *The Manufactured Crisis*. New York: Longman.

Bernbaum, G. (1977) *Knowledge and Ideology in the Sociology of Education*. London: Macmillan.

Bernstein, B. (1971) On the classification and framing of educational knowledge. In M.F.D. Young (ed.) *Knowledge and Control*. London: Macmillan, pp. 47–69.

Bernstein, B. (1973) Class and pedagogies: visible and invisible. In *Class, Codes and Control*, Volume 3. London: Routledge and Kegan Paul, pp. 116–156.

Best, R. (1983) *We've All Got Scars*. Bloomington, IN: Indiana University Press.

Bettie, J. (2003) *Women Without Class*. Berkeley, CA: University of California Press.

Beynon, J. (1985) *Initial Encounters in the Secondary School*. Lewes: Falmer.

Beynon, J. (1987) Miss Floral mends her ways. In L. Tickle (ed.) *The Arts in Education*. London: Croom Helm, pp. 80–120.

Beynon, J. and Atkinson, P. (1984) Pupils as data gatherers. In S. Delamont (ed.) *Readings on Interaction in the Classroom*, London: Methuen, pp. 255–272.

Biddle, B.J. and Saha, L. (2002) *The Untested Accusation*. Westport, CT: Ablex.

Bissinger, H.G. (1990) *Friday Night Lights*. New York: Da Capo Press.

Blishen, E. (1948) *Roaring Boys*. Harmondsworth: Penguin.

Boellstorff, T. (2008) *Coming of Age in Second Life*: *An anthropologist explores the virtually human*. Princeton, NJ: Princeton University Press.

Bourdieu, P. (1984) *Distinction*. Cambridge: Polity.

Bourdieu, P. (1988) *Homo Academicus*. Cambridge: Cambridge University Press.

Bourdieu, P. (1996) *The State Nobility*. Cambridge: Polity.

Bourdieu, P. (1998) *Practical Reason*. Cambridge: Polity.

Bourdieu, P. (1999) *The Weight of the World*. Cambridge: Polity.

Bourdieu, P. (2001) *Masculine Domination*. Cambridge: Polity.

Bourgois, P. (1996) *In Search of Respect*. Cambridge: Cambridge University Press.

Brady, I. (2000) Anthropological poetics. In N.K. Denzin and Y. Lincoln (eds) (2000) *Handbook of Qualitative Research*, 2nd edition. Thousand Oaks: Sage, pp. 949–979.

Brady, I. (2005) Poetics for a planet. In N. Denzin and Y. Lincoln (eds) *Handbook of Qualitative Research*, 3rd edition. Thousand Oaks, CA: Sage, pp. 979–1026.

Brady, I. (2009) How to die in the desert. *International Review of Qualitative Research*, 2, 1, 155–161.

Brown, K.M. (1991) *Mama Lola*. Berkeley, CA: University of California Press.

Brown-Saracino, J., Thurk, J. and Fine, G.A. (2008) Beyond groups: seven pillars of peopled ethnography in organisations and communities. *Qualitative Research*, 8, 5, 547–567.

Brown, P., Green, A. and Lauder, H. (2001) *High Skills*. Oxford: Oxford University Press.

Brown, R. (ed.) (1973) *Knowledge, Education and Cultural Change*. London: Tavistock.

Browning, B. (1998) *Infectious Rhythm*. New York: Routledge.

Brunvand, J.H. (1983) *The Vanishing Hitchhiker*. London: Picador.

Brunvand, J.H. (1984) *The Choking Doberman*, New York: W.N. Norton.

Bryan, K.A. (1980) Pupil perception of transfer. In A. Hargreaves and L. Tickle (eds) *Middle Schools*. London: Harper and Row, pp. 228–246.

Bullivant, B.M. (1978) *The Way of Tradition*. Melbourne: ACER.

Burgess, R.G. (1983) *Experiencing Comprehensive Education*. London: Methuen.

Burgess, R.G. (ed) (1984) *The Research Process in Educational Settings*. London: Falmer.

Burgess, R.G. (ed.) (1985a) *Field Methods in the Study of Education*. London: Falmer.

Burgess, R.G. (ed.) (1985b) *Strategies of Educational Research*. London: Falmer.

Burgess, R.G. (1987) Studying and restudying Bishop McGregor School. In G. Walford (ed.) *Doing Sociology of Education*. Lewes: Falmer.

Burke, J.L. (1995) *In the Electric Mist with the Confederate Dead*. London: Orion.

Burnett, J. H. (1969) Ceremony, rites and economy in the student system of an American high school. Reprinted in S. Delamont (ed.) (2012) *Ethnographic Methods in Education*. London: Sage. Four volumes, Volume II, pp. 17–30.

Byrne, E. (1975) Inequality in education. *Educational Review*, 27, 3, 179–191.

Canaan, J. (1987) A comparative analysis of American suburban cliques. In G. Spindler and L. Spindler (eds) *Interpretive Ethnography of Education*. Hillsdale, NJ: Erlbaum, pp. 385–408.

Casanova, U. (1991) *Elementary School Secretaries*. Newbury Park, CA: Corwin Press.

Casanova, U. (2010) *Sí Se Puede*. New York: Teachers College Press.

Cazden, C. (1986) Classroom discourse. In M. Wittrock (ed.) *Handbook of Research on Teaching*, 3rd edition. New York: Collier-Macmillan, pp. 432–463.

Chang, H. (2008) *Autoethnography as Method*. Walnut Creek, CA: Left Coast Press.

Chang, P.J. and Rosiek, J. (2003) Anti-colonialist antinomies in a biology lesson. *Curriculum Inquiry*, 33, 3, 251–290.

Cicourel, A. and Kitsuse, J.I. (1963) *The Educational Decision Makers*. New York: Bobbs-Merrill.

Clarke, A. and Star, S.L. (2008) The social world framework. In E.J. Hackett et al. (eds) *The Handbook of Science and Technology Studies*. Cambridge, MA: MIT Press, pp. 113–137.

Clifford, J. and Marcus, G.E. (eds) (1986) *Writing Culture*. Berkeley, CA: University of California Press.

Clough, P. (1992) *The End(s) of Ethnography*. Newbury Park, CA: Sage.

Clough, P. (2002) Poetic performance given at the ASA conference, in the SSSI stream, Chicago.

Coffey, A. (1999) *The Ethnographic Self*. Thousand Oaks, CA: Sage.

Coffey, A. and Atkinson, P.A. (1996) *Making Sense of Qualitative Data*. Thousand Oaks, CA: Sage.

Coffey, A. and Delamont, S. (2000) *Feminism and the Classroom Teacher*. London: Falmer.

Coleman, J. (1961) *The Adolescent Society*. New York: The Free Press.

Connolly, P. (1998) *Racism, Gender and Identity in Young Children*. London: Routledge.

Connolly, P. (2004) *Boys and Schooling in the Early Years*. London: Routledge Falmer.

Corrigan, P. (1979) *Schooling the Smash Street Kids*. London: Macmillan.

Cortazzi, M. (1991) *Primary Teaching: How It Is*. London: David Fulton.

Cortazzi, M. (1993) *Narrative Analysis*. London: Falmer Press.

Cortazzi, M. and Jin, Lixian (2012) Approaching narrative analysis with 19 questions. In S. Delamont (ed.) *Handbook of Qualitative Research in Education.* Cheltenham: Elgar, pp. 474–488.

Cottrell, S. (2004) *Professional Music Making in London.* Aldershot: Ashgate.

Coulthard, M. (1974) Approaches to the study of classroom interaction. *Educational Review*, 22, 1, 38–50.

Cowan, J. (1991) Going out for coffee? In P. Loizos and E. Papataxiarchis (eds) *Contested Identities.* Princeton, NJ: Princeton University Press, pp. 180–201.

Coxon, A.P.M. (1983) A cookery class for men. In A. Murcott (ed.) *The Sociology of Food and Eating.* Aldershot: Gower, pp. 172–177. Reprinted in S. Delamont (ed.) (2012) *Ethnographic Methods in Education.* London: Sage. Four volumes, Volume III, pp. 223–230.

Crompton, R. (1995) Trajectoires femininas dans la banque et la pharmacie. *Les Cahiers du Mage*, 1, 1, 63–74.

Crosnoe, R. (2011) *Fitting In, Standing Out.* Cambridge: Cambridge University Press.

Crossley, N. (1995) Merleau Ponty, the elusive body and carnal sociology. *Body and Society*, 1, 1, 43–663.

Cusick, P. (1973) *Inside High School.* New York: Holt, Rinehart and Winston.

Darmanin, M. (1990) *Sociological Perspectives on Schooling in Malta.* Unpublished PhD Thesis. Cardiff: Cardiff University.

Datnow, A. (1997) Using gender to preserve tracking's status hierarchy. *Anthropology and Education Quarterly*, 28, 2, 204–228. Reprinted in S. Delamont (ed.) (2012) *Ethnographic Methods in Education.* London: Sage. Four volumes, Volume IV, pp. 317–339.

Datnow, A. (1998) *The Gender Politics of Educational Change.* London: Falmer Press.

Davidson, J. (1997) *Courtesans and Fishcakes.* London: Harper Collins.

Davies, L. (1984) *Pupil Power.* London: Falmer.

Davies, W.B.(1995) Bernstein on classrooms. In P.A. Atkinson, W.B. Davies and S. Delamont (eds) *Discourse and Reproduction.* Cresskill, NJ: Hampton, pp. 137–158.

Delamont, S. (1978a) The contradictions in ladies' education. In S. Delamont and L. Duffin (eds) *The Nineteenth-Century Woman.* London: Croom Helm, pp. 134–163.

Delamont, S. (1978b) The domestic ideology and women's education. In S. Delamont and L. Duffin (eds) *The Nineteenth Century Woman.* London: Croom Helm, pp. 164–187.

Delamont, S. (1981) All Too Familiar? *Educational Analysis*, 3, 1, 69–84. Reprinted in S. Delamont (ed.) (2012) *Ethnographic Methods in Education.* London: Sage. Four volumes, Volume I, pp. 279–294.

Delamont, S. (1983a) *Interaction in the Classroom*, 2nd edition. London: Methuen.

Delamont, S. (1983b) The ethnography of transfer. Part IV of M. Galton and J. Willcocks (eds) *Moving from the Primary Classroom.* London: Routledge, pp. 97–153.

Delamont, S. (1984) Debs, dollies, swots and weeds. In G. Walford (ed.) *British Public Schools.* London: Falmer, pp. 65–86.

Delamont, S. (1987) The primary teacher 1945–1990: myths and realities. In S. Delamont (ed.) *The Primary School Teacher.* London. Falmer, pp. 3–20.

Delamont, S. (1989) *Knowledgeable Women.* London: Routledge.

195

Delamont, S. (1990) *Sex Roles and the School* (2nd edition) London: Routledge.

Delamont, S. (1993) Distant dangers and forgotten standards. *Women's History Review*, 1, 2, 233–252.

Delamont, S. (1998) You need the leotard. *Sport, Education and Society*, 3, 1, 5–18.

Delamont, S. (1999) Gender and the discourse of derision. *Research Papers in Education*, 14, 1, 3–21.

Delamont, S. (2000) The anomalous beasts. *Sociology*, 34, 1, 95–112.

Delamont, S. (2002) *Fieldwork in Educational Settings*, 2nd edition. London: Falmer.

Delamont, S. (2003) *Feminist Sociology*. London: Sage.

Delamont, S. (2005a) No place for women among them. *Sport, Education and Society*, 10, 3, 305–320.

Delamont, S. (2005b) Four great gates. *Research Papers in Education*, 20, 1, 85–100.

Delamont, S. (2006a) The smell of sweat and rum. *Ethnography and Education*, 1, 2, 161–176.

Delamont, S. (2006b) Where the boys are. *Waikato Journal of Education*, 11, 1, 7–26

Delamont, S. (2008) Confessions of a ragpicker. In S. Delamont and P. Atkinson (eds) *Gender and Research*. Volume 3: *Feminist Methods*. London: Sage, pp. 317–329.

Delamont, S. (2010) Neopagan narratives. *Sociological Research Online* 14, 5, 15. Available at: http://www.socresonline.org.uk/14/5/18.html.

Delamont, S. (ed.) (2012a) *Ethnographic Methods in Education*. Four volumes. London: Sage.

Delamont, S. (ed.) (2012b) *Handbook of Qualitative Research in Education*. Cheltenham: Edward Elgar.

Delamont, S. (2012c) The parochial paradox. In K. Anderson-Levitt (ed.) *Anthropologies of Education*. New York: Berghahn, pp. 49–70.

Delamont, S. and Atkinson, P.A. (1990) 'Waxing eloquent'. *Teaching and Teacher Education*, 6, 2, 111–125.

Delamont, S. and Atkinson, P.A. (1995) *Fighting Familiarity*. Cresskill, N.J.: Hampton Press.

Delamont, S., Atkinson, P.A. and Parry, O. (2000) *The Doctoral Experience*. London: Falmer.

Delamont, S., Atkinson, P. and Pugsley, L (2010) The concept smacks of magic. *Teaching and Teacher Education*, 26, 1, 3–10.

Delamont, S. and Galton, M. (1980) The first weeks of middle school. In A. Hargreaves and L. Tickle (eds) *Middle Schools*. London: Harper and Row, pp. 207–227.

Delamont, S. and Galton, M. (1986) *Inside the Secondary Classroom*. London: Routledge.

Delamont, S. and Galton, M. (1987) Anxieties and anticipations: pupils' views of transfer to secondary school. In A. Pollard (ed.) *Children and their Primary Schools*. Falmer: London, pp. 236–251.

Delamont, S. and Stephens, N. (2008) Up on the roof. *Cultural Sociology* 1, 2, 57–74.

de Marrais, K.B. (1998) (ed.) *Inside Stories*. Mahwah, NJ: Erlbaum.

Denham, C. and Lieberman, A. (1980) *Time on Task*. Washington, DC: NIE.

De Nora, T. (2000) *Music in Everyday Life*. Cambridge: Cambridge University Press.

Denscombe, M. (1984a) Keeping 'em quiet. In S. Delamont (ed.) *Readings on Interaction in the Classroom*. London: Methuen, pp. 134–159.

Denscombe, M. (1984b) *Classroom Control*. London: Allen and Unwin.

Denzin, N. (2003) *Performance Ethnography*. Thousand Oaks, CA: Sage.

Denzin, N. (2009) Apocalypse now. *International Review of Qualitative Research*, 2, 2, 331–344.

Denzin, N. and Lincoln, Y. (eds) (1994) *Handbook of Qualitative Methods*. Thousand Oaks, CA: Sage.

Denzin, N. and Lincoln, Y. (eds) (2000) *Handbook of Qualitative Methods*, 2nd edition. Thousand Oaks, CA: Sage.

Denzin, N. and Lincoln, Y. (eds) (2005) *Handbook of Qualitative Methods*, 3rd edition. Thousand Oaks, CA: Sage.

Denzin, N.K., Lincoln, Y and Smith, L.T. (eds) (2008) *Handbook of Critical and Indigenous Methodologies*. Thousand Oaks, CA: Sage.

Desmond, M. (2006) Becoming a firefighter. *Ethnography*, 7, 4, 387–421. Reprinted in S. Delamont (ed.) (2012) *Ethnographic Methods in Education*. London: Sage. Four volumes, Volume II, pp. 275–306.

Deyhle, D. (1998) The role of the applied anthropologist: Between schools and the Navaho Nation. In K. Bennett De Marrais (ed.) *Inside Stories*. Mahwah, NJ: Erlbaum, pp. 35–48.

Dicks, B., Mason, B., Coffey, A., Atkinson, P.A. (2005) *Qualitative Research and Hypermedia*. London: Sage.

Dimitriadis, G, (2008) *Studying Urban Youth Culture*. New York: Peter Lang.

Dimitriadis, G. (2011) *Critical Dispositions Evidence and Expertise in Education*. New York: Routledge.

Donetto, S. (2012) Medical students and patient-centred clinical practice. *British Journal of Sociology of Education*, 33, 3, 431–450.

Donohue, J.J. (2002) Wave people: the martial arts and the American imagination. In D.E. Jones (ed) *Combat, Ritual and Performance*. Westport, CT: Praeger. pp. 65–80.

Downey, G. (2005) *Learning Capoeira*. New York: Oxford University Press.

Edmondson, R. (1984) *Rhetoric in Sociology*. London: Macmillan.

Edwards, A.E., Fitz, J. and Whitty, G. (1989) *The State and Private Education*. Lewes: Falmer.

Eisner, E. (1997) The promise and perils of alternative forms of data representation. *Educational Researcher*, 26, 6, 4–10.

Eisner, E. (2001) Concerns and aspirations for qualitative research in the new millennium. *Qualitative Research*, 1, 2, 135–145.

Eisner, E. and Peshkin, A. (eds) (1990) *Qualitative Inquiry in Education*. New York: Teachers College Press.

Ellis, B. (2001) *Aliens, Ghosts and Cults*. Jackson, MS: University Press of Mississippi.

Ellis, C. (2002) Shattered lives. *Journal of Contemporary Ethnography*, 31, 4, 375–410.

Ellis, C. (2009) Telling tales on neighbours. *International Review of Qualitative Research*, 2, 1, 3–28.

Ellis, C. and Bochner, A. (eds) (1996) *Composing Ethnography*. Walnut Creek, CA: Alta Mira Press.

Ellis, C. and Bochner, A. (2000) Autoethnography, personal narrative, reflexivity. In N. Denzin and Y. Lincoln (eds) *Handbook of Qualitative Research*, 2nd edition. Thousand Oaks, CA: Sage, pp.733–768.

Entwistle, J. (2009) *The Aesthetic Economy of Fashion*. Oxford: Berg.

197

Ericsson, K.A., Krampe, R.T. and Tesch-Romer, C. (1993) The role of deliberate practice in the acquisition of expert performance. *Psychological Review*, 100, 3, 363–406.

Erickson, F. (2006) Studying side by side. In G. Spindler and L. Hammond (eds) *Innovations in Educational Ethnography*. Mahwah, NJ: Erlbaum, pp. 235–258.

Fabian, J. (1983) *Time and the Other*. New York: Columbia University Press.

Faubion, J.D. and Marcus, G.E. (eds) (2009) *Fieldwork is Not What it Used to Be*. Ithaca, NY: Cornell University Press.

Fehr, C. (2008) Are smart men smarter than smart women? In A.M. May (ed.) *The 'Woman Question' and Higher Education*. Cheltenham: Edward Elgar, pp. 102–108.

Fincham, B., McGuinness, M. and Murray, L. (eds) (2010) *Mobile Methodologies*. London: Palgrave.

Finders, M.J. (1997) *Just Girls*. New York: The Teachers College Press.

Fine, G.A. (1981) Rude words. *Maledicta*, 5, 51–68.

Fine, G.A. (1983) *Shared Fantasy*. Chicago: University of Chicago Press.

Fine, G.A. (1985) Occupational aesthetics. *Urban Life*, 14, 1, 3–32. Reprinted in S. Delamont (ed.) (2012) *Ethnographic Methods in Education*. London: Sage. Four volumes, Volume III, pp. 231–250.

Fine, G.A. (1987) *With the Boys*. Chicago: The University of Chicago Press.

Fine, G.A. (ed.) (1995) *A Second Chicago School?* Chicago: The University of Chicago Press.

Fine, G.A. (1996) *Kitchens*. Berkeley, CA: University of California Press.

Fine, G.A. (1998) *Morel Tales*. Cambridge, MA. Harvard University Press.

Fine, G.A. (2001) *Gifted Tongues*. Princeton: Princeton University Press.

Fine, G.A. (2003) Towards a peopled ethnography. *Ethnography*, 4, 1, 41–60.

Fine, G.A. (2004) *Everyday Genius*. Chicago: The University of Chicago Press.

Fine, G.A. (2007) *Authors of the Storm*. Chicago: The University of Chicago Press.

Flanders, N.A. (1970) *Analysing Teaching Behaviour*. New York. Addison-Wesley.

Foley, D. (1996) The silent Indian as cultural production. In B. Levinson, D. Foley and D. Holland (eds) *The Cultural Production of the Educated Person*. Albany, NY: SUNY Press, pp. 79–92.

Foley, D.A., Levinson, B.A., Hurtig, J. (2001) Anthropology goes inside: The new educational ethnography of ethnicity and gender. In W.G. Secada (ed.) *Review of Research in Education*, 25, 37–98. Washington, DC: AERA.

Ford, J. (1969) *Social Class and the Comprehensive School*. London: Routledge and Kegan Paul.

Fordham, S. (1993) 'Those loud Black girls'. *Anthropology and Education Quarterly*, 24, 1, 3–32.

Fordham, S. (1996) *Blacked Out*. Chicago: The University of Chicago Press.

Forsey, M.G. (2010) Ethnography as participant listening. *Ethnography*, 11, 4, 558–572.

Foster, P., Gomm, R. and Hammersley, M. (1996) *Constructing Educational Research*. London: Falmer.

Fox, I. (1984) The demand for a public school education. In G. Walford (ed.) *British Public Schools*. Lewes: Falmer Press, pp. 45–64.

Fraleigh, S.H. and Hanstein, P. (eds) (1999) *Researching Dance*. London: Dance Books Ltd.

Frank, A. (2010) In defence of narrative exceptionalism. *Sociology of Health and Illness*, 32, 4, 665–667.

Frazer, E. (1993) Talking about class in a girls' public school. In G. Walford (ed.) *The Private Schooling of Girls*. London: Woburn Press, pp. 127–152.

Frosch, J.D. (1999) Dance ethnography. In S.H. Fraleigh and P. Hanstein (eds) (1999) *Researching Dance*. London: Dance Books Ltd., pp. 249–282.

Furlong, V.J. (1976) Interaction sets in the classroom. In M. Stubbs and S. Delamont (eds) *Explorations in Classroom Observation*. Chichester: Wiley, pp. 23–44.

Galton, M., Simon, B. and Croll, P. (1980) *Inside the Primary Classroom*. London: Routledge and Kegan Paul.

Galton, M. and Simon, B. (1980) (eds) *Progress and Performance in the Primary Classroom*. London: Routledge and Kegan Paul.

Gamradt, J. (1998) 'Studying Up' in educational anthropology. In K. Bennett de Marrais (ed.) *Inside Stories*. Mahwah; NJ: Erlbaum, pp. 67–78.

Garfinkel, H. (1967) *Studies in Ethnomethodology*. Englewood Cliffs, NJ: Prentice-Hall.

Geer, B. (1964) First days in the field. In P. Hammond (ed.) *Sociologists at Work*. New York: Basic Books, pp. 372–398. Reprinted in S. Delamont (ed.) (2012) *Ethnographic Methods in Education*. London: Sage. Four volumes, Volume I, pp. 243–262.

Geer, B. (1966a) Notes on occupational commitment. *School Review*, 74, 1, 31–47.

Geer, B. (1966b) Occupational commitment and the teaching profession. *School Review*, 77, 1, 31–47.

Geer, B. (ed.) (1972) *Learning to Work*. Beverley Hills, CA: Sage.

Geertz, C. (1973) *The Interpretation of Cultures*. New York: Basic Books.

Gewirtz, S., Ball, S.J. and Bowe, R. (1995) *Markets, Choice and Equity in Education*. Buckingham: Open University Press.

Gibson, M. (1988) *Accommodation without Assimilation*. Ithaca, NY: Cornell University Press.

Gilbert, G.N. and Mulkay, M. (1984) *Opening Pandora's Box*. Cambridge: Cambridge University Press.

Gillborn, D. and Youdell, D. (2000) *Rationing Education*. Buckingham: Open University Press.

Gladwell, M. (2009) *Outliers*. Harmondsworth: Penguin.

Glaser, B. and Strauss, A.L. (1965) *Awareness of Dying*. Chicago: Aldine.

Goffman, E. (1959) *The Presentation of Self in Everyday Life*. New York: Doubleday Anchor.

Goffman, E. (1963) *Stigma*. Harmondsworth: Penguin Books.

Gordon, C.W. (1957) *The Social System of the High School*. Glencoe, IL: The Free Press.

Gordon, J.A. (2009) Children of the *danchi*: a Japanese primary school for Newcomers. *Ethnography and Education*, 4, 2, 165–179.

Grant, G. (1988) *The World We Created at Hamilton High*. Cambridge, MA: Havard University Press.

Greenwood, D.M. (1994) *Holy Terrors*. London: Hodder Headline.

Greenwood, S. (2000) *Magic, Witchcraft and the Otherworld*. Oxford: Berg.

Gubrium, J. and Holstein (eds) (2005) *Handbook of Interviewing*. Thousand Oaks, CA: Sage.

Gupta, A. and Ferguson, J. (eds) (1997) *Anthropological Locations*. Berkeley, CA: University of California Press.

Gustafson, K. (2009) Us and them – children's identity work and social geography in a Swedish school yard. *Ethnography and Education*, 4, 1, 1–16.

Hafferty, F.W. (1988) Cadaver stories. *Journal of Health and Social Behaviour*, 29, 4, 344–356.

Hafferty, F.W. (1991) *Into the Valley*. New Haven, CT: Yale University Press.

Hagedorn, K.J. (2001) *Divine Utterances*. Washington, DC: Smithsonian Institution Press.

Hall, T., Lashua, B., and Coffey, A. (2008) Sounds and the everyday in qualitative research. *Qualitative Inquiry*, 14, 6, 1017–14.

Halsey, A.H., Heath, A. and Ridge, J.M. (1980) *Origins and Destinations*. Oxford: Clarendon Press.

Hammersley, M. (1980) Classroom ethnography, *Educational Analysis*, 2, 1, 47–74. Reprinted in S. Delamont (ed.) (2012) *Ethnographic Methods in Education*. London: Sage. Four volumes, volume I, pp. 75–106.

Hammersley, M. (1982) The sociology of classrooms. In A. Hartnett (ed.) *The Social Sciences in Educational Studies*. London: Heinemann, pp. 227–242.

Hammersley, M. (2001) Whose side was Becker on? *Qualitative Research*, 1, 1, 91–110.

Hammersley, M. (2008) *Questioning Qualitative Inquiry*. London: Sage.

Hammersley, M. (2010) Research, Art or Politics? *International Review of Qualitative Research*, 3, 1, 5–10.

Hammersley, M. and Atkinson, P.A. (2007) *Ethnography*, 3rd edition. London: Routledge.

Hamilton, M. (2007) *In Search of the Blues*. London: Jonathan Cape.

Hanna, J.L. (1982) Public social policy and the children's world. In G. Spindler (ed.) *Doing the Ethnography of Schooling*. New York: Holt, Rinehart and Winston, pp. 316–355.

Hargreaves, A. (1984) Contrastive rhetoric and extremist talk. In A. Hargreaves and P. Woods (eds) *Classroom and Staffrooms*. Milton Keynes: Open University Press.

Hargreaves, A. (1986) *Two Cultures of Schooling*. Lewes: Falmer.

Hargreaves, D. (1967) *Social Relations in a Secondary School*. London: Routledge and Kegan Paul.

Hargreaves, D.H. (1982) *The Challenge for the Comprehensive School*. London: Routledge and Kegan Paul.

Hargreaves, L. and Galton, M. (2002) *Transfer from the Primary Classroom 20 Years On*. London: Routledge.

Haywood, C. and Mac an Ghaill, M. (1996) Schooling masculinities. In M. Mac an Ghaill (ed.) *Understanding Masculinities*. Buckingham: Open University Press. pp. 50–60.

Heap, J. (1985) Discourse in the production of classroom knowledge, *Curriculum Enquiry*, 15, 245–279.

Heath, S.B. (1982) Questioning at home and at school. In G. Spindler (ed.) *Doing the Ethnography of Education*. New York: Holt, Rinehart and Winston, pp. 102–131.

Heath, S.B. (1983) *Ways with Words*. Cambridge: Cambridge University Press.

Heath, S.B. (2012) *Words at Work and Play*. Cambridge: Cambridge University Press.

Hess, G.A. (1999) Keeping educational anthropology relevant. *Anthropology and Education Quarterly*, 30, 4, 404–412.

Herzfeld, M. (1983) Semantic slippage and moral fall. *Journal of Modern Greek Studies*, 1, 161–172.

Herzfeld, M. (1985) *The Poetics of Manhood*. Princeton, NJ: Princeton University Press.

Herzfeld, M. (1991) *A Place in History*. Princeton, NJ: Princeton University Press.

Herzfeld, M. (2004) *The Body Impolitic*. Chicago: The University of Chicago Press.

Herzfeld, M. (2009) The cultural politics of gesture. *Ethnography*, 10, 2, 131–152.

Hey, V. (1997) *The Company She Keeps*. Buckingham: Open University Press.

Heyl, B. (1979) *The Madam as Entrepreneur*. New Brunswick, NJ: Transaction.

Heyl, B. (2012) The madam as teacher. In S. Delamont (ed.) *Ethnographic Methods in Education*. London: Sage: Four volumes, Volume III, pp. 251–264.

Hilsum, S. and Cane, B.S. (1971) *The Teacher's Day*. Slough: NFER.

Ho, Karen (2009) *Liquidated*. Durham, NC: Duke University Press.

Holland, D. C. and Eisenhart, M.A. (1992) *Educated in Romance*. Chicago: The University of Chicago Press.

Hollingshead, A.B. (1947) *Elmtown's Youth*. New York: John Wiley and Sons.

Hollingshead, A.B. (1975) *Elmtown's Youth and Elmtown Revisited*. New York: Wiley.

Hurston, Z.N. (1935) *Mules and Men*. New York: Lippincott. 1990 edition: New York: Harper Perennial.

Hutton, R. (1999) *The Triumph of the Moon*. Oxford: Oxford University Press.

Hutton, R. (2006a) How myths are made. In R. Hutton (ed.) *Witches, Druids and King Arthur*. Hambledon: Continuum, pp. 1–38.

Hutton, R. (2006b) Living with witchcraft. In R. Hutton (ed.) *Witches, Druids and King Arthur*. Hambledon: Continuum, pp. 259–294.

Hymes, D. (1996) *Ethnography, Linguistics, Narrative Inequality*. London: Taylor and Francis.

Ikeda, K. (1998) *A Room Full of Mirrors*. Stanford: Stanford University Press.

Jackson, P. (1968) *Life in Classrooms*. New York: Holt, Rinehart and Winston.

Jacob, E. (1987) Qualitative research traditions. *Review of Educational Research*, 57, 1, 1–50.

James, A. (2001) Ethnography in the study of children and childhood. In P.A. Atkinson, A. Coffey, S. Delamont, J. Lofland and L. Lofland (eds.) *Handbook of Ethnography*. London: Sage. pp. 246–257.

James, A., Hockey, J. and Dawson, A. (eds) (1997) *After Writing Culture*. London: Routledge.

Jamous, H. and Peloille, B. (1970) Professions or self-perpetuating systems? In J.A. Jackson (ed.) *Professions and Professionalisation*. Cambridge: Cambridge University Press, pp. 111–152.

Jeffery, P. (1979) *Frogs in a Well*. London: Zed Books.

Jennings, G., Brown, D. and Sparkes, A.C. (2010) It can be a religion if you want. *Ethnography*, 11, 4, 533–557.

Jones, Ricky, L. (2004) *Black Haze: Violence, Sacrifice, and Manhood in Black Greek-Letter Fraternities*. Albany, NY: State University of New York Press.

Jones, S.H. (2005) Autoethnography. In N. Denzin and Y. Lincoln (eds) *Handbook of Qualitative Research*, 3rd edition. Thousand Oaks, CA: Sage, pp. 703–792.

Karabel, J. and Halsey, A.H. (eds) (1977) *Power and Ideology in Education*. New York: Oxford University Press.

Karweit, N.L. (1981) Time in School. In R.G. Corwin (ed.) *Research in Educational Organisations*. Greenwich, CT: JAI Press.

Katz, J. (2001) From how to why. *Ethnography*, 2, 4, 443–474.

Katz, J. (2002) From how to why: on luminous description, Pt 2. *Ethnography*, 3, 1, 63–90.

Kendall, L. (2000) Oh No! I'm a nerd! *Gender and Society*, 14, 2, 256–74.

Kenna, M. (1992) Changing places and altered perspectives. In J. Okely and H. Callaway (eds) *Anthropology and Autobiography*. London: Routledge.

King, A.R. (1967) *The School at Mopass*. New York: Holt, Rinehart and Winston.

Knapp, M. and Knapp, H. (1976) *One Potato, Two Potato*. New York: W. Norton.

Kusenbach, M. (2003) Street phenomenology: the go-along as ethnographic research tool. *Ethnography*, 4, 455–485.

Kusenbach, M. (2012) Mobile methods. In S. Delamont (ed.) (2012) *Handbook of Qualitative Research in Education*. Cheltenham: Edward Elgar, pp. 252–264.

Lacey, C. (1970) *Hightown Grammar*. Manchester: Manchester University Press.

Lambart, A. (1982) Expulsion in context, In R. Frankenberg (ed) *Custom and Conflict in British Society*. Manchester: Manchester University Press. pp. 188–208. Reprinted in S. Delamont (ed.) *Ethnographic Methods in Education*. Volume 4. London: Sage. pp. 187–204.

Lande, B. (2007) Breathing like a soldier. In C. Shilling (ed.) *Embodying Sociology*. Oxford: Blackwell, pp. 95–108.

Lareau, A. (1996) Common problems in fieldwork. In A. Lareau and J. Shultz (eds) *Journeys through Ethnography*. Boulder, CO: Westview Press, pp. 195–236.

Lareau, A. (2003) *Unequal Childhoods*. Berkeley, CA: University of California Press.

Larkin, Ralph W. (2007) *Comprehending Columbine*. Philadelphia: Temple University Press.

Lash, S. and Urry, J. (1994) *Economies of Signs and Space*. London: Sage.

Lave, J. and Wenger, E. (1991) *Situated Learning*. Cambridge: Cambridge University Press.

Leacock, E. (1969) *Teaching and Learning in City Schools*. New York: Basic Books.

Leacock, S. and Leacock, R. (1975) *Spirits of the Deep*. New York: Doubleday.

Lefkowitz, B. (1998) *Our Guys: The Glen Ridge Rape and the Secret Life of the Perfect Suburb*. New York: Vintage Books.

Levinson, B.A., Foley, D.E., Holland, D.C. (eds) (1996) *The Cultural Production of the Educated Person*. Albany NY: SUNY Press.

Lewis, J.L. (1992) *Ring of Liberation*. Chicago: University of Chicago Press.

Lightfoot, Sara L. (1983) *The Good High School*. New York: Basic Books.

Lofland, L (1975) The 'Thereness' of women. In M. Millman (ed.) *Another Voice*. New York: Doubleday Anchor.

Lofland, J. and Lofland, L. (2005) *Analysing Social Settings*, 3rd edition. Belmont, CA: Wadsworth.

Loizos, P. (1981) *The Heart Grown Bitter*. Cambridge: Cambridge University Press.

Long, C. M. (2006) *A New Orleans Voudou Priestess*. Talahassie, FL: University Press of Florida.

Mac an Ghaill, M. (1994) *The Making of Men*. Buckingham: Open University Press.

Magliocco, S. (2004) *Witching Culture*. Philadelphia: University of Pennsylvania Press.

Mannay, D. (2011) Making the familiar strange. *Qualitative Research*, 11, 1, 1–19.

Mannay, D. (2013) Keeping close and spoiling revisited. *Gender and Education*, 25, 1, 91–107.

Mannix, D. (1951) *Memoirs of a Sword Swallower*. London: Hamish Hamilton.

Marion, J.S. (2008) *Ballroom*. Oxford: Berg.

Markham, A. (1998) *Life Online: Researching Real Experience in Virtual Space*. Walnut Creek, CA: Alta Mira Press.

Marquese, M. (1994) *Anyone But England*. London: Verso.

Mathieson, M. (1973) *The Preachers of Culture*. London: Allen and Unwin.

May, A. M. (ed.) (2008) *The 'Woman Question' and Higher Education: Perspectives on Gender and Knowledge Production in America*. Cheltenham: Edward Elgar.

McCulloch, K. (2007) Living at sea. *Ethnography and Education*, 2, 3, 289–304.

McDonald, M. (1989) *We Are Not French*! London: Routledge.

McNamara, D. (1980) The outsider's arrogance. *British Educational Research Journal*, 6, 2, 113–126.

McPherson, G.H. (1972) *Small Town Teacher*. Cambridge, MA: Harvard University Press.

Mead, M. (1943) Our educational emphasis in primitive perspective. In S. Delamont (ed.) (2012) *Ethnographic Methods in Education*. London: Sage. Four volumes, Volume 1, pp. 3–12.

Measor, L. (1984) Gender and the sciences. In M. Hammersley and P. Woods (eds) *Life in Schools*. Milton Keynes: The Open University Press, pp. 89–107.

Measor, L. and Woods, P. (1983) The interpretation of pupil myths. In M. Hammersley (ed.) *The Ethnography of Schooling*. Driffield, Yorkshire: Nafferton Books, pp. 55–76.

Measor, L. and Woods, P. (1984) *Changing Schools*. Milton Keynes: Open University Press.

Mellor, D. (2003) *Playground Romance*. Unpublished PhD thesis, Cardiff: Cardiff University.

Mellor, D. and Delamont, S. (2011) Old anticipations, new anxieties? *Cambridge Journal of Education* 41, 3, 333–34.

Merryfield, M.M. (2000) Why aren't teachers being prepared to teach for diversity, equity and global interconnections? *Teaching and Teacher Education*, 16, 4, 429–444.

Merton, D.E. (2005) Transitions and 'trouble': rites of passage for suburban girls. *Anthropology and Education Quarterly*, 36, 2, 132–48.

Metz, M. (1978) *Classrooms and Corridors*. Berkeley, CA: University of California Press.

Metz, M. (1984) Editor's Foreword. *Sociology of Education*, 57, 2, 429–444.

Middleton, S. (2001) *Educating Researchers*. Wellington: New Zealand Association for Educational Research.

Miller, Daniel and Slater, Don (2000) *The Internet*. Oxford: Berg.

Moffat, M. (1989) *Coming of Age in New Jersey*. New Brunswick, NJ: Rutgers University Press.

Mueller, J. and O'Connor, C. (2007) Telling and retelling about 'self' and 'others'. *Teaching and Teacher Education*, 23, 6, 840–856.

Murphy, J.M. (1993) *Santeria: African Spirits in America*. Boston: Beacon Press.

Nader, L. (1975) Up the anthropologist – perspectives gained from studying up. In D. Hymes (ed.) *Reinventing Anthropology*. New York: Vintage Books, pp. 284–312.

O'Connor, E. (2007) Embodied knowledge in glassblowing. In C. Shilling (ed.) *Embodying Sociology*. Oxford: Blackwell, pp. 126–141.

Myers, W.B. (2008) Straight and white. *Qualitative Inquiry* 14, 1, 160–171.

O'Hagan, A. (1995) *The Missing*. London: Picador.

Orellana, M.E. and Thorne, B. (1998) Year-round schools and the politics of time. *Anthropology and Education Quarterly*, 29, 4, 446–472.

Ortner, S. (2002) 'Burned like a tattoo'. High School social categories and 'American culture'. *Ethnography*, 3, 2, 115–148. Reprinted in S. Delamont (ed.) (2012) *Ethnographic Methods in Education*. London: Sage. Four volumes, Volume II, pp. 57–86.

Ortner, S.B. (2003) *New Jersey Dreaming*. Durham, NC: Duke University Press.

Paechter, C. (2000) *Changing School Subjects*. Buckingham: Open University Press.

Palonsky, S.B. (1975) Hempies and squeaks, truckers and cruisers: A participant observer study in a city high school. *Educational Administration Quarterly* 11, 2, 86–103. Reprinted in S. Delamont (ed) *Ethnographic Methods in Education* Volume 4. London: Sage, pp. 83–100.

Papageorgiou, D. (2007) Field research on the run. In A. McLean and A. Leibing (eds) *The Shadow Side of Fieldwork*. Oxford: Blackwell, pp. 221–238.

Park, Roberta (1987) Sport, gender and society in a transatlantic Victorian perspective. In J. A. Mangan and R. Park (eds) *From 'Fair Sex' to Feminism*. London: Cass, pp. 58–96.

Parker, H. (1974) *View from the Boys*. Newton Abbott: David and Charles.

Parker, R. (2006) *School Days*. London. No Exit Press.

Parman, S. (1998) Making the familiar strange: The anthropological dialogue of George and Louise Spindler. In George Spindler and Louise Spindler (eds) *Fifty Years of Anthropology and Education 1950–2000*. Mahwah: NJ: Lawrence Erlbaum, pp. 393–416. Reprinted in S. Delamont (ed.) (2012) *Ethnographic Methods in Education*. London: Sage. Four volumes, volume I, pp. 319–340.

Patrick, J. (1973) *A Glasgow Gang Observed*. London: Eyre Methuen.

Pelissier, C. (1991) The anthropology of teaching and learning. *Annual Review of Anthropology*, 20: 75–95.

Peshkin, A. (1972) *Kanuri Schoolchildren*. New York: Holt, Rinehart and Winston.

Peshkin, A. (1978) *Growing Up American*. Chicago: the University of Chicago Press.

Peshkin, A. (1982) *The Imperfect Union*. Chicago: The University of Chicago Press.

Peshkin, A. (1986) *God's Choice*. Chicago: The University of Chicago Press.

Peshkin, A. (1991) *The Color of Strangers, The Color of Friends*. Chicago: The University of Chicago Press.

Peshkin, A. (1994) *Growing up American*, 2nd edition. Chicago: The University of Chicago Press.

Peshkin, A. (1997) *Places of Memory*. Mahwah, NJ: Erlbaum.

Peshkin, A. (2001) *Permissable Advantage*? New York: Routledge.

Peterson, W.A. (1964) Age, teachers's role and the institutional setting. In B.J. Biddle and W. Ellena (eds) *Contemporary Research on Teacher Effectiveness*. New York: Holt, Rinehart and Winston, pp. 264–315.

Petrone, R. (2010.)'You have to get hit a couple of times'. *Teaching and Teacher Education*, 26, 1, 119–127. Reprinted in S. Delamont (ed.) (2012) *Ethnographic Methods in Education*. London: Sage. Four volumes, Volume II, pp. 307–326.

Phillips, S.U. (1982) Learning the 'cant'. In G. Spindler (ed.) *Doing the Ethnography of Education*. New York. Holt, Rinehart and Winston, pp. 176–209.

Poulos, C. (2010) Transgressions. *International Review of Qualitative Research*, 3, 1, 67–88.

Phillips, S.U. (1983) *The Invisible Culture*. New York: Holt Rinehart and Winston.

Powell, K. (2006) Inside-out and Outside-In. Participant observation in *Taiko* drumming. In G. Spindler and L. Hammond (eds) *Innovations in Educational Ethnography*. Mahwah, NJ: Erlbaum, pp. 33–64.

Power, S., Edwards, A., Whitty, G., Wigfall, V. (2003) *Education and the Middle Class*. Buckingham: Open University Press.

Price, A. (1973) *Colonel Butler's Wolf*. Newton Abbott: Crime Fiction Book Club.

Prior, L. (2012) The role of documents in social research. In S. Delamont (ed.) *Handbook of Qualitative Research in Education*. Cheltenham: Edward Elgar, pp. 426–438.

Prout, A. (1997) *Children's Bodies*. London: Macmillan.

Proweller, A. (1998) *Constructing Female Identities*. Albany, NY: SUNY Press.

Puddephatt, A.J., Shaffir, W. and Kleinknecht, S.W. (2009) (eds) *Ethnographies Revisited*. London: Routledge.

Pugach, M.C. (1998) *On the Border of Opportunity*. Mahwah, NJ: Erlbaum.

Pugsley, L. (1998) 'Throwing your brains at it', *International Studies in the Sociology of Education*, 8, 8, 71–90.

Pugsley, L. (2004) *The University Challenge*. Aldershot: Ashgate.

Raissiguier, C. (1994) *Women Becoming Workers*. New York: SUNY Press.

Raley, J.D. (2006) Finding safety in dangerous places. In G. Spindler and L. Hammond (eds) *Innovations in Educational Ethnography*. Mahwah, NJ: Erlbaum, pp. 127–168.

Reay, D., Crozier, G., James, D. (2011) *White Middle Class Identities and Urban Schooling*. Basingstoke: Palgrave.

Reed-Danahay, D. (1987) Farm children at school. *Anthropological Quarterly*, 60, 2, 83–89.

Reed-Danahay, D. (1996) *Education and Identity in Rural France*. Cambridge: Cambridge University Press.

Reed-Danahay, D. (2005) *Locating Bourdieu*. Bloomington, IN: Indiana University Press.

Reed-Danahay, D. and Anderson-Levitt, K. (1991) Backward country, troubled city? *American Ethnologist*, 18, 3, 546–565. Reprinted in S. Delamont (ed.) (2012) *Ethnographic Methods in Education*. London: Sage. Four volumes, Volume II, pp. 31–56.

Renold, E. (2005) *Girls, Boys and Junior Sexualities*. London: Routledge Falmer.

Richardson, L. (1990) *Writing Strategies*. Newbury Park, CA: Sage.

Richardson, L. (1994) Writing: A method of inquiry. In N.K. Denzin, and Y. Lincoln (eds) *Handbook of Qualitative Research*. Thousand Oaks, CA: Sage, pp. 516–529.

Richardson, L. (2008) My dinner with Lord Esqy. *Qualitative Inquiry* 14, 1, 13–7.

Rideout, V.J. Foehr, U.G. and Roberts, D.F. (2012) *Generation M: Media in the Lives of 8–18, The New York Times,* 10/6/2012.

Riseborough, G. (1988) Pupils, recipe knowledge, curriculum, and the cultural production of class, ethnicity and patriarchy. *British Journal of Sociology of Education*, 9, 1, 39–54. Reprinted in S. Delamont (ed.) (2012) *Ethnographic Methods in Education*. London: Sage. Four volumes, Volume III, pp. 67–84.

Riseborough, G. (1992) The Cream Team: an ethnography of BTEC national diploma (catering and hotel management) students in a tertiary college. *British Journal of Sociology of Education*, 13, 2, 215–245.

Riseborough, G. (1993) GBH – the Gobbo Barmy Army. In I. Bates and G. Riseborough (eds) *Youth and Inequality*. Buckingham: Open University Press, pp. 160–228.

Robertson, R. and Whyte, K. (2005) Globalisation. In C. Calhoun, C. Rojek and B. Turner (eds) *The Sage Handbook of Sociology* London: Sage. pp. 345–366.

Rogers, S.C. (1991) *Shaping Modern Times in Rural France*. Princeton, NJ: Princeton University Press.

Ronai, C.R. (1996) My mother is mentally retarded. In C. Ellis and A. Bochner (eds) *Composing Ethnography*. Walnut Creek, CA: Alta Mira, pp. 109–131.

Rose, S. (1988) *Keeping Them out of the Hands of Satan*. New York: Routledge and Kegan Paul.

Rosiek, J. (2006) Toward teacher education that takes the study of culture as foundational. In G. Spindler and L. Hammond (eds) *Innovations in Educational Ethnography*. Hillside, NJ: Erlbaum, pp. 259–286.

Roth, J. (1963) *Timetables*. Indianapolis, IN: Bobbs-Merrill.

Ruhleder, K. (2000) The virtual ethnographer: Fieldwork in distributed electronic environments. *Field Methods*, 12, 1, 3–17.

Rutter, M. et al. (1979) *Fifteen Thousand Hours*. London: Open Books.

Sabin, P.C. (2007) On sentimental education among college students. *Teachers College Record*, 109, 7, 1682–1704.

Salamone, S.D. (1986) *In the Shadow of the Holy Mountain*. Boulder, CO: East European Monographs.

Salz, J. (1998) Why was everyone laughing at me? In J. Singleton (ed.) *Learning in Likely Places*. Cambridge: Cambridge University Press, pp. 85–103.

Savage, M. (2010) *Identities and Social Change in Britain since 1940*. Oxford: Oxford University Press.

Sconzert, K., Lazzetto, D. and Purkes, S. (2000) Small-town college to big-city school. *Teaching and Teacher Education*, 16, 4, 465–490.

Scott, S. (2004) Researching shyness. *Qualitative Research*, 4, 1, 91–105.

Scott, S. (2007) *Shyness and Society*. Basingstoke: Palgrave.

Scott, S. (2009) *Making Sense of Everyday Life*. Cambridge: Polity.

Seeger, A. (2008) Theories forged in the crucible of action. In G. Barz and T.J. Cooley (eds) *Shadows in the Field*, 2nd edition. Oxford: Oxford University Press, pp. 271–288.

Serbin, L (1978) Teachers, peers and play preferences. In B. Sprung (ed.) *Perspectives on Non-Sexist Early Childhood Education*. New York: Teachers College Press, pp. 79–93.

Sewell, T. (1997) *Black Masculinities and Schooling*. Stoke on Trent: Trentham Books.

Seyer-Ochs, I. (2006) Lived landscapes of the Fillmore. In G. Spindler and L. Hammond (eds) *Innovations in Educational Ethnography*. Mahwah, NJ: Erlbaum, pp. 169–232.

Sharp, R. and Green, A. (1976) *Education and Social Control*. London: Routledge and Kegan Paul.

Shibutani, T. (1955) Reference groups as perspectives. *American Journal of Sociology* 60, 3, 562–569.

Shibutani, T. (1966) *Improvised News*. Indianapolis, IN: Bobbs-Merrill.

Shilling, C. (2007) Sociology and the body. In C. Shilling (ed.) *Embodying Sociology*. Oxford: Blackwell, pp. 1–18.

Shumar, W. (1997) *College for Sale*. London: Falmer.

Sikes, P., Measor, L. and Woods, P. (1982) *Teacher Careers*. London: Falmer.

Sinclair, S. (1996) *Making Doctors*. Oxford: Berg.

Singleton, J. (1967) *Nichu: A Japanese School*. New York: Holt, Rinehart and Winston.

Singleton, J. (1998a) Craft and art education in Mashiko pottery workshops. In J. Singleton (ed.) *Learning in Likely Places*. Cambridge: Cambridge University Press, pp. 122–133.

Singleton, J. (ed.) (1998b) *Learning in Likely Places*. Cambridge: Cambridge University Press.

Singleton, J. (1999) Reflecting on the reflections. *Anthropology and Education Quarterly*, 30, 4, 455–459. Reprinted in S. Delamont (ed.) (2012) *Ethnographic Methods in Education*. London: Sage. Four volumes, volume I, pp. 341–346.

Siwatu, K.O (2007) Preservice teachers' culturally responsive self-efficacy and outcome expectancy beliefs. *Teaching and Teacher Education*, 23, 7, 1086–1101.

206

Slater, C. (1986) *Trail of Miracles*. Berkeley, CA: University of California Press.

Slater, C. (1990) *City Steeple, City Streets*. Berkeley, CA: University of California Press.

Smilde, D. (2007) *Reasons to Believe*. Berkeley, CA: University of California Press.

Smith, L.M. and Geoffrey, W. (1968) *The Complexities of an Urban Classroom*. New York: Holt, Rinehart and Winston.

Smith, L. M. and, Keith, P. (1971) *Anatomy of Educational Innovation*. London: Wiley.

Smith, L.M., Kleine, P.E., Prunty, J.P. and Dwyer, D.C. (1986) *Educational Innovation*. London: Falmer Press.

Smith, L.M., Prunty, J.P., Dwyer, D.C. and Kleine, P.E. (1987) *The Fate of an Innovative School*. London: Falmer Press.

Smith, L.M., Dwyer, D.C., Prunty, J.P. and Kleine, P.E. (1988) *Innovation and Change in Schooling*. London: Falmer Press.

Solomon, J. (1991) School laboratory life. In B.E. Woolnough (ed.) *Practical Science*. Milton Keynes: Open University Press, pp. 101–111.

Sparkes, A. (1996) The fatal flaw. *Qualitative Inquiry*, 2, 463–494.

Spencer, J. (1989) Anthropology as a kind of writing. *Man*, 24, 145–164.

Spencer, J. (2001) Ethnography after postmodernism. In P. Atkinson, A. Coffey, S. Delamont, J. Lofland, and L. Lofland (eds). *Handbook of Ethnography*. London: Sage, pp. 443–452 .

Spindler, G. (1955) *Education and Anthropology*. Stanford: Stanford University Press.

Spindler, G. (1967) *Education and Culture*. New York: Holt, Rinehart and Winston.

Spindler, G. (ed.) (1982) *Doing the Ethnography of Education*. New York: Holt, Rinehart and Winston.

Spindler, G. (ed.) (2000) *Fifty Years of Anthropology and Education*. Mahwah, NJ: Erlbaum.

Spindler, G. and Hammond, L. (eds) (2006) *Innovations in Educational Ethnography*. Mahwah, NJ: Erlbaum.

Spindler, G. and Spindler, L. (1982) Roger Harker and Schonhausen. In G. Spindler (ed.) *Doing the Ethnography of Schooling*. New York: Holt, Rinehart and Winston, pp. 20–47. Reprinted in S. Delamont (ed.) (2012) *Ethnographic Methods in Education*. London: Sage. Four volumes, volume I, pp. 295–318.

Spindler, G. and Spindler, L. (eds) (1987) *Interpretive Ethnography of Education*. Hillside, NJ: Erlbaum.

Spradley, J. (1969) *Guests Never Leave Hungry*. London: Yale University Press.

Spradley, J. (1979) *Ethnographic Interviewing*. New York: Holt, Rinehart and Winston.

Spradley, J. and Mann, B. (1975) *The Cocktail Waitress*. New York: Wiley.

Star, S.L. (1989) The structure of ill-structured solutions: Boundary objects and heterogeneous distributed problem solving. In L. Gasser and M. Huhns (eds) *Distributed Artificial Intelligence*. San Mateo, CA: Morgan Kaufman, pp. 37–54.

Star, S.L. (2010) This is not a boundary object: reflections on the origin of a concept. *Science, Technology and Human Values*, 35, 6, 600–617.

Star, S.L. and Griesemer, J.R. (1989) Institutional ecology, 'translations' and boundary objects. *Social Studies of Science*, 19, 4, 387–420.

Stephens, N., Atkinson, P.A., and Glasner, P. (2008) The UK Stem Cell Bank as performative architecture, *New Genetics and Society*, 27, 2, 87–95.

Stephens, N. and Delamont, S. (2006a) Balancing the *berimbau*. *Qualitative Inquiry*, 12, 1, 316–339.

Stephens, N. and Delamont, S. (2006b) Samba no mar. In P. Vannini and D. Waskul (eds) *Body/Embodiment*. Aldershot: Ashgate, pp. 109–122.

Stephens, N. and Delamont, S. (2009) They start to get *malicia*. *British Journal of Sociology of Education*, 30, 5, 537–548.

Stephens, N. and Delamont, S. (2010) Vim de Bahia pra lhe ver. In Fincham, B. et al. (eds) (2010) *Mobile Methodologies*. Basingstoke: Palgrave, pp. 85–102.

Stinchcombe, A. (1964) *Rebellion in a High School*. Chicago: Quadrangle.

Stoller, P. (1989) *The Taste of Ethnographic Things*. Philadelphia: University of Pennsylvania Press.

Stoller, P. (1997) *Sensuous Scholarship*. Philadelphia: University of Pennsylvania Press.

Suchman, L. (1994) Working relations of technology production and use. *Computer Supported Cooperative Work*, 2, 1, 21–39. Reprinted in D. Mackenzie and J. Wajcman (eds) (1999) *The Social Shaping of Technology*. Buckingham: Open University Press.

Sussman, L. (1977) *Tales out of School*. Philadelphia, PA: Temple University Press .

Swain, J. (2003) How young schoolboys became somebody, *British Journal of Sociology of Education*, 24, 3, 299–314.

Tester, K. (ed.) (1994a) *The Flâneur*. London: Routledge.

Tester, K. (1994b) Introduction. In K. Tester (ed.) *The Flâneur*. London: Routledge, pp. 1–21.

Thomas, C. (2010) Negotiating the contested terrain of narrative methods in illness contexts. *Sociology of Health and Illness*, 32, 4, 647–661.

Thompson, F. (1937/2007) *Thompson's Cricket Verses* (ed. E.V. Lucas) Oxford: Oxford University Press. Reprinted in In D.R. Allen (ed.) (2000) *A Breathless Hush: The MCC Anthology of Cricket Verse*. London: Methuen, p. 154.

Thrift, N. (2006) Reinventing invention. *Economy and Society*, 35, 3, 279–306.

Tight, M. (2002) Editorial. *Studies in Higher Education*, 27, 3, 261–262.

Tillman-Healy, L. (1996) A secret life in a culture of thinness. In C. Ellis and A. Bochner (eds) *Composing Ethnography*. Walnut Creek, CA: Alta Mira Press, pp. 76–108.

Timmons-Flores, M. (2009) Navigating contradictory communities of practice in learning to teach for social justice. *Anthropology and Education Quarterly*, 38, 4, 380–404.

Tinkler, P. and Jackson, C. (2004) *The Doctoral Examination Process*. Maidenhead: Open University Press.

Tobin, J. (1998) Tango and the scandal of homosocial desire. In W. Washabaugh (ed.) *The Passion of Music and Dance*. Oxford: Berg, pp. 79–102.

Tooley, J. (1998) *Educational Research*. London: OFSTED.

Trix, F. (1993) *Spiritual Discourse*. Philadelphia: University of Pennsylvania Press.

Turner, R.H. (1960) Modes of social ascent through education: sponsored and contest mobility. In A.H. Halsey, J. Floud and C.A. Anderson (eds) *Education, Economy and Society*. New York: The Free Press, pp. 121–139.

Twigger, R. (1989) *Angry White Pyjamas*. London: Phoenix.

Urry, J. (2007) *Mobilities*. Cambridge: Polity.

Valle, I. and Weiss, E. (2010) Participation in the figured world of graffiti. *Teaching and Teacher Education*, 26, 1, 128–135.

Valli, L. (1986) *Becoming Clerical Workers*. London: Routledge.

Van Gennep, A. (1909) *The Rites of Passage*. English edition published 1960, Chicago: The University of Chicago Press.

Varenne, H. (2007a) Alternative anthropological perspectives on education. *Teachers College Record*, 109, 7, 1539–1544.

Varenne, H. (2007b) Difficult collective deliberations. *Teachers College Record*, 109, 7, 1559–1588. Reprinted in S. Delamont (ed.) (2012) *Ethnographic Methods in Education*. London: Sage. Four volumes, Volume I, pp. 347–356.

Viera, A.L.B.M. (2004) *Capoeira and the Game of Life*. Lisbon: Privately Printed.

Vollen, L. and Ying, C. (eds) (2008) *Voices From the Storm*. San Francisco: McSweeney's Books.

Vulliamy, G. (1976) What counts as school music? In G. Whitty and M. Young (eds) *Explorations in the Politics of School Knowledge*. Driffield: Nafferton, pp. 19–34.

Vos, G. de (2011) A meeting with the devil at the crossroads. *Contemporary Legend Series*, 3, 1, 119–159.

Wacquant, L. (2004) *Body and Soul*. London: Oxford University Press.

Wafer, J. (1991) *The Taste of Blood*. Philadelphia: University of Pennsylvania Press.

Wainwright, S. and Turner, B. (2004) Epiphanies of embodiment. *Qualitative Research*, 4, 3, 311–337.

Walford, G. (1984) (ed.) *British Public Schools*. Lewes: Falmer.

Walford, G. (1986) *Life in Public Schools*. London: Methuen.

Walford, G. (1991) (ed.) *Doing Educational Research*. London: Routledge.

Walford, G. (1994) (ed.) *Researching the Powerful in Education*. London: UCL Press.

Walker, J.C. (1988) *Louts and Legends*. Sydney: Allen and Unwin.

Walker, R. and Adelman, C. (1976) Strawberries. In M. Stubbs and S. Delamont (eds) *Explorations in Classroom Observation*. Chichester: Wiley. pp. 133–150.

Walsh, D. (1998) Incomplete stories. In K. Bennett de Marrais (ed.) *Inside Stories*. Mahwah, NJ: Erlbaum, pp. 185–196.

Ward, M. (1999) Managing student culture and culture shock. *Anthropology and Education Quarterly*, 30, 2, 228–237.

Ward, M. (2004) *Voodoo Queen*. Jackson, MS: University Press of Mississippi.

Watson, C. (2012) Analysing narratives. In S. Delamont (ed.) *Handbook of Qualitative Research in Education*. Cheltenham: Elgar, pp. 460–473.

Wax, M. and Wax, R. (1971) Great tradition, little tradition and formal education. In M. Wax, S. Diamond and F. Gearing (eds) *Anthropological Perspectives on Education*. New York, Basic Books, pp. 3–27.

Weaver-Hightower, M. (2003) The 'boy turn' in research on gender and education. *Review of Educational Research*, 73, 4, 471–498.

Weiler, K. (1988) *Women Teaching for Change*. New York: Bergin and Garvey.

Weis, L. (1990) *Working Class Without Work*. New York: Routledge.

Weis, L. (2004) *Class Reunion*. New York: Routledge.

Whiteside, T. and Mathieson, M. (1971) The secondary modern school in fiction. *British Journal of Educational Studies*. xix, 3, 283–29.

Williams, M. (2006) *Virtually Criminal*. London: Routledge.

Willis, P. (1977) *Learning to Labour*. Farnborough: Gower.

Willson, M. (2010) *Dance Lest We All Fall Down*. Seattle: University of Washington Press.

Wilson, E. (1991) *The Sphinx in the City*. London: Sage.

Wilson, E. (2001) *The Contradictions of Culture*. London: Sage.

Winkle-Wagner, R. (2009) *The Unchosen Me*. Baltimore: The Johns Hopkins University Press.

Wolcott, H.F. (1967) *A Kwakiutl Village and School*. New York: Holt, Rinehart and Winston.

Wolcott, H.F. (1977 [2005]) *Teachers versus Technocrats*. Eugene, OR: Centre for Educational Policy and Management, University of Oregon. (Reprinted, 2005, by Walnut Creek, CA: Alta Mira Press).

Wolcott, H.F. (1981) Confessions of a 'trained' observer. In T.S. Popkewitz and B.R. Tabachnik (eds) *The Study of Schooling*. New York: Praeger, pp. 247–263. Reprinted in S. Delamont (ed.) (2012) *Ethnographic Methods in Education*. London: Sage. Four volumes, volume I, pp. 263–278.

Wolcott, H.F. (1983) Adequate schools and inadequate education: The life history of a sneaky kid. *Anthropology and Education Quarterly*, 14, 1, 3–32.

Wolcott, H.F. (2002a) *Sneaky Kid and its Aftermath*. Walnut Creek, CA: Alta Mira Press.

Wolcott, H.F. (2002b) Ethnography? Or Educational Travel Writing? In Y. Zou and E.T. Trueba (eds) *Ethnography and Schools*. Lanham, MA: Rowman and Littlefield, pp. 27–48.

Woodhead, C. (1998) Academia gone to seed. *New Statesman* (20 March), pp. 51–52.

Woodruff, E.A. and Curtner-Smith, M.D. (2007) Transitionary from elementary to secondary school: American pupils' scary stories and physical education folklore. *Sport, Education and Society*, 12, 4, 415–430.

Woodward, K. (2008) Hanging out and hanging about. *Ethnography*, 9, 4, 536–560.

Wright, C. (1996) School processes – an ethnographic study. In J. Eggleston, David Dunn and Mahdu Anjali (eds) *Education for Some*. Stoke on Trent: Trentham Books, pp. 127–180.

Wulff, H. (1998) *Ballet Across Borders*. Oxford: Berg.

Wylie, W. (1951) *Village in the Vaucluse*. Cambridge, MA: Harvard University Press.

Yeo, Wee Loon (2010) Belonging to 'Chinatown'. *International Studies in Sociology of Education*, 20, 1, 53–64.

Young, M.F.D. (1971) Introduction. In M.F.D. Young (ed.) *Knowledge and Control*. London: Collier-Macmillan, pp. 1–17.

Young, M.F.D. (1976) The schooling of science. In G. Whitty and M. Young (eds) *Explorations in the Politics of School Knowlege*. Driffield: Nafferton, pp. 47–62.

Zerubavel, E. (1979) *Patterns of Time in Hospital Life*. Chicago: The University of Chicago Press.

Zerubavel, E. (1981) *Hidden Rhythms*. Chicago: The University of Chicago Press.

Zerubavel, E. (2003) *Time Maps*. Chicago: The University of Chicago Press.

index

Abraham, J. 114, 117
absences 8, 129
Abu-Lughod, L. 90–1
academics and lecturers
  age, and educational role 49
  research obligations 187
  self-efficacy 23
  subject-dependent timetables 60–1
Adam, B. 45
Adelman, C. 139
Adler, P. 3, 78, 111, 179
Adler, P. A. 3, 78, 111, 179
aesthetic market place 104–5
African-American religions 33–4, 43
African Americans
  adolescents and rap music 106
  boxing trainers and training 9, 148, 176
  boys' rejection of racial embodiment
    94, 97
  children's perceived lack of language 175
  class, and children's sense of agency 54
  class, and parents' control over time 55
  Delta Blues 31–2
  female college students 17, 109, 117, 123
  folklore study 10, 26, 63, 128
  fraternities and sororities 79, 109, 124–5
  pupils' lived landscapes 38
  Trackton community 64–5, 162
  urban school failure 3
African-Brazilian religions 154, 155
African-Brazilian slaves 144
African-Brazilian tradition 28 *see also*
  capoeira
African-Caribbean religions 155
African-Caribbean standpoint 20
African-Caribbeans
  anti-school boys 114
  girls 'interaction sets' 125
age
  and children's academic 'progress' 50
  and Japanese theatrical roles 48
  and performativity 103
  and teacher–pupil relations 17–18, 72

Aggleton, P. 117
Albas, C. 156
Albas, D. 156
Alert Bay, British Columbia 27
Allan, A. J. 116
American Anthropological Association 28
Anderson, L. 185, 186
Anderson-Levitt, K. 19, 50
Anglos, New Mexico 112
anthropology
  fieldwork compared with sociological
    27, 161–2
  'luminous' description 6
  mobile methods 79
  use of ethnography 2
anthropology of education 1–2, 7, 8
  and the familiarity problem 14
  focus on anti-school pupils 113
  ignorance of sociology of
    education, 3–4, 13
  neglect of non-school education 14, 15
  neglect of sensory material 147, 148
  setting schools in communities 39
  and the study of knowledge 165, 169
  usefulness of *flâneur* concept 29
Anthropology of Education Quarterly 14
apprenticeships 21
Argentina 102
Ashburton, evocation 32–3
Asian-American pupils 38
Assunção, M. R. 73
Atkins, A. 33, 34
Atkinson, P. A. 13, 20, 22, 32, 39–40, 57–9,
    69–70, 71, 86–7, 93, 125, 130, 132,
    134, 137, 140, 141, 179, 186, 187
audio-visual recordings 93
Australia 115, 149, 159
  teachers' use of education research 8
  see also Lubavitcher Jewish School,
    Melbourne
autoethnography 5, 136, 148–9, 179–80
  capoeira crisis two example 183–5,
    186, 188